How Mary Beth Draws Dogs and Accidentally Builds a Business

Written and illustrated by

Philip Copitch, Ph.D.

Written and illustrated by Philip Copitch, Ph.D.

HERE TO SERVE YOU:

Hutzpah Press titles are available in quantity discounts for promotions, premiums, and fundraisers.

FOR FURTHER INFORMATION PLEASE CONTACT:

HUTZPAH PRESS
Geri Copitch, Sr. Editor
PO BOX 400
IGO CA 96047-0400

Dr. Phil's websites:
Business: www.CopitchInc.com

Cartoon: www.copitch.com

Dr. Phil's cartoons are available on shirts, mouse pads, cards, and lots more. See www.copitch.com

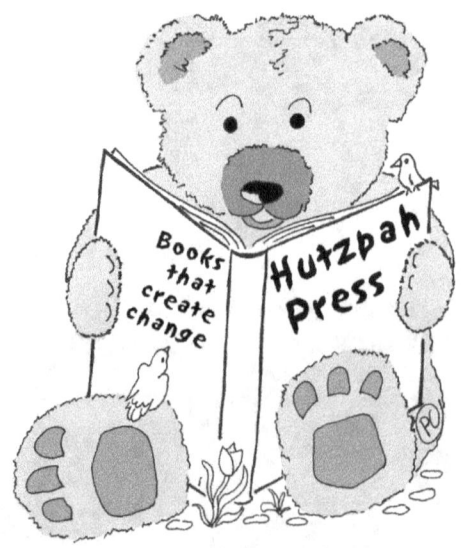

Dedication

Thanks Geri, the love of my life!

I do appreciate that you put up with my sense of humor.

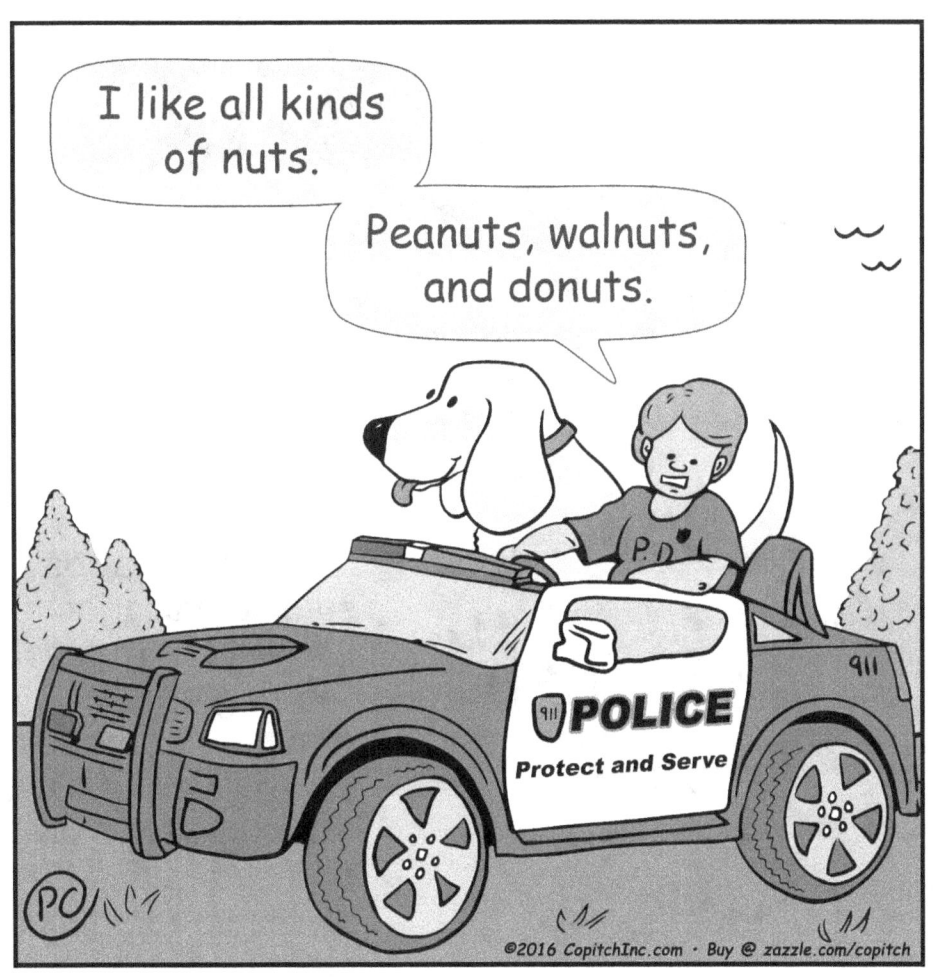

Chapter 1

Mary Beth Schmendrick has always loved hats. Ever since she was a little, little, girl, Mary Beth figured that if toes needed socks, then heads needed hats.

Now that Mary Beth is a girl of 9, she almost always wears a hat. She has hundreds of hats. Hats of all sorts. She owns a fancy dress hat that she could wear to meet the Queen of England. She has a tattered old derby she could wear to a horse racetrack, if she knew where one was.

Mary Beth loves her collection of baseball caps from teams across America. And army hats. She has lots of soldier type hats.

She also has a men's size 8 hat like the ones bad guys in old movies wore. She even has a nursing cap that her grandma wore during the war.

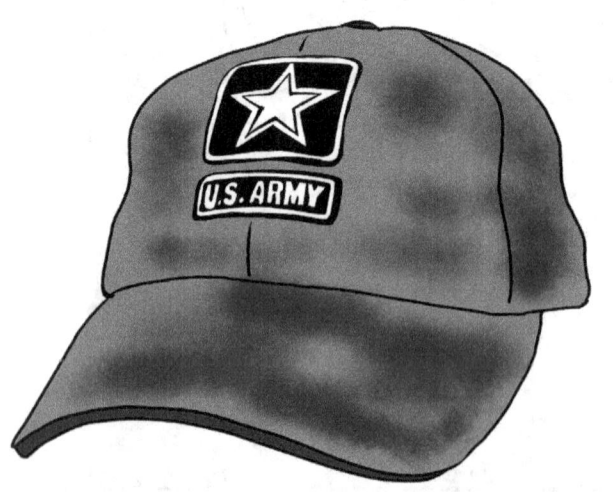

Mary Beth knew she looked good in hats because lots of adults, even adults she didn't know, would call out, "Hey kid, you look good in a hat," as they walked by.

On the first day of summer vacation, the one between third grade and fourth grade, Mary Beth went to her mother and asked, "Can I have some money so I can go to the thrift store and buy a hat?"

Mary Beth's mom was cleaning out her teacher's bag, which is what all teachers do the first day of summer vacation.

"I don't have any spare change, I guess you'll have to get a job," Mom said, without looking up from her pile of many books, papers, pencils, erasers, and that zip lock bag filled with emergency sugar packets, one crumpled unused but not new napkin, three aspirin, a hair tie, and four paper clips.

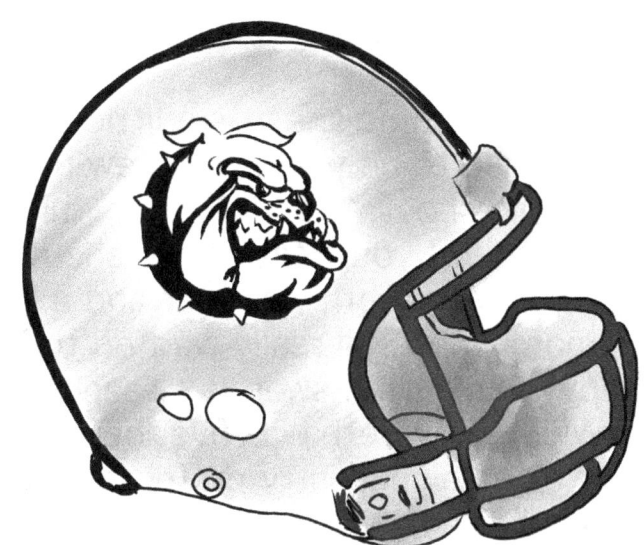

Mary Beth was disappointed with her mom's answer, so she went to her dad's lab in the garage.

"Dad, can I have some money for a hat?" she said, with her best polite smile.

"I can't stop what I'm mixing, honey," he said, as he poured blue goop from one flask into another that was filled with green fizzy yuck. "This reagent waits for no man."

"Mom said I should get a job."

Dad was very distracted by the purple bubbling slime that smelled like a combination of duck poop and Aunt Rosa's Christmas morning coffee breath.

"That sounds like a fine idea, honey," Dad said.

"OK," Mary Beth said, as she headed out of the lab to go find a job.

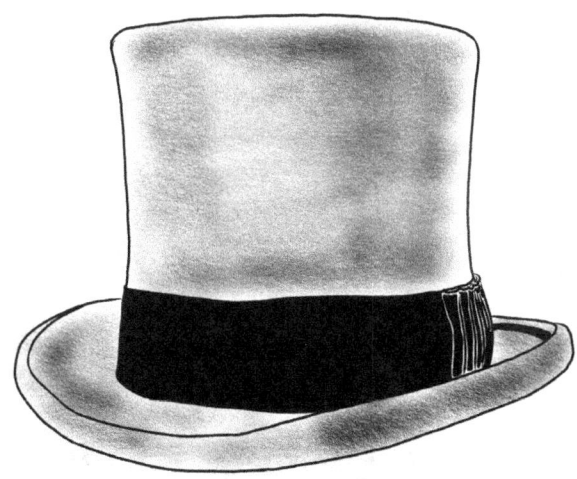

Chapter 2

From the time she was a little girl, adults asked Mary Beth what she wanted to be when she grew up. When she was four years old she would shout, "Hat!" But she quickly stopped saying that because adults look at you weird if you shout, "Hat!" at them.

When Mary Beth was four and a half she would say, "Teacher, like my mom." She still really wanted to be a hat, but her mom looked so happy when she answered, "Teacher, like my mom."

When Mary Beth was five, her dad asked her, "Why don't you want to be a chemistry professor like me?" So, for a while she told adults that she wanted to be a chemistry teacher. This made both Mom and Dad smile, even though Mary Beth had no idea what a teacher would teach to a chemistry.

When Mary Beth turned seven, she got a book full of cartoons. It made her laugh, and she enjoyed sharing the funny drawings with her friends. One day, while Mary Beth was copying cartoon characters out of the book, a thought came to her, *I know what I want to be when I grow up.*

A few days later, when Aunt Hilda asked her, "What do you want to be when you grow up?" Mary Beth happily announced, "I want to be a cartoonist. A cartoonist that draws hats."

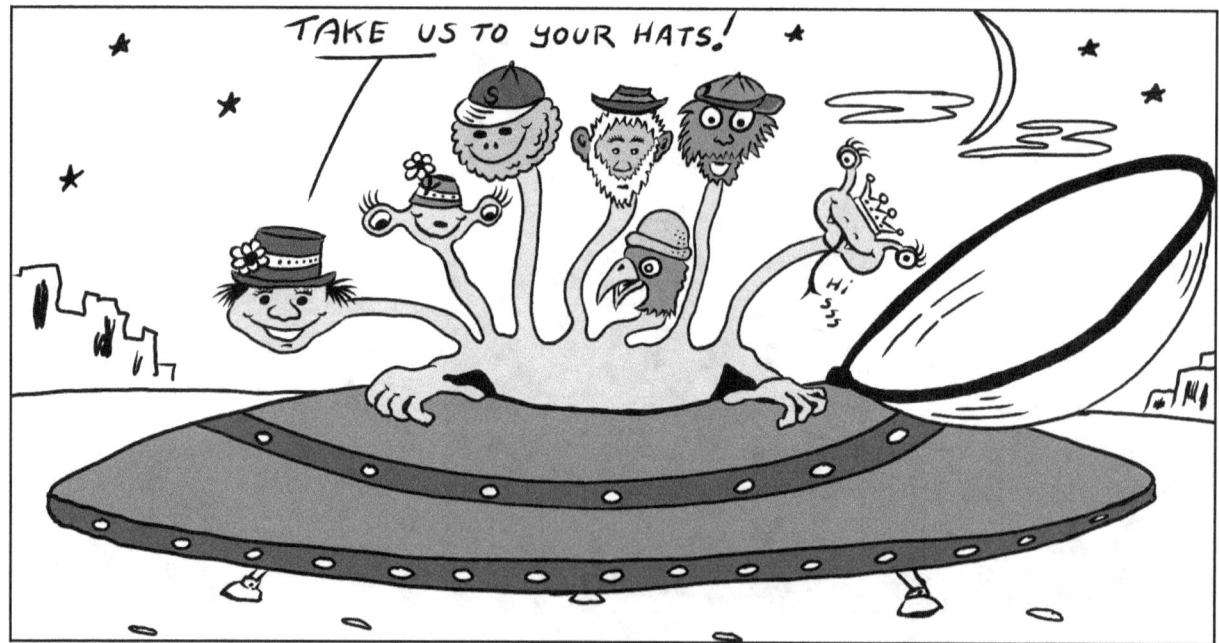

Mary Beth's first cartoon

Chapter 3

"Mom and Dad say I have to get a job," Mary Beth told her best friend in the whole world—as well as a few other planets like Jupiter, Mars, and Venus. Jazz, the German Shepherd Dog, exhaled all bored like, as if she didn't understand what Mary Beth was talking about.

Mary Beth was sitting on the porch holding her drawing pad and explaining her problems to Jazz.

"I have to make money so I can buy hats," Mary Beth said.

Jazz perked up and looked straight at her. Mary Beth drew a cartoon thought bubble on a piece of paper and filled it in with what she thought Jazz was thinking. "Draw me!" Mary Beth took the thought bubble and put it up by Jazz's head. She was right. Jazz wanted Mary Beth to draw her.

Mary Beth smiled as she drew Jazz.

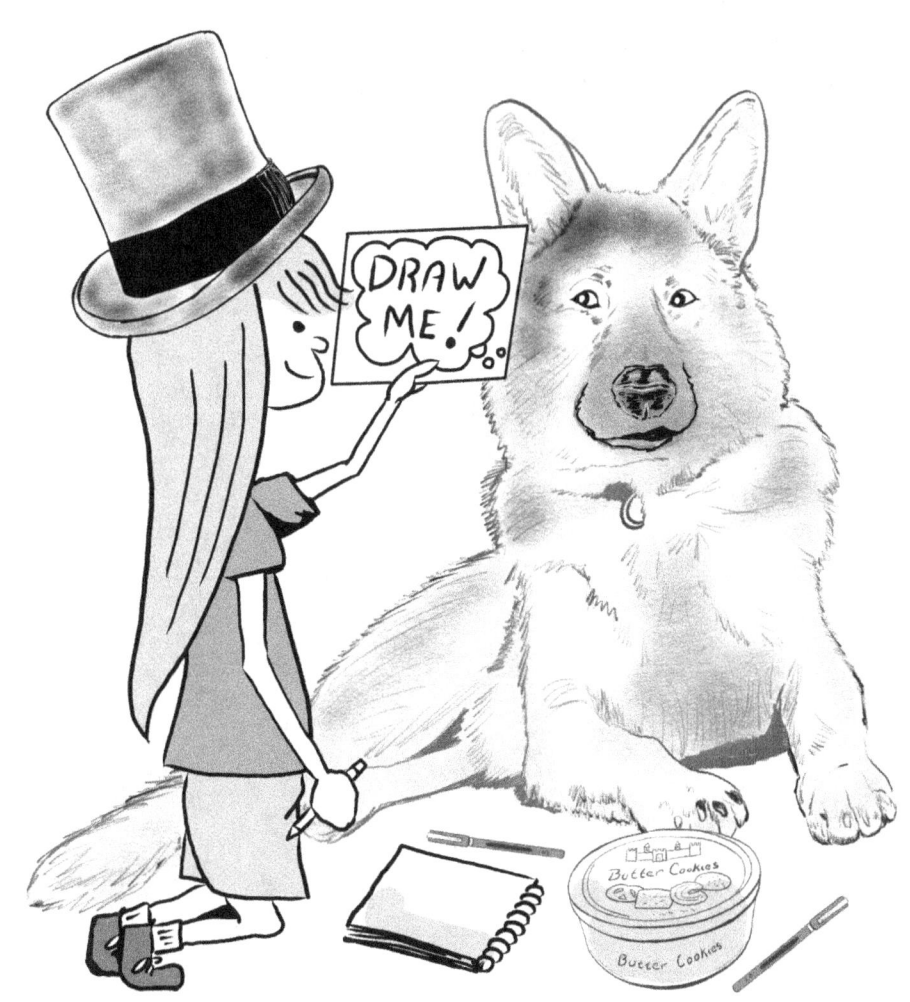

Chapter 4

Just as Mary Beth was finishing her cartoon of Jazz she heard, "Hi, Mary Beth."

It was the postman delivering the mail. "That's really nice," he said. "You're really good at drawing."

Mary Beth explained that she was trying to figure out how to make money so she could buy a hat.

A big smile crossed the postman's face.

"If you have Jazz saying, 'Hi, Mr. Villa', instead of 'draw me', I'll give you a quarter for it. My mail truck could use some art on its dashboard."

"Really, oh wow! Can I have it for you tomorrow?" Mary Beth asked.

"That sounds great," Mr. Villa said. "See you tomorrow." He patted Jazz on the head and walked off to deliver the mail.

Mary Beth drew her very best. She did a pencil drawing to get the art just the way she wanted it. Then she used a black pen to make the lines of her art stand out. After all the black lines were inked in correctly she gently erased all the pencil lines. Mary Beth used the side of her pencil to lightly add shades of gray. The drawing made Mary Beth and Jazz very happy.

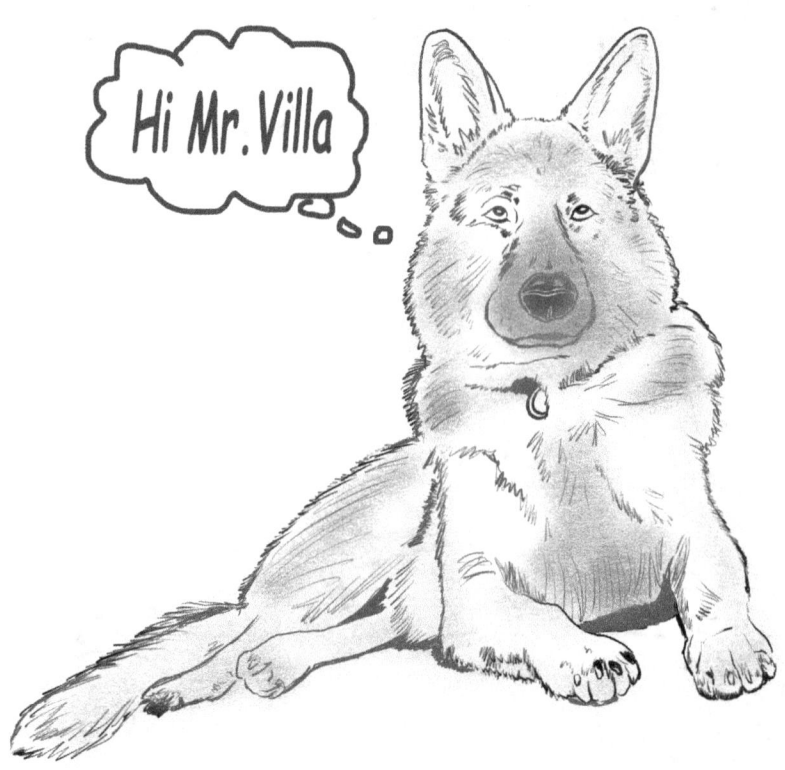

Chapter 5

The next day, Mr. Villa smiled happily at the drawing.

"I love it," he said, "but it isn't finished."

"Finished?" Mary Beth said.

"Sure, an artist always signs her work," Mr. Villa said.

"Oh, I should have known that," Mary Beth said.

With her favorite pen, Mary Beth signed her cartoon with her initials, MBS. Then she put a hat on the M.

Mr. Villa handed Mary Beth a shiny new quarter. "Congratulations! You are now a professional artist."

"Wow, thanks Mr. Villa," Mary Beth whispered, as she stared at her shiny new quarter. *It's from New Jersey.*

"What do you think of this?" Mary Beth asked Jazz. To find out what Jazz thought she drew a thought bubble and put it up by Jazz's head. Jazz was thinking, "You have a job!"

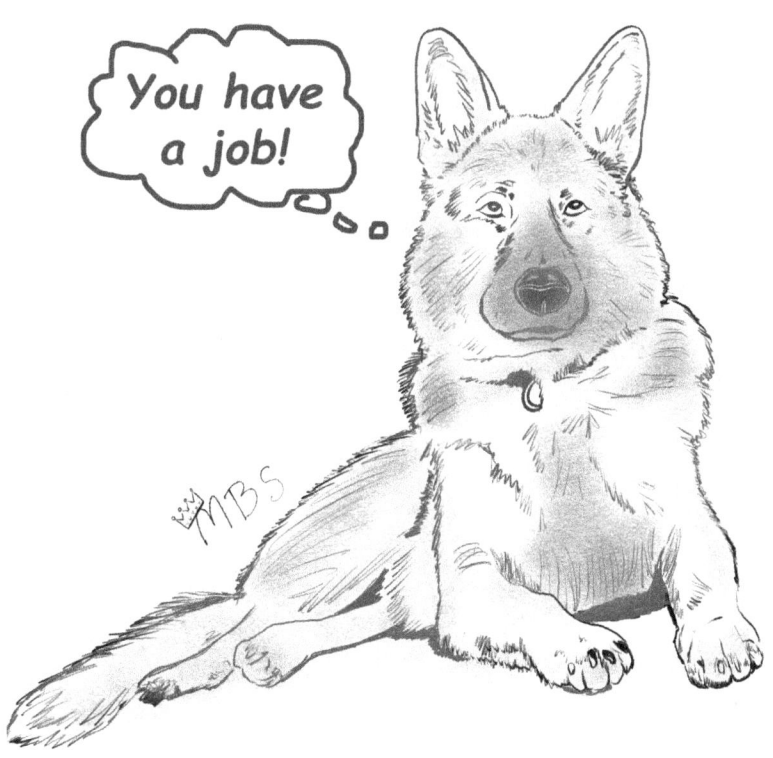

Chapter 6

Now that Mary Beth had a job she needed to figure out how to sell her drawings.

Mary Beth had a good idea about how to draw stuff, she just didn't know how to sell the stuff she drew.

Mary Beth had a tin Butter Cookie container from two Christmases ago. She kept her pencils, erasers, and a few pens in it. She also had a small ruler and a few jar caps of different sizes. She used the ruler if she needed to draw a very straight line, and the jar tops allowed her to draw very round circles of different sizes.

Mary Beth had loads of "scrap" paper that her dad kept in a pile on the shelf by the computer printer in his lab. They had lots of words and math on one side, but the other side was perfect for drawing. Every now and then, Mary Beth needed paper that she could draw on both sides. Like when she drew birthday cards or get well cards. When she needed new paper she knew she could always find it in the front slot of the computer printer. Her dad always kept lots of new paper for her there.

Mary Beth figured that if she was going to sell her art, she should draw it on new paper. So, she went out to her dad's lab and took all the new paper out of the printer. Now she had hundreds of sheets, more than enough to start a business.

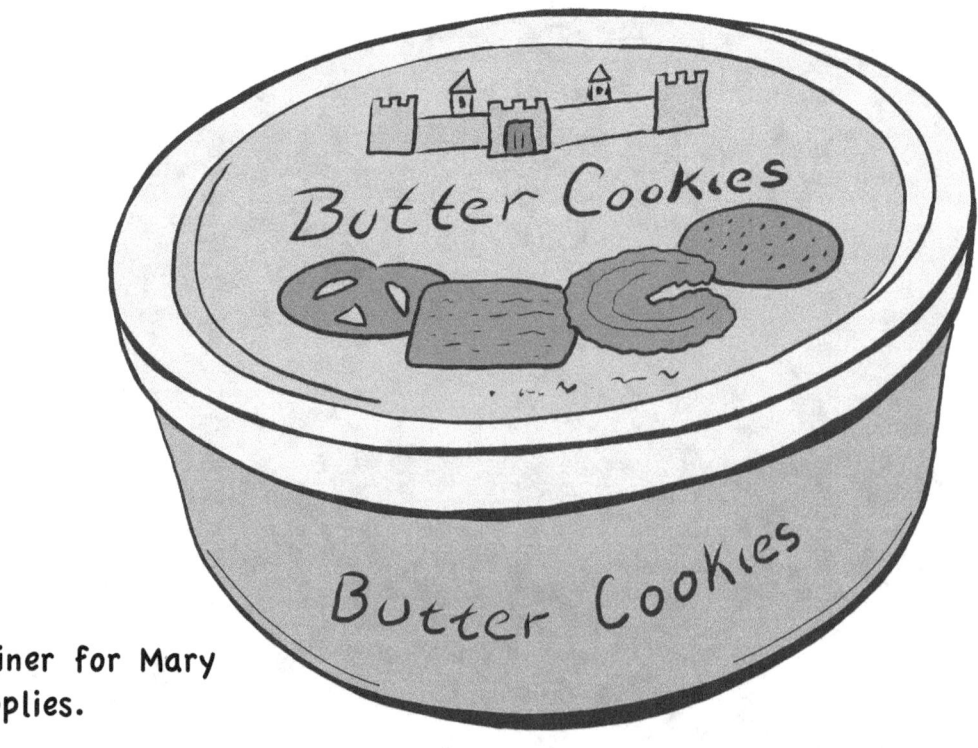

Storage container for Mary Beth's art supplies.

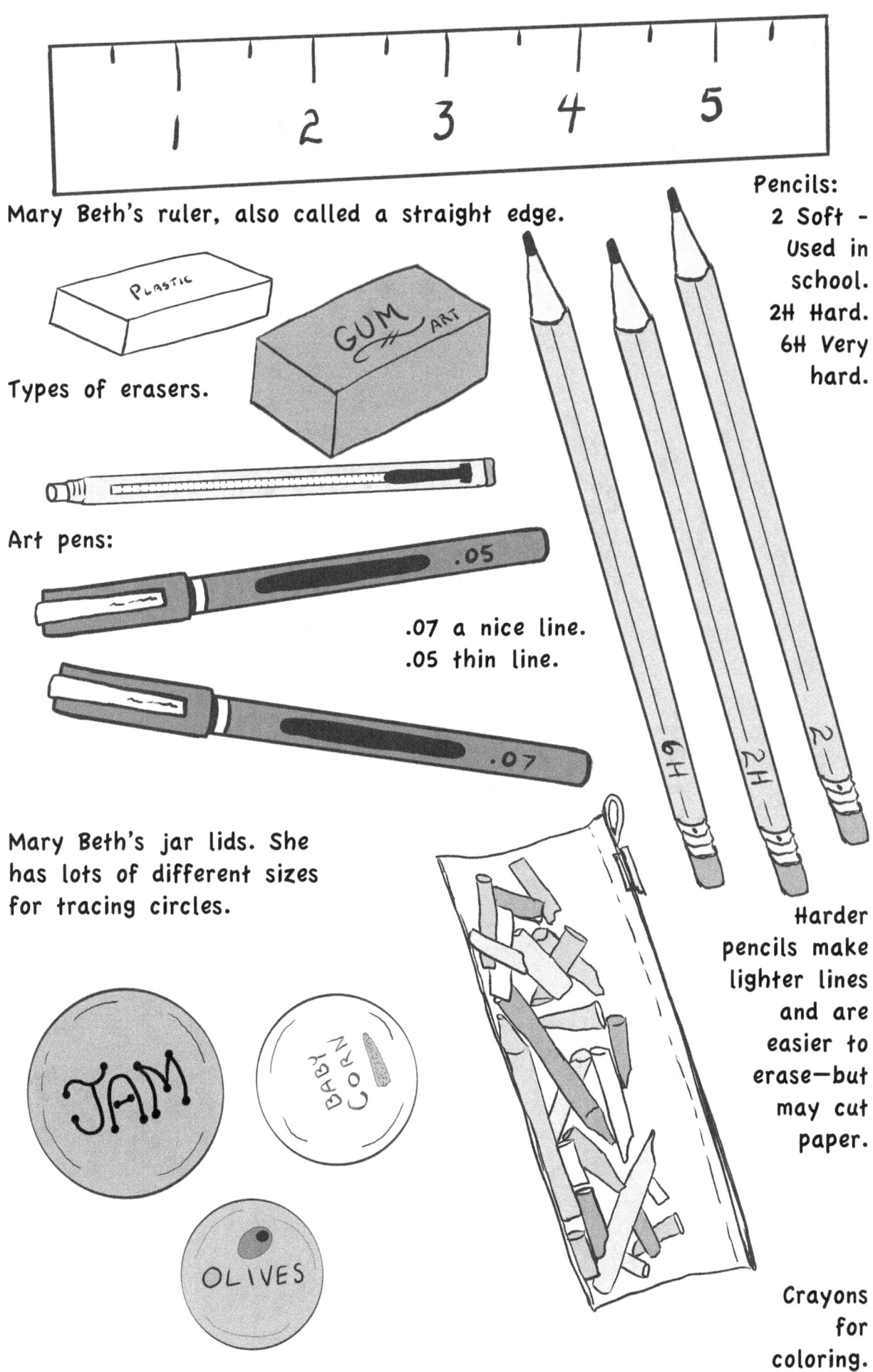

1 2 3 4 5

Mary Beth's ruler, also called a straight edge.

PLASTIC

Types of erasers.

GUM ART

Art pens:

.05

.07 a nice line.
.05 thin line.

.07

Pencils:
2 Soft –
Used in
school.
2H Hard.
6H Very
hard.

6H 2H 2

Mary Beth's jar lids. She
has lots of different sizes
for tracing circles.

JAM

BABY CORN

OLIVES

Harder
pencils make
lighter lines
and are
easier to
erase—but
may cut
paper.

Crayons
for
coloring.

Chapter 7
How to draw a pug
This is Puddles the Proud Pug

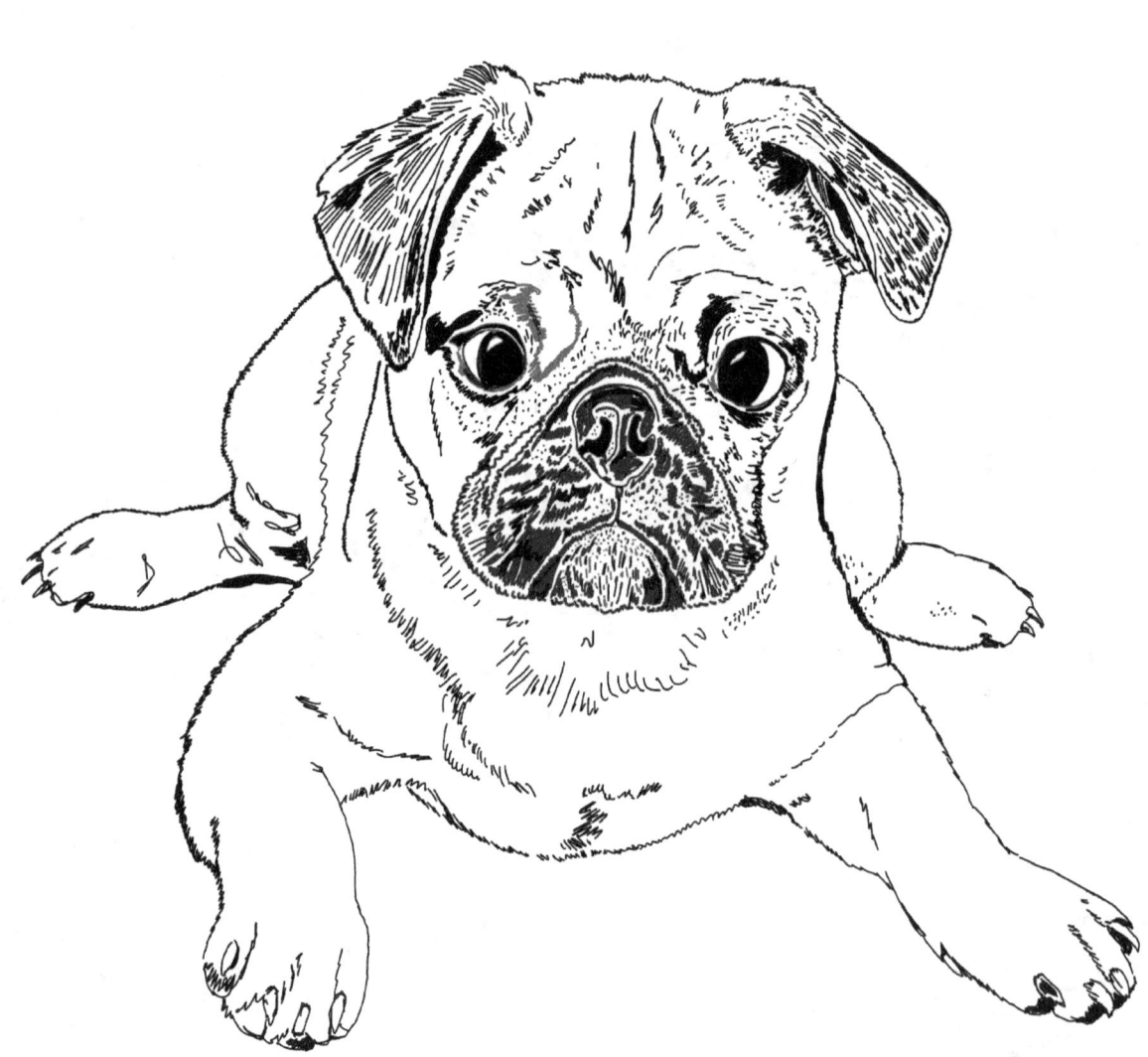

Puddles lived next door with her mommy, Mrs. O'Day. Mrs. O'Day loved Puddles and liked to feed him people cookies. When Mary Beth saw Puddles napping on his back porch she decided to practice drawing him. She also knew that there was a good chance that Mrs. O'Day might come out to play and bring cookies for Puddles and her.

Puddles woke up as Mary Beth was sketching him. He just stared at her. Puddles was a relaxed dog. He liked naps and food.

When Mrs. O'Day came out to play, she said, "Hi, Mary Beth, would you like some cookies and a juice box?"

"Thanks, Mrs. O'Day," Mary Beth said, without looking up from her art.

"What are you doing?" Mrs. O'Day asked.

"I have a new job, actually my first ever job. I draw dogs and sell my drawings," Mary Beth said.

"I'd love a drawing of Puddles," Mrs. O'Day smiled and said. "How much does it cost?"

"Not that much. I want to buy a hat," Mary Beth said.

"Sounds good," Mrs. O'Day said, as she went back into the house. "If I like it, I'll pay you a dollar for a drawing of my Puddles."

A few minutes later, Mary Beth said to Puddles, "Did your mommy say a dollar? Wow, she must really love you."

Advice from Mary Beth on how to draw Puddles.

The rough sections of
Puddles. Remember, draw
lightly with a pencil.

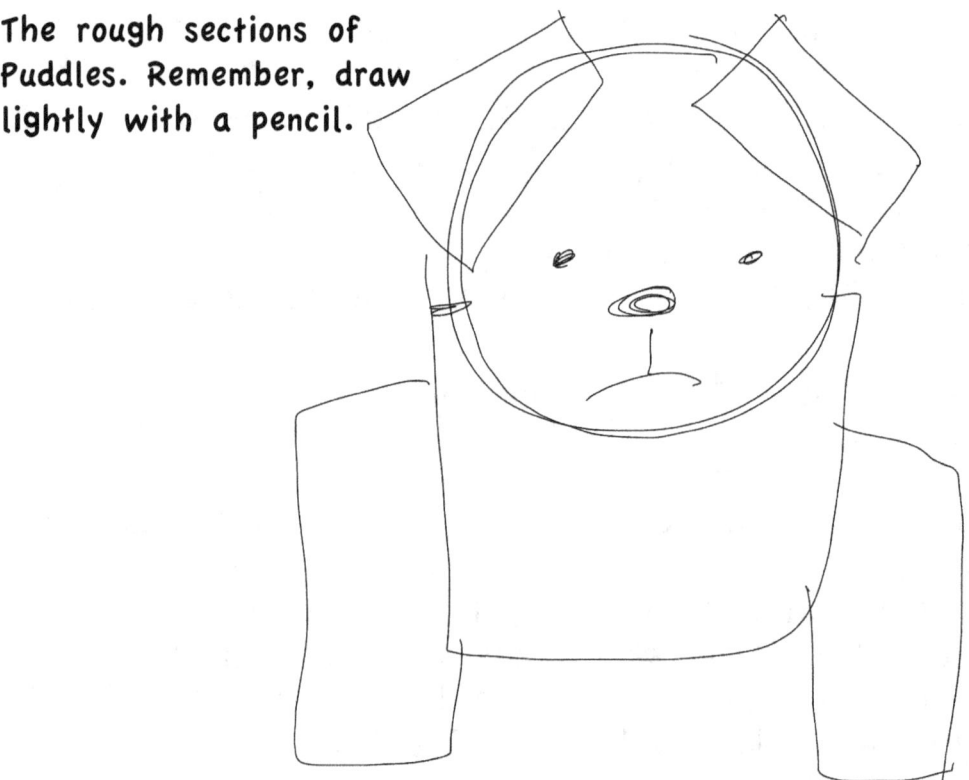

Puddles' ears and
eyes are about
here.

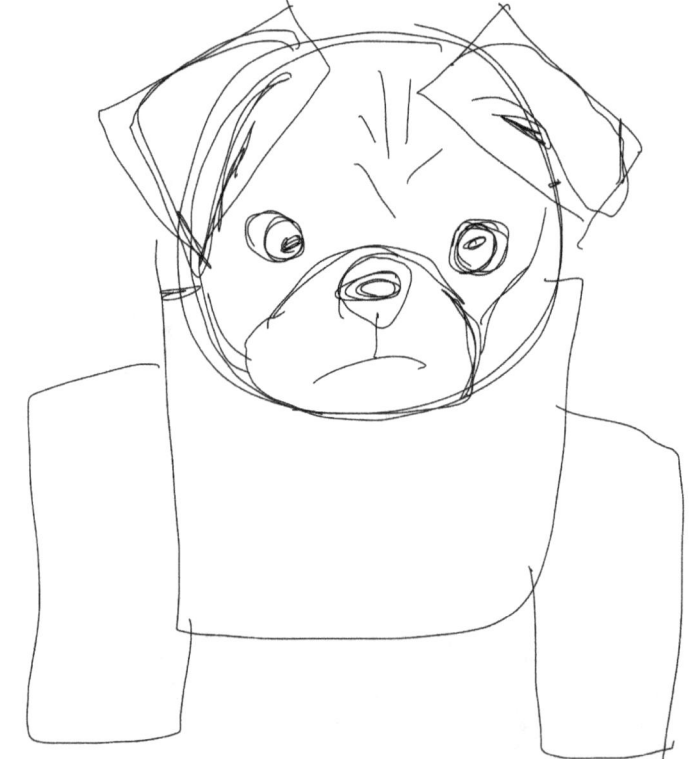

His legs need to be less boxy. He is lying down and relaxing.

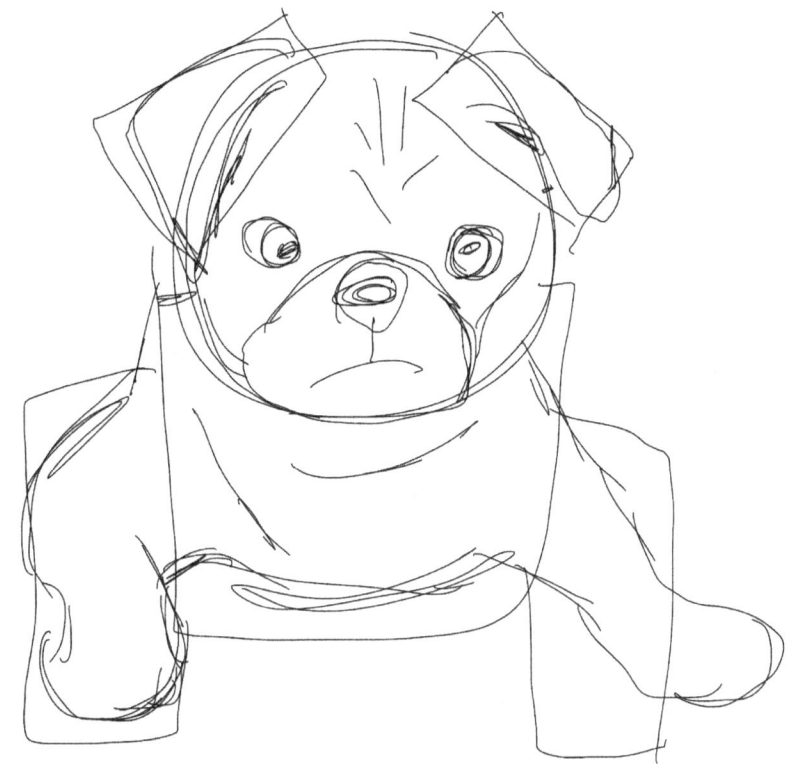

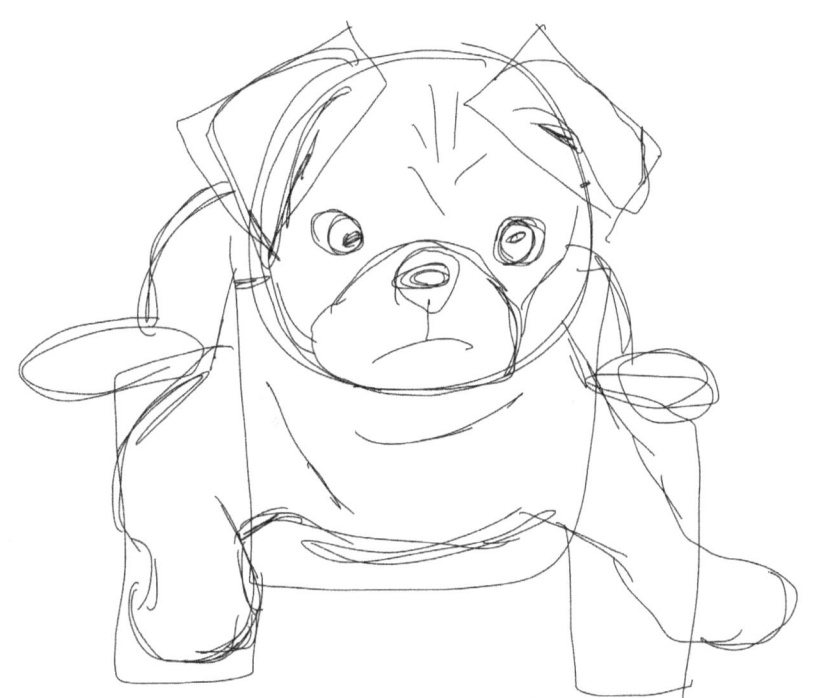

At this point I want to erase some of my first boxy guidelines.

Wow, after I cleaned up my lines, I noticed that
I left off the top of Puddles' head. OOOPS! Sorry
Puddles. But it is easy to fix.

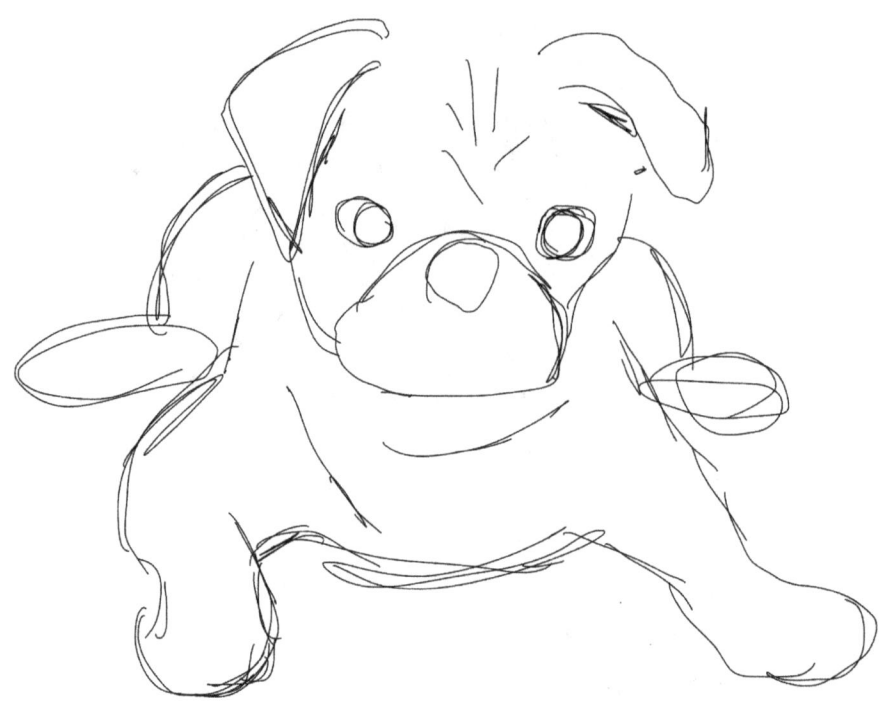

Now we draw more detail. Still drawing with a pencil. A lot of
drawing is really erasing the pencil lines you don't need any more.

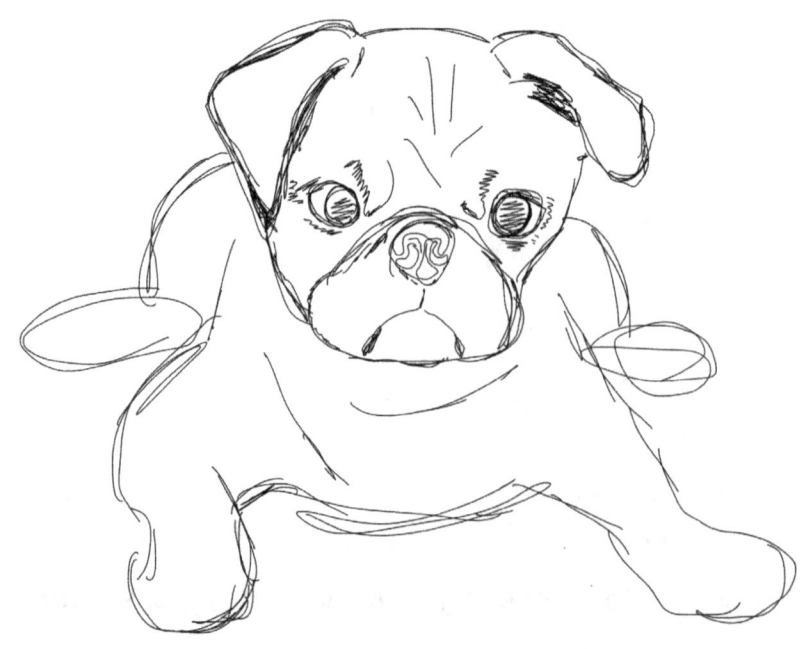

And even more detail.

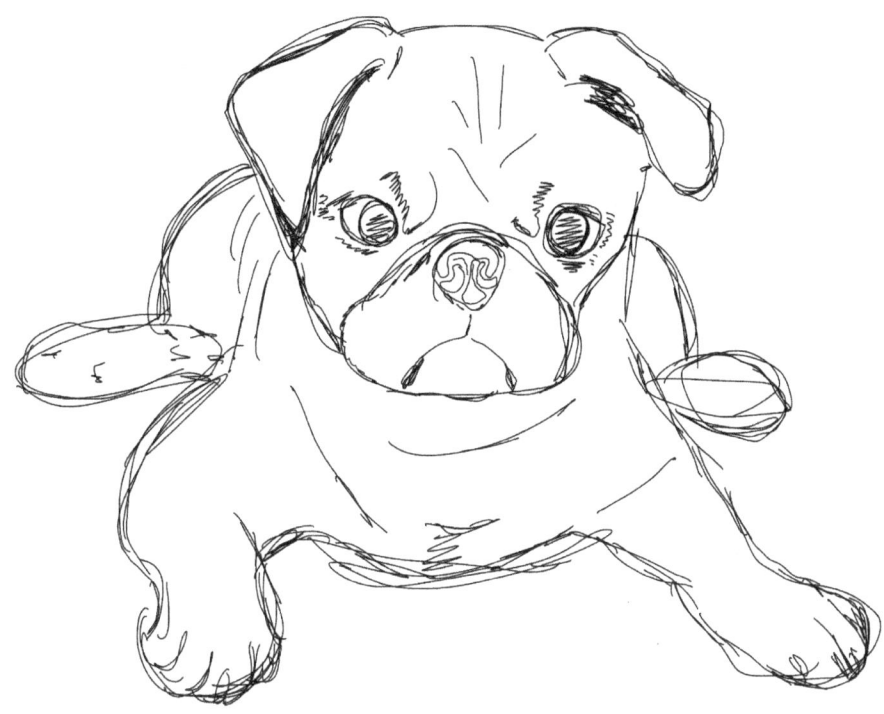

Now we are ready to pen over our pencil lines. Puddles the Proud Pug has scruffy fur. We want to add this texture to our art.

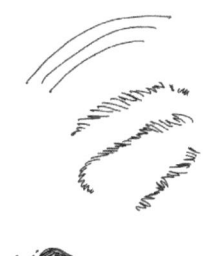
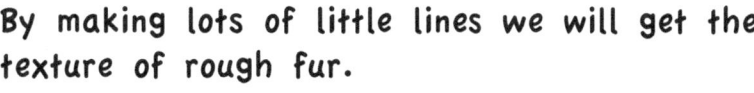

Straight lines do not give us the texture we will need.

By making lots of little lines we will get the texture of rough fur.

Because Puddles' nose is almost totally black we have to use blotches and dots to simulate Puddles' snout. The black dots allow us to fake light black without drawing Puddles' nose as a big black blob. The blotches and the dots let us see the black and the almost black parts of his snout.

Ear   Top of head

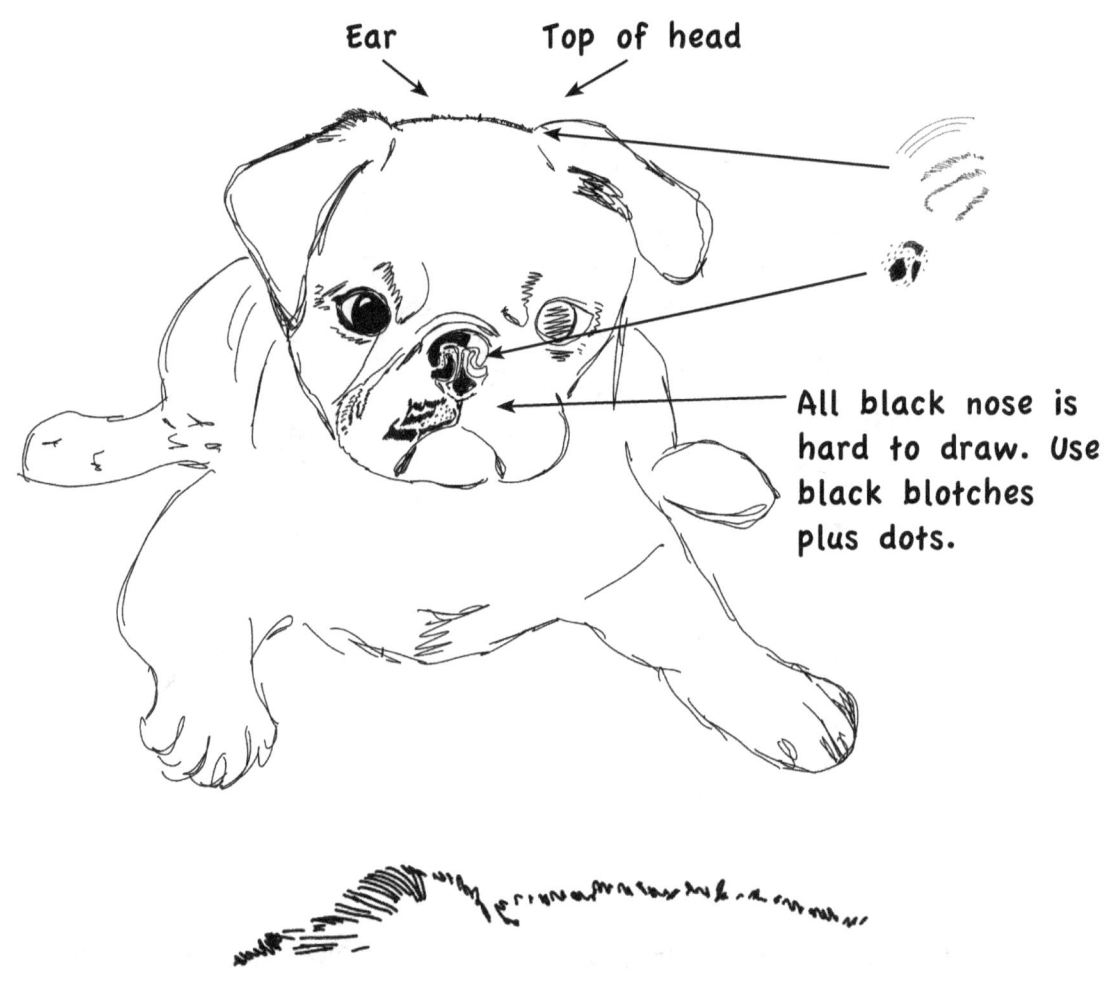

All black nose is
hard to draw. Use
black blotches
plus dots.

Take your time.

You will have to draw
lots of little lines, dark
blotches, and black dots.
But, it's worth it.

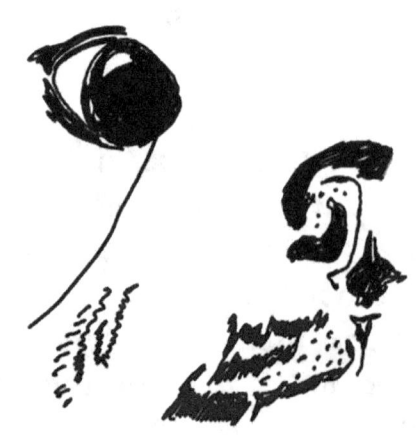

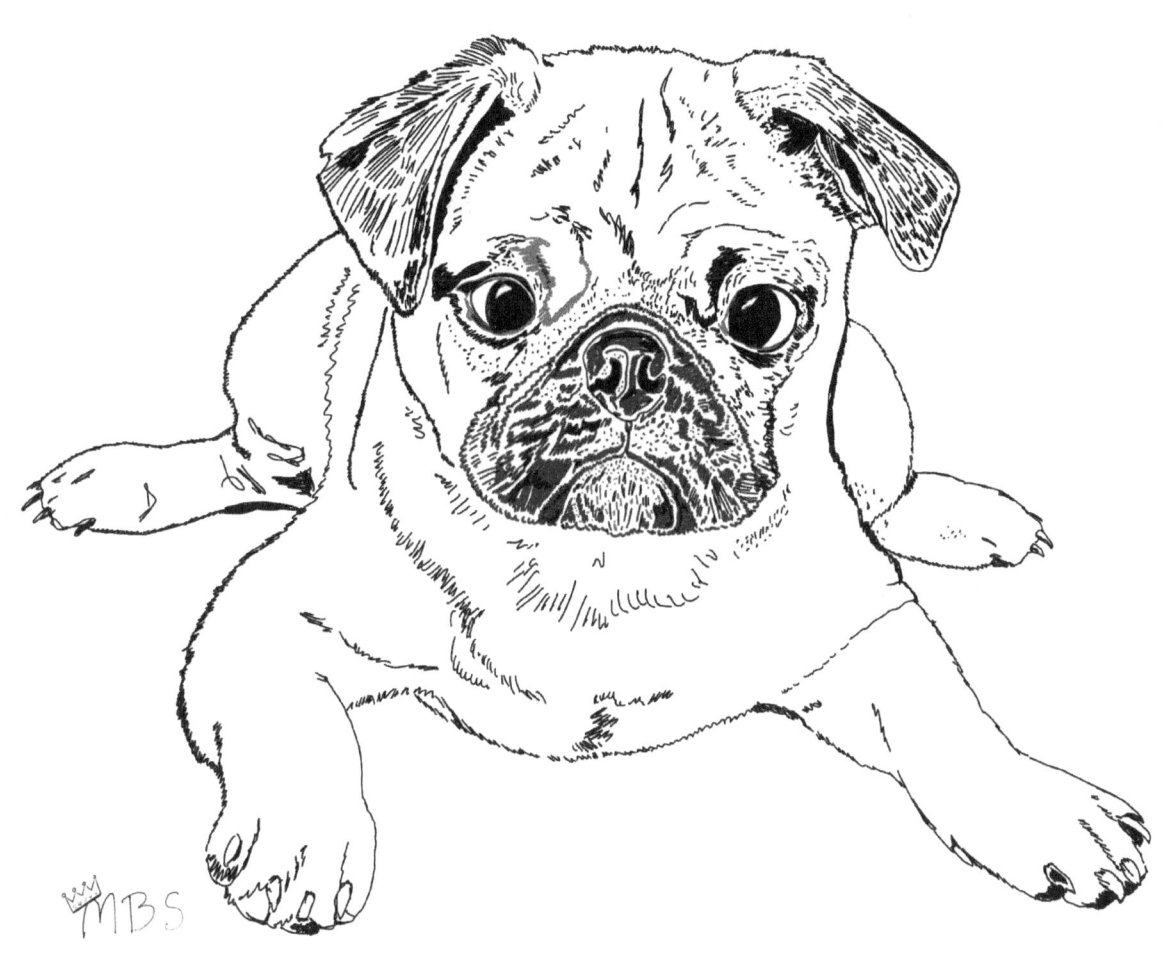

When Mary Beth was done with the drawing, she knocked on the door. Mrs. O'Day loved the drawing and kept saying, "Puddles, look at how cute you are." Mrs. O'Day gave Mary Beth a one dollar bill, two cookies, and a fun size bag of pretzels.

"Thanks, Mary Beth," Mrs. O'Day said. "I'm going to put this in a frame."

Mary Beth patted Puddles on the head, "See you later."

Puddles just stared at Mary Beth's cookies and drooled a little.

Chapter 8
How to draw a St. Bernard Dog

This is Washburn. He is a happy fellow. He weighs 240 pounds before dinner and 262.5 pounds after.

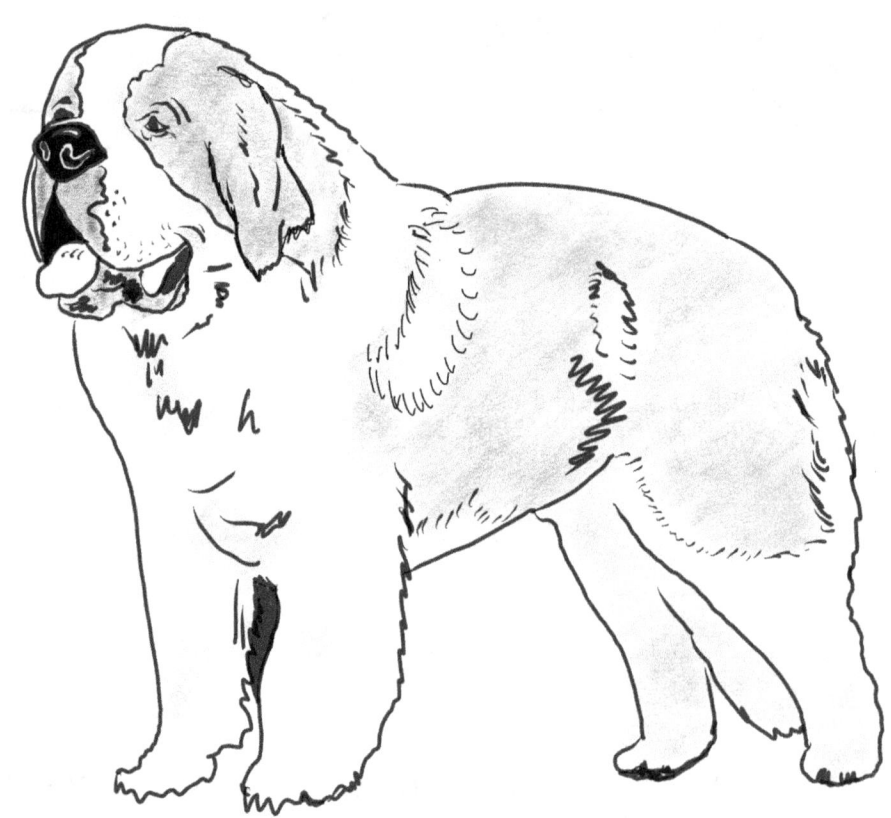

Washburn spent a lot of time lying under a giant oak tree in his backyard. Mary Beth liked Washburn because he was humongous but not scary. He did slobber though, but that was only really disgusting when Mr. Peterson was bringing him his dinner.

One day, Mary Beth was reading her read aloud homework to Washburn when Mr. Peterson came home. As the car pulled into the driveway Washburn started to smack his lips in anticipation of dinner. Washburn had extra large lips. At the back of his mouth, a slime started to build. It started to hang out of his mouth. It got longer and longer. Mr. Peterson called the really long ones "flingerflangers." 'Cause when Washburn shook his giant head the flingerflanger would be launched into flight. Head over heels it would fling. Whatever it landed on got flingerflangered; slimed by twelve inches of Washburn spit that wrapped around you and jiggled. It was thick, warm, and overly sticky. It only came off with a scrubbing in the bathtub.

This day it was worse. Washburn must have been super hungry. The flingerflangers were fourteen inches long, when he shook his rotund noggin, they swayed and got longer. They grew to sixteen inches on either side of Washburn's cheeks. Mary Beth hid behind Mr. Peterson who had no place to hide. He did his best to cover himself by flailing his arms about.

Then it happed, the flingerflangers grew to seventeen inches. Washburn shook his head harder, Mr. Peterson yelled, "No!" as the flingerflangers flung. They elongated up and around but never let go of Washburn's giant back lips. They flung around his huge snout picking up speed as they got even longer. They wrapped not once, but twice. The sound "splat" rang out as first one then the other landed on Washburn's wide fuzzy forehead. When he blinked his eyelashes made the phlegm move up and down. Washburn flingerflangered himself.

As Mr. Peterson unwrapped flingerflangers from Washburn's face, Mary Beth pondered that this was only the seventh grossest thing she had seen in her life, so she decided that she had no need to throw up.

"It is best to save throwing up for the grossest stuff," she told Mr. Peterson who didn't seem to hear.

While Mr. Peterson was hosing off Washburn's face, Mary Beth told him about her job. He was happy to buy a drawing of Washburn, as long as there were no flingerflangers.

Advice from Mary Beth on how to draw Washburn.

Rough drawing. We use circles and blocks to give us
an idea of the whole dog. This is done with a very
light pencil touch. Remember, all the pencil lines will
be erased, so the lighter the better.

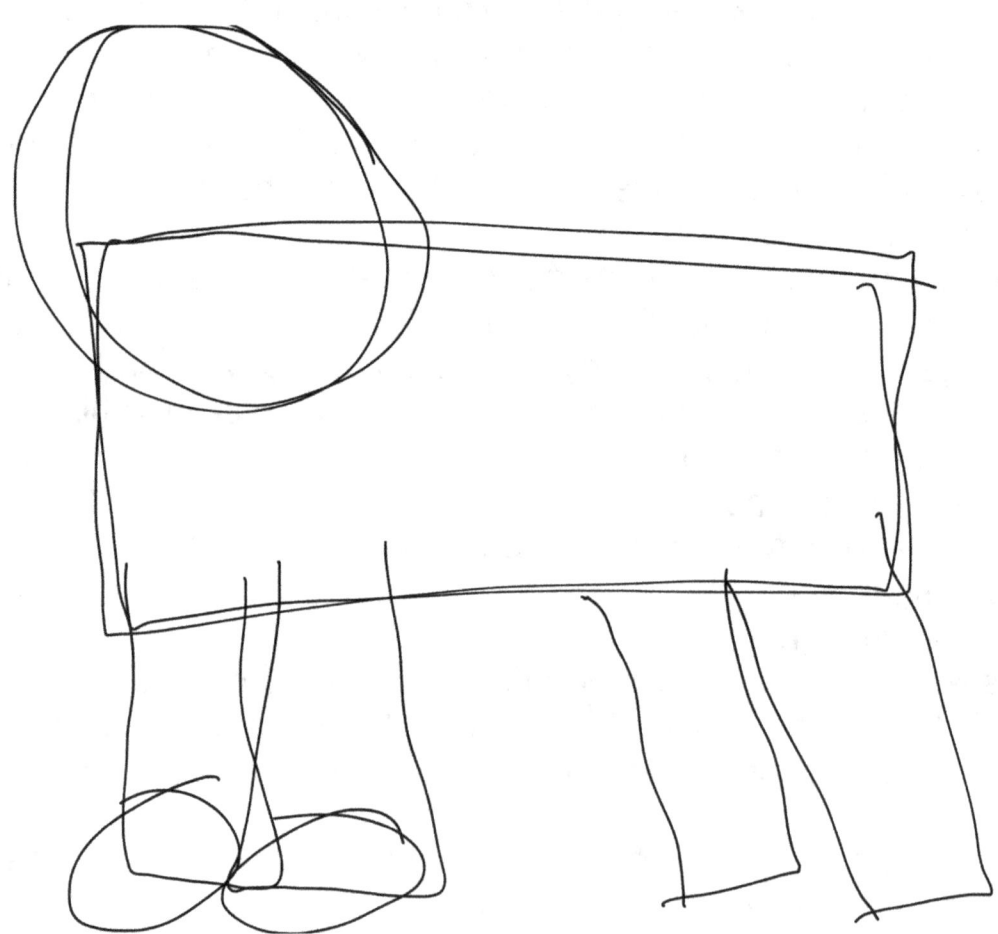

Now we lightly start to draw in the head shape.

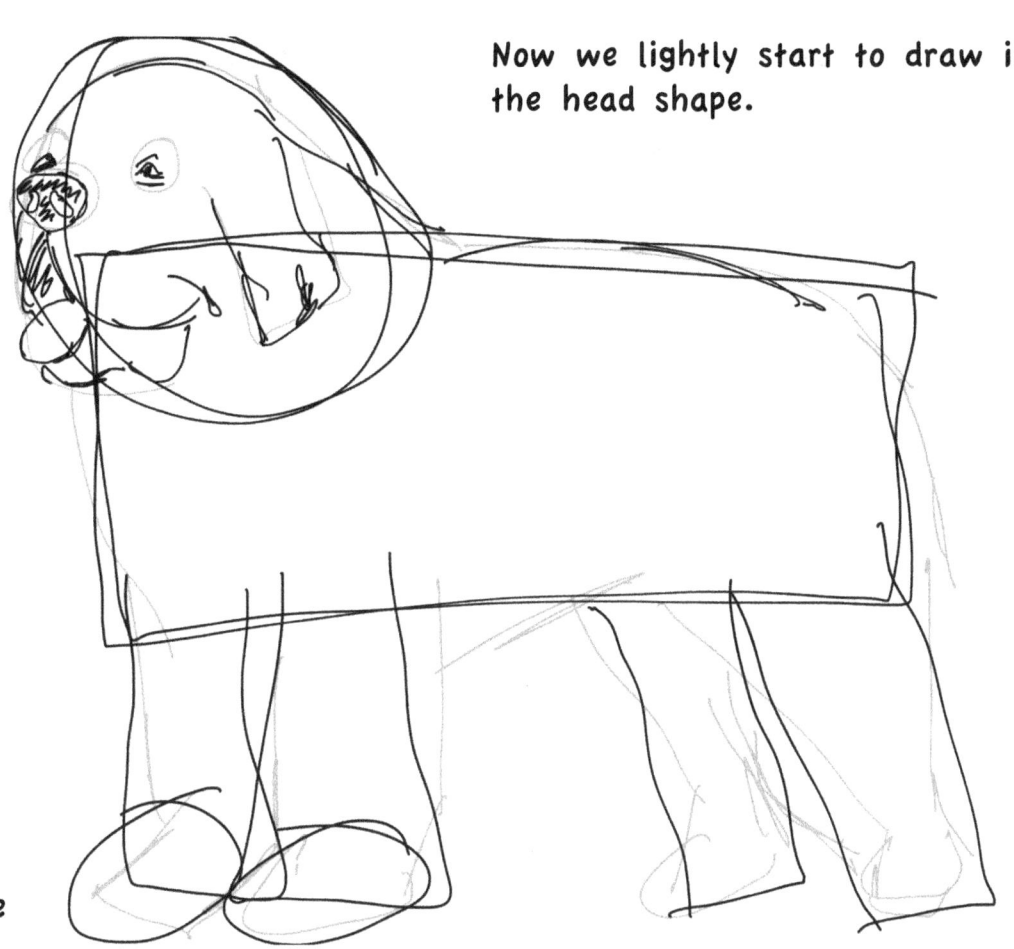

And the body shape.

Gently erase the boxy guides. This makes it easier to see what we are doing.

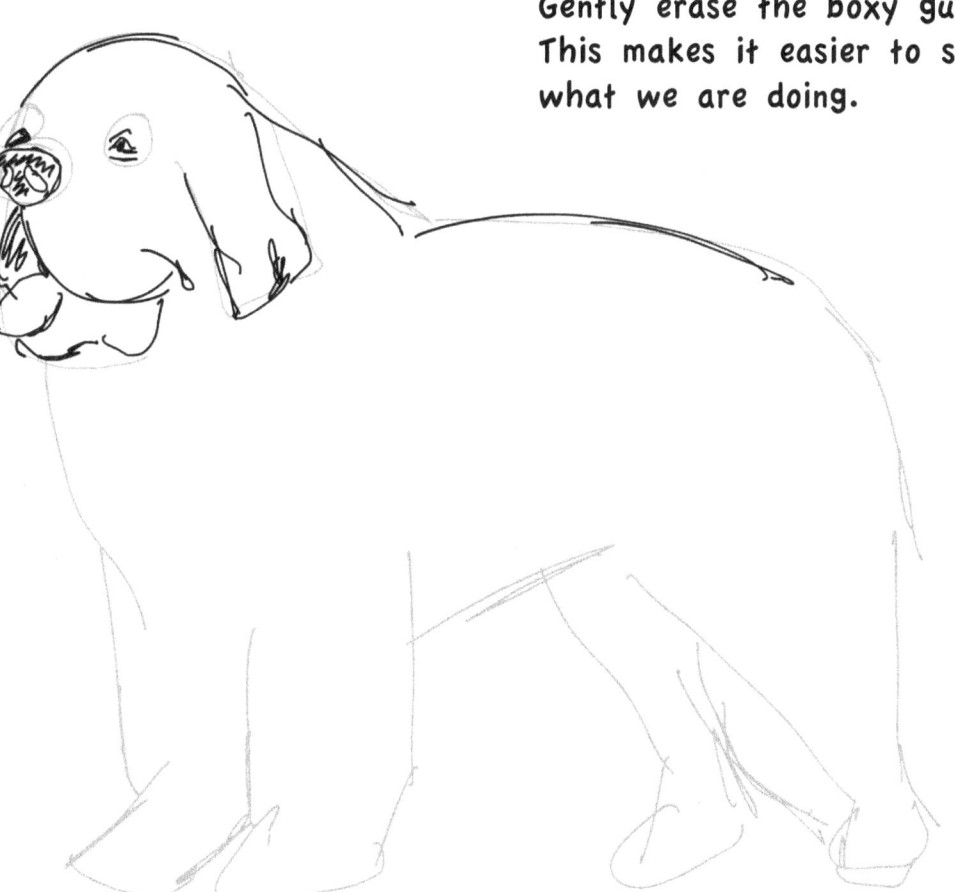

A lot of drawing is erasing.

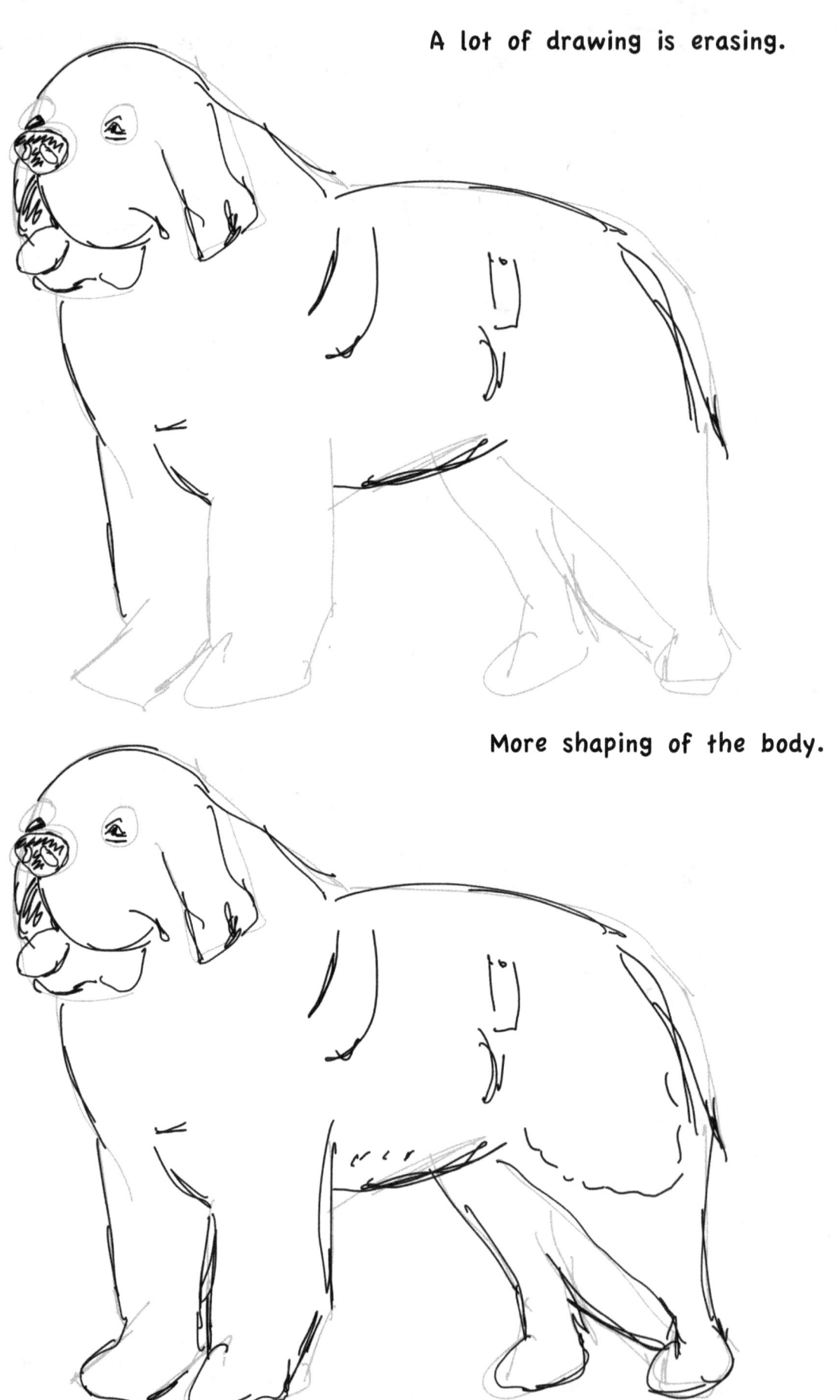

More shaping of the body.

Now we pen over the lines we like.

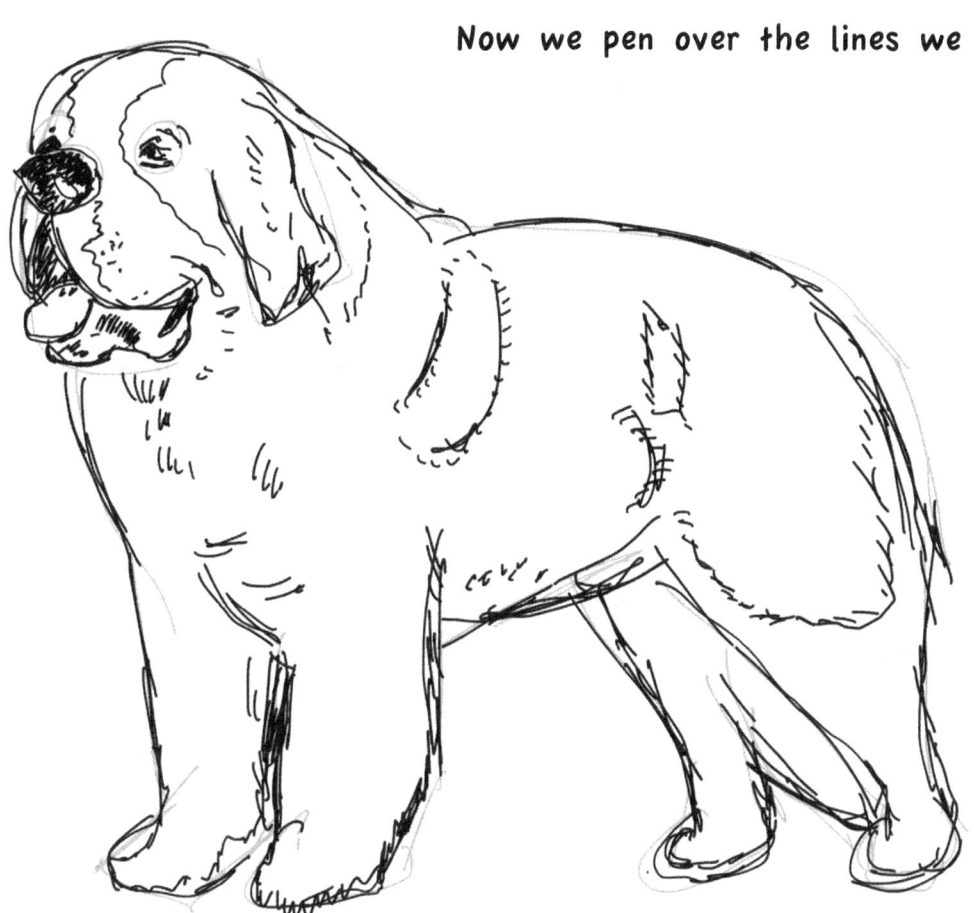

Carefully erase the pencil.

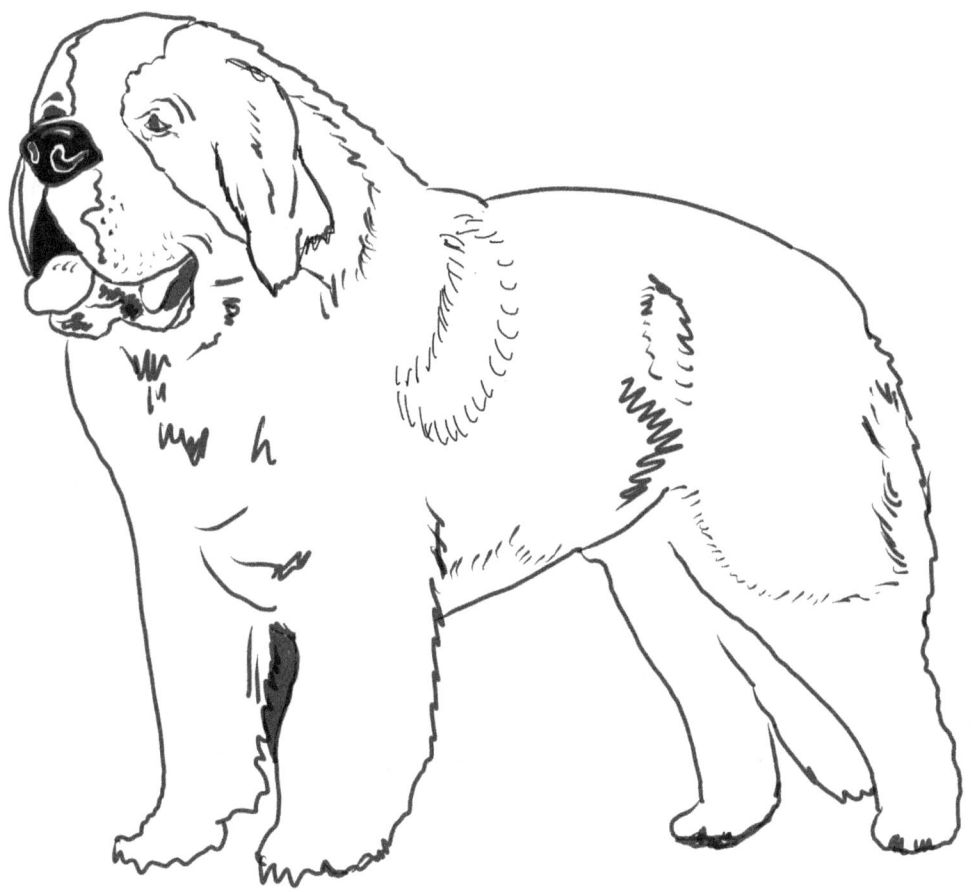

Our St. Bernard is looking good. Now we can shade in gray or use colored pencils to add color.

We can shade the body by using the side of our pencil point. It is usually better to go over your shading many times to make it darker instead of pressing hard with your pencil.

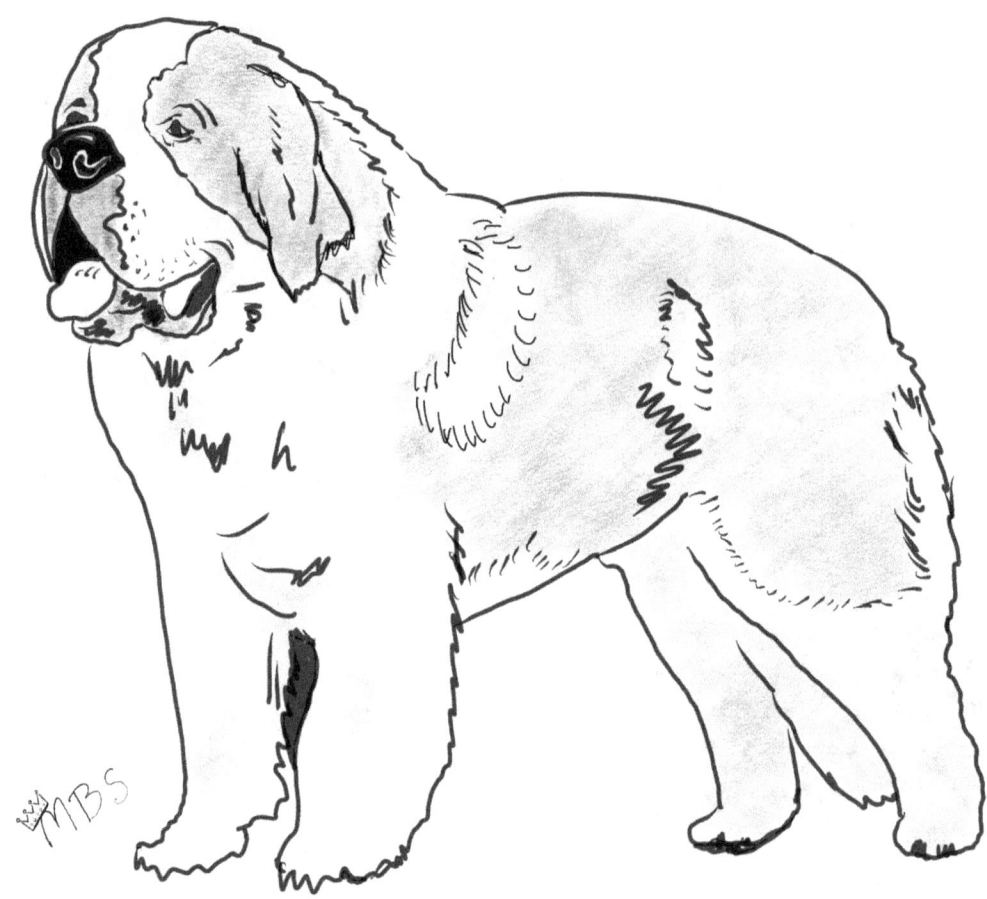

Mr. Peterson loved Mary Beth's drawing of Washburn. When he found out that his neighbor, Mrs. O'Day, had paid a dollar he said, "Washburn is a magnificent dog, so much bigger than Puddles. I think $5.00 seems about right."

Mary Beth walked home with her new $5.00 bill. She didn't know what to think. She drew Washburn on the same size paper as she did Puddles. She liked making $5.00. She had never made $5.00 before. She thought, *I wonder how many hats I can get for $5.00?*

Chapter 9
How to draw a Bulldog

This is Mrs. Harrington, the Bulldog. She is a powerful dog for her size. She is all muscle and charm. A little mischievous but never naughty.

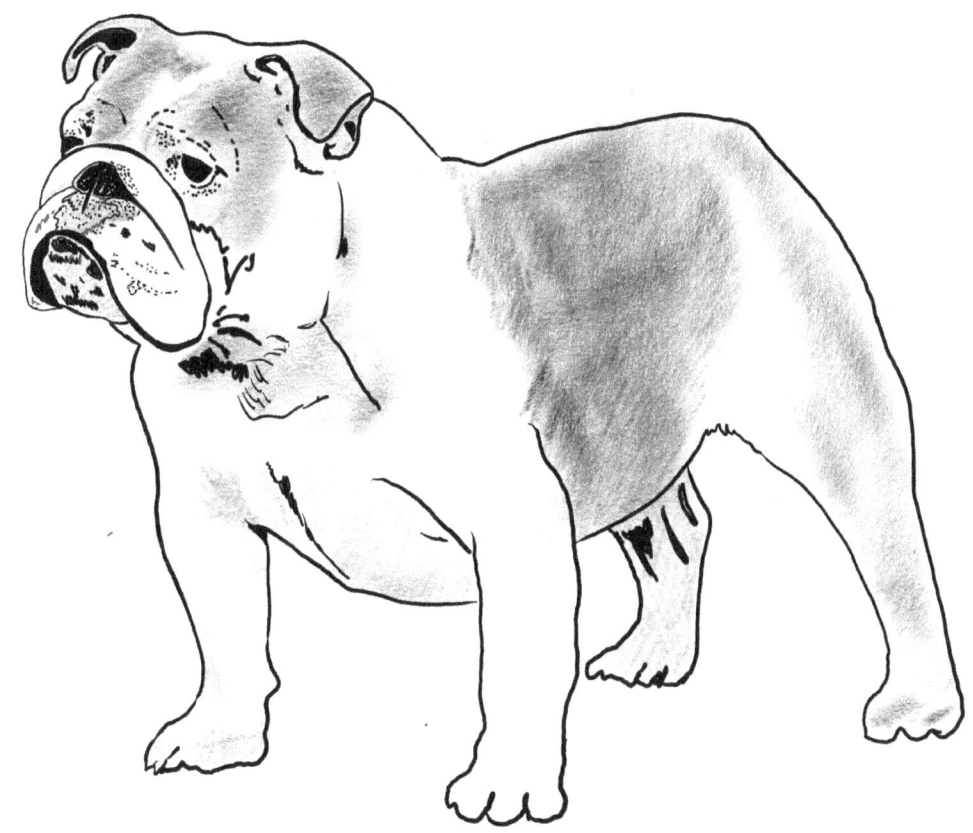

Mrs. Harrington was a Bulldog. She was proud and strong and always acted like a dignified lady—except for the way she sneezed. Her sneeze was not ladylike. It was more military cannon like.

Mrs. Harrington's sneeze was a grand performance. First she screwed up her face while standing stiffly at attention. Then she performed two warm up sneezes, little snotty toots, followed by ten quick eye blinks and lots of throat swallows. At this point, Mrs. Harrington was ready for the grand finale. She took a deep breath and *cachoooooo*. Stuff came out with such force her whole body was blown backwards: two inches if she was on carpet, five if she was on the kitchen tile. Following the eruption, Mrs. Harrington looked around rapidly, barking, as if she was trying to figure out where all that cannon noise came from.

Mrs. Harrington was sleeping in her backyard by the signs that read PIZZA and By the Slice. Mrs. Harrington's dad owned a pizza parlor over by the high school. It was a fun place with video games and large bathrooms that echoed. He also had a huge trailer for selling pizza at the football games and on the 4th of July.

Mary Beth sat down and started to draw Mrs. Harrington. As a model, Mrs. Harrington was better than most. She stood calmly and only once tried to help draw by gnawing on Mary Beth's favorite 2H pencil.

"Hi, Mary Beth," the Pizza King said. "What you up to?"

"I'm a business woman. I draw dogs for money."

"Draw dogs do ya, how fun. And people pay you?"

"Yep, my mom says that I have to make money if I want to buy hats, because she doesn't have any money."

Mary Beth showed her drawing of Mrs. Harrington to Mr. King.

"Wow, that's pretty good, how much?"

"How much do you want to give me for it?" Mary Beth smiled.

"Wow, I see I'm up against a shrewd negotiator. How about a trade?" Mr. King said.

"A trade?"

"Sure, business owners trade services all the time. How about if I give you a large pizza for your drawing of the best dog in the whole wide world."

"I don't buy pizza, I'm a kid. My mom buys the pizza."

"Oh, you're a good negotiator. OK, my final offer: three large pizzas, but not a penny more. You can take your family out for dinner."

"That would be fun. OK, I guess," Mary Beth thought out loud.

A few minutes later, Mr. King gave her three pizza gift certificates.

When she got home, Mary Beth told her mom that she wasn't sure if she made a good trade.

"Mary Beth, you seem to have a knack for business. A large pizza at Pizza King is over twenty bucks. You sold your drawing for well over $60. Do you want to take your old tired mommy and daddy out for pizza tonight?"

"Sure," Mary Beth said. "I wonder if I can get one of those paper hats that says PIZZA KING, like the employees get to wear?"

Advice from Mary Beth on how to draw Mrs. Harrington.

We start with a rough drawing. We use blocks to give us an idea of the whole dog. This is done with a very light pencil touch. Remember all the pencil lines will be erased so the lighter the better.

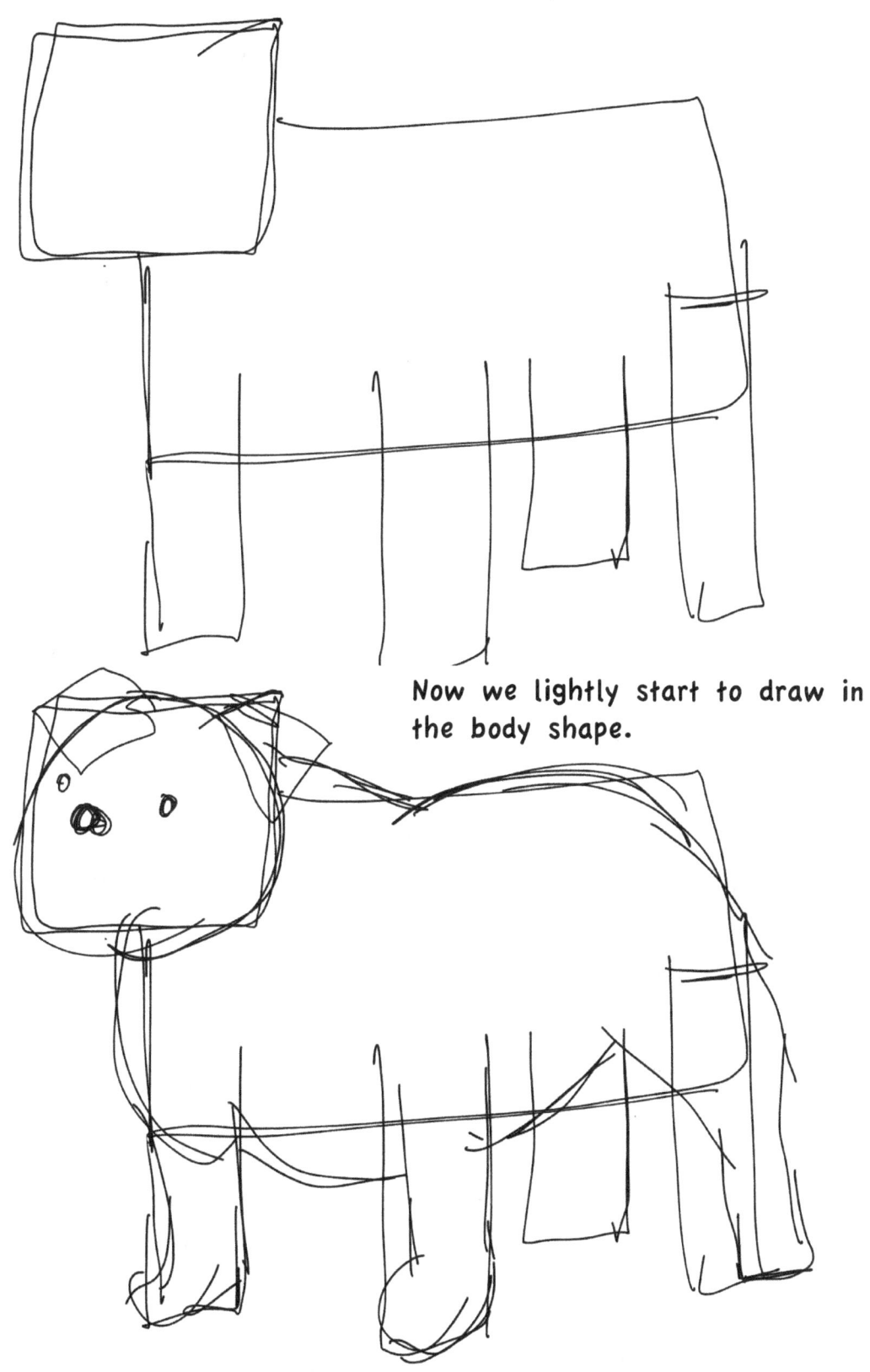

Now we lightly start to draw in the body shape.

Gently erase the boxy guides. This makes it easier to see what we are doing as we add a little detail to Mrs. Harrington's face.

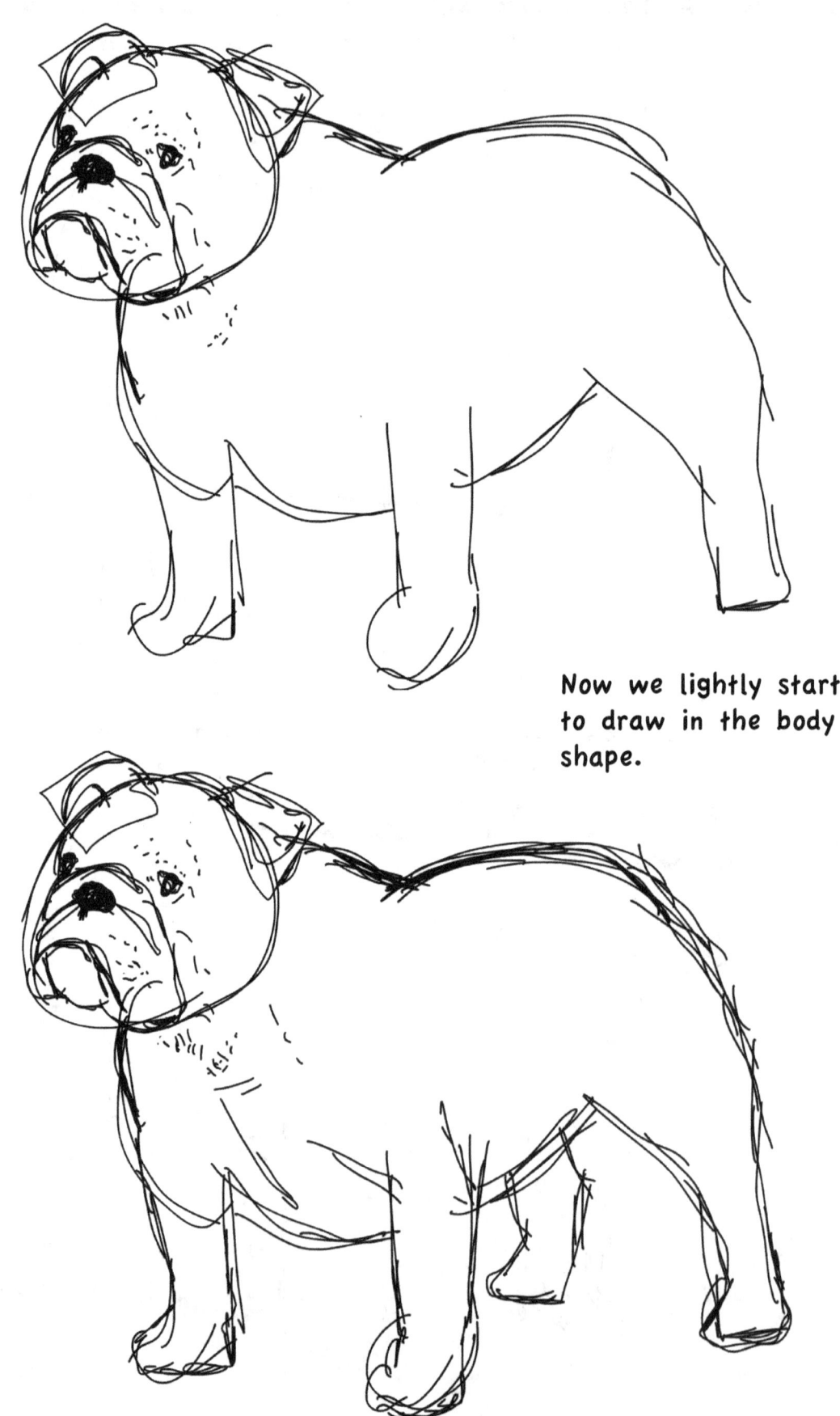

Now we lightly start to draw in the body shape.

More shaping of the body.

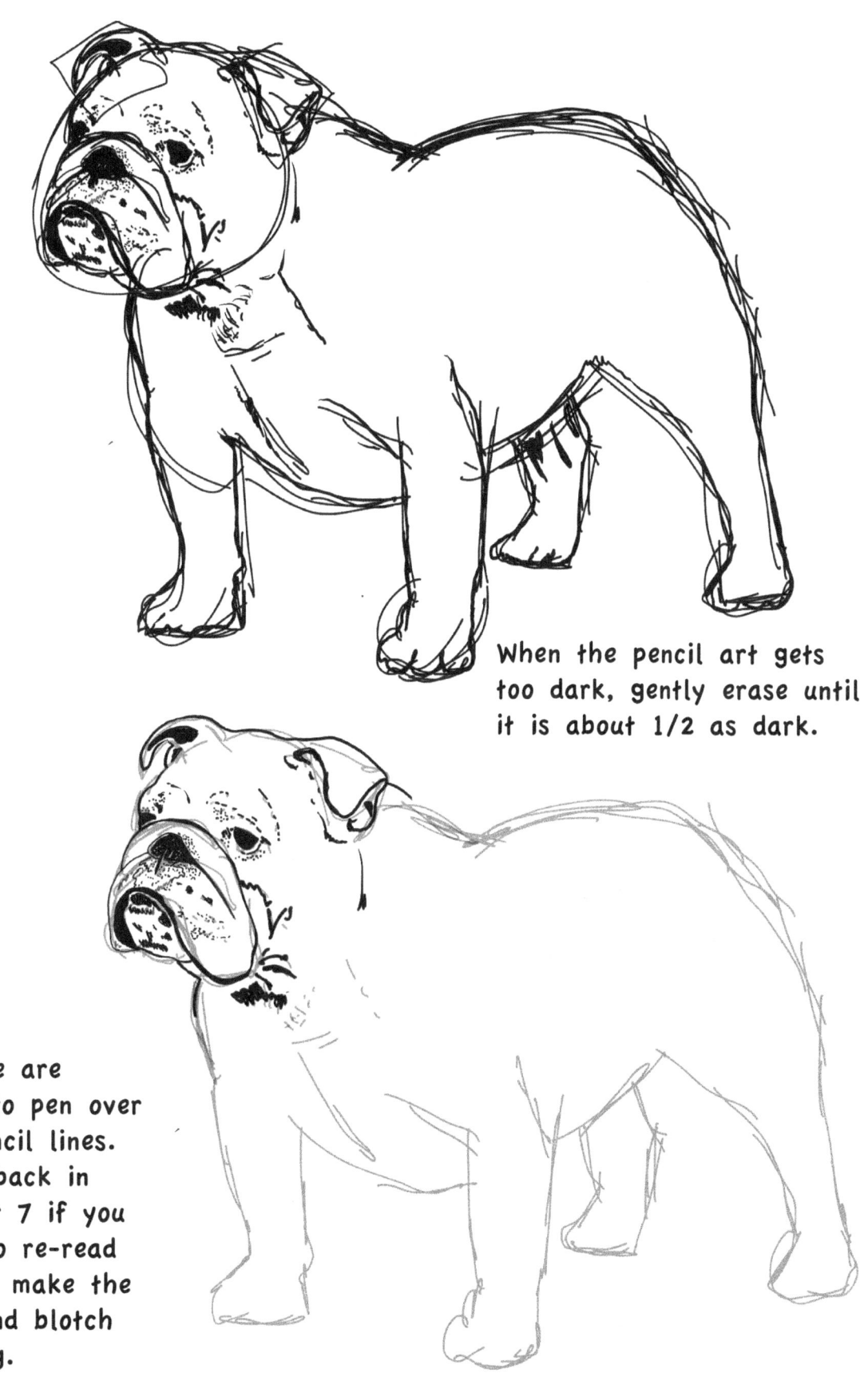

When the pencil art gets too dark, gently erase until it is about 1/2 as dark.

Now we are ready to pen over our pencil lines. Check back in Chapter 7 if you want to re-read how to make the nose and blotch coloring.

More shaping of the body with the pen.

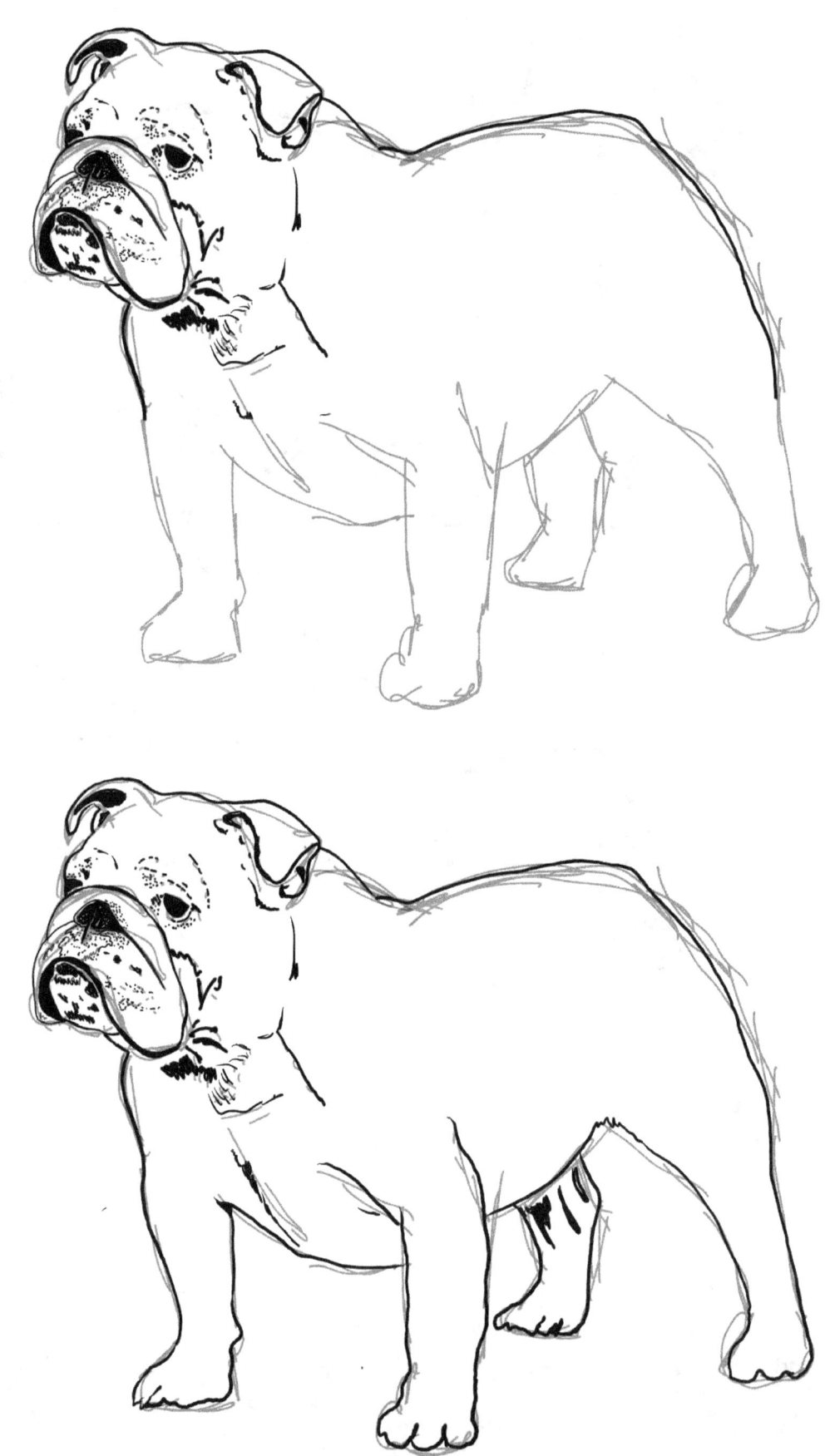

Now we are ready to erase the guidelines. This allows Mrs. Harrington to jump off the page...

even though she is too much of a lady to actually jump.

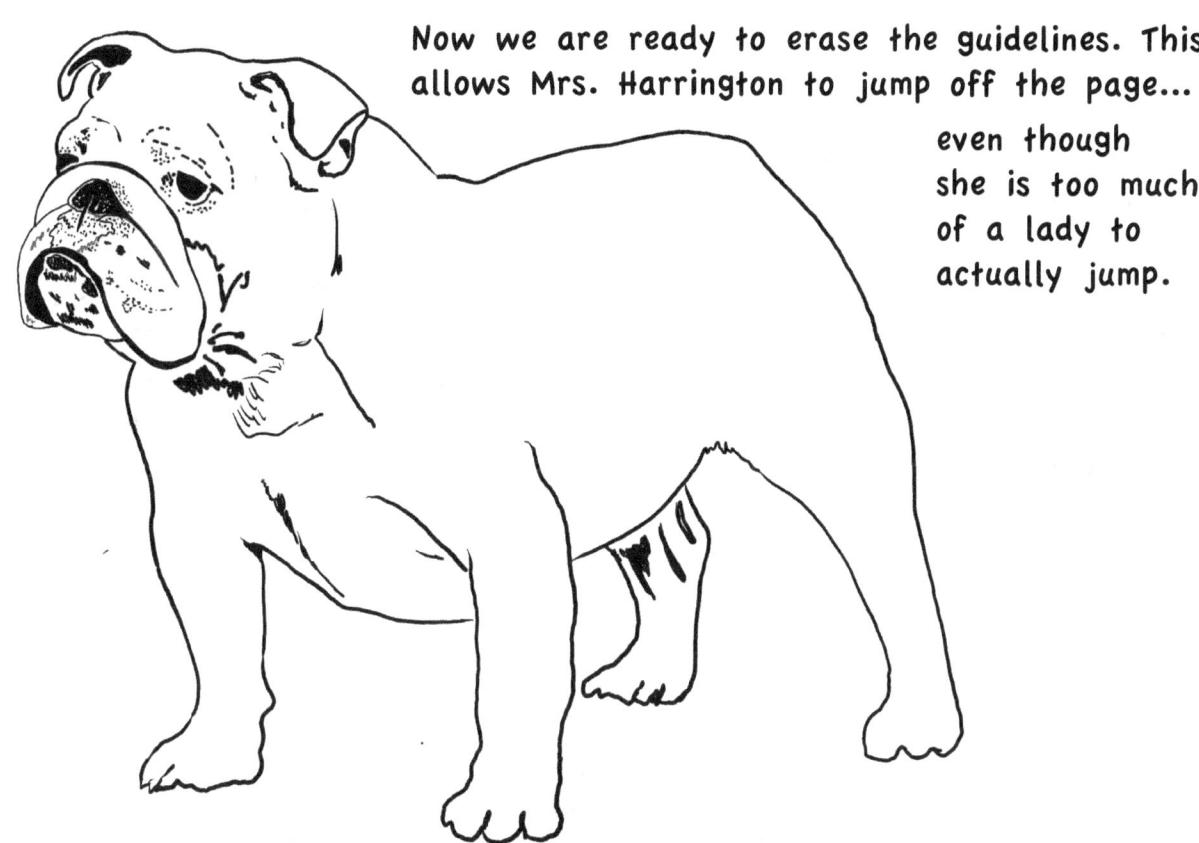

We can shade the body by using the side of our pencil point. It is usually better to go over your shading many times to make it darker instead of pressing hard with your pencil one time.

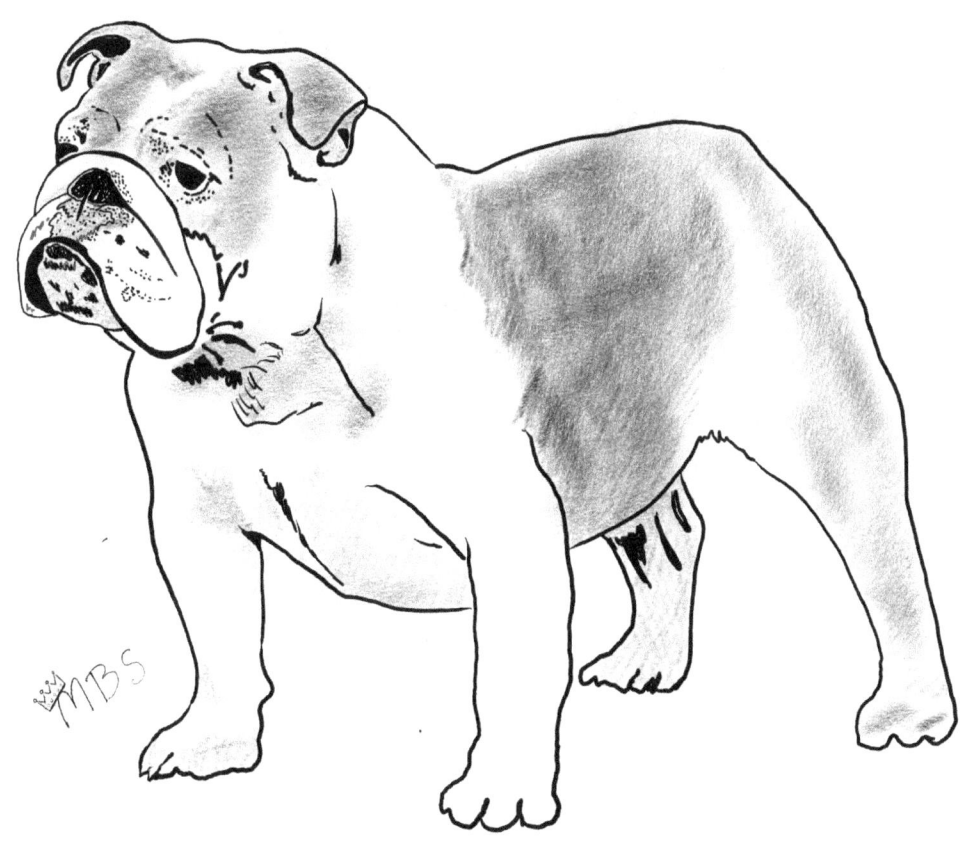

Chapter 10
How to draw a Beagle

This is Barry the Beagle. He is a puppy not even one year old. Mary Beth wanted to draw a portrait of Barry. A portrait drawing tends to be only the head, face, and shoulders of your model. Mary Beth chose to draw a portrait of Barry because he has dreamy eyes. By only drawing Barry's head, she had enough room on the page to show how adorable Barry truly is.

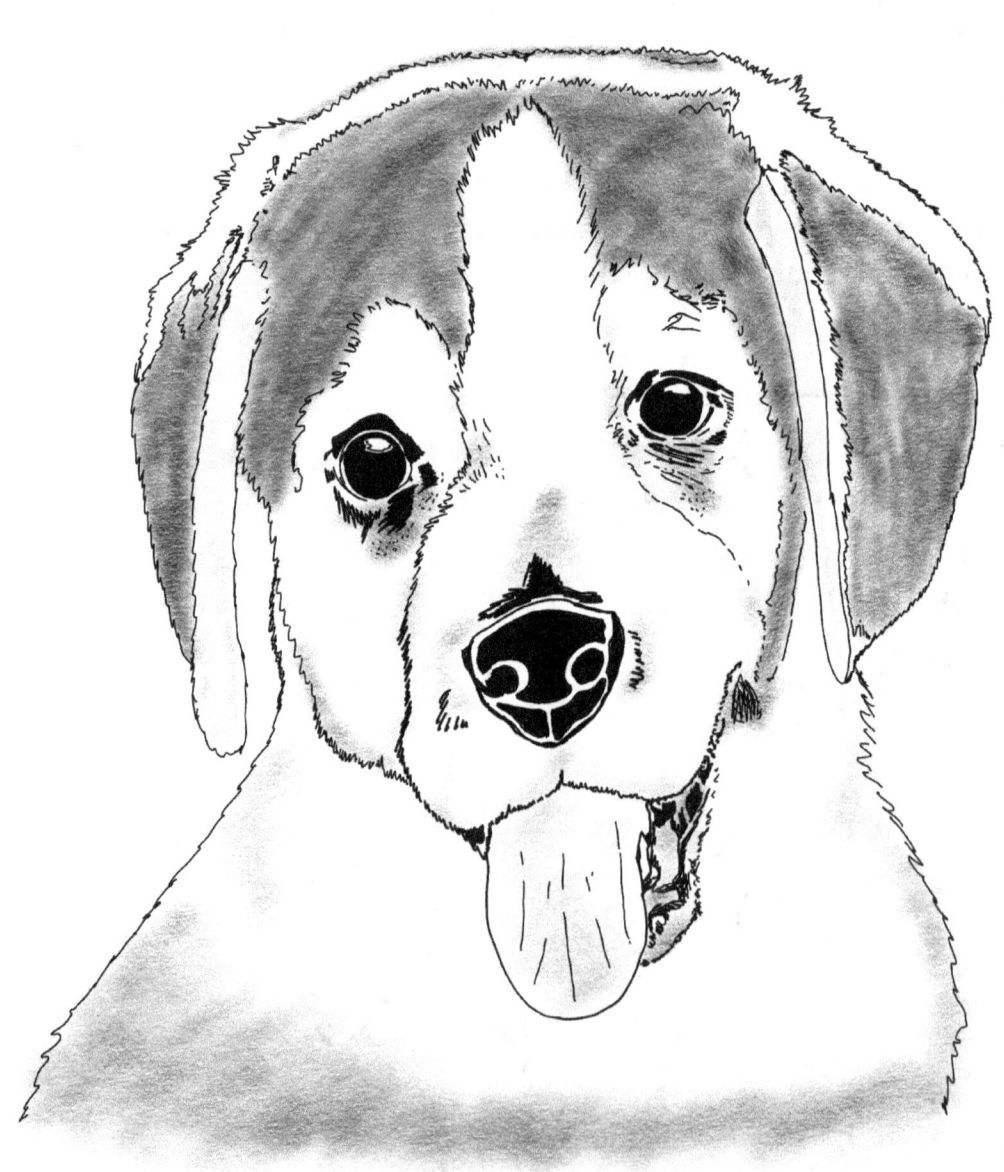

It was a nice summer day so Mary Beth went down to the park at the end of the cul-de-sac. The rules at the park insisted that dogs must be on a leash. Mary Beth and Jazz think this is a dumb rule so Mary Beth puts a leash on Jazz, but doesn't hold it. Instead, she drapes it over Jazz's back like a boring decoration.

As she sat on the swing, Mary Beth saw Juanita and her new puppy, Barry.

"Nice hat, Mary Beth. Are you working at Pizza King now?" Juanita asked, with a huge smile.

"Nah, Mr. King gave me a few the other night. He even gave me two hairpins to hold them on my head," Mary Beth said.

"I've always liked your style, MB."

"Thanks, but I have a problem. Now that you're in high school I figure you know lots," Mary Beth said.

"I hope I can help. What's up?"

"I've started a dog drawing business, but when people ask me how much I charge, I don't ever seem to know."

"I've been working at the county fair selling giant corn dogs on a stick. I don't know how they got the price, but it's too much. $6.50 for a corn dog! But we sell a lot. The manager doesn't talk about the price, but he barks constantly about upsell," Juanita said, with a scrunched face.

"Upsell," Mary Beth repeated.

"Yeah, the manager is a broken record. He says the same two things like a million times a shift. 'If you have time to lean, you have time to clean' and 'Always upsell!'"

"Upsell?"

"You know, when the customer orders a corn dog you have to say, 'Do you want fries with that, sir?' If they say 'yes', you upsell again, 'Do you want a drink with that, sir?'"

"So as I sell you one thing, I sell you more of something else. Like, Juanita do you want a drawing of Barry?"

"Yeah, actually I do," Juanita smiled. "Can you draw his dreamy eyes?"

"Sure, and do you want fries with that, ma'am?"

The two girls hugged and giggled.

"I don't see fries being a good upsell," Juanita said, "but maybe you could offer to do dog drawings on Christmas or Get Well cards?"

Jazz and Barry laid next to each other gently rubbing faces.

Advice from Mary Beth on how to draw Barry the Beagle

Let's start with a circle to show where the model's head goes. Then we add a large plus sign to help figure out where the eyes will go. The plus is a little lower than half way down the head. A second circle shows where the snout goes.

Here we have the idea of a head, snout, and floppy ears.

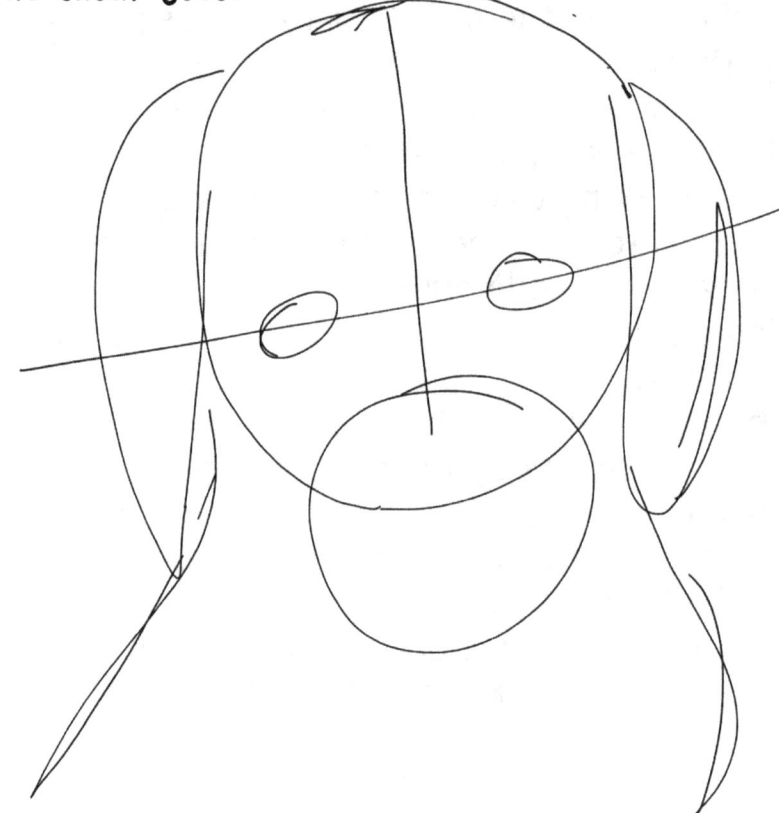

A few more very light lines help us see Barry's basic shape.

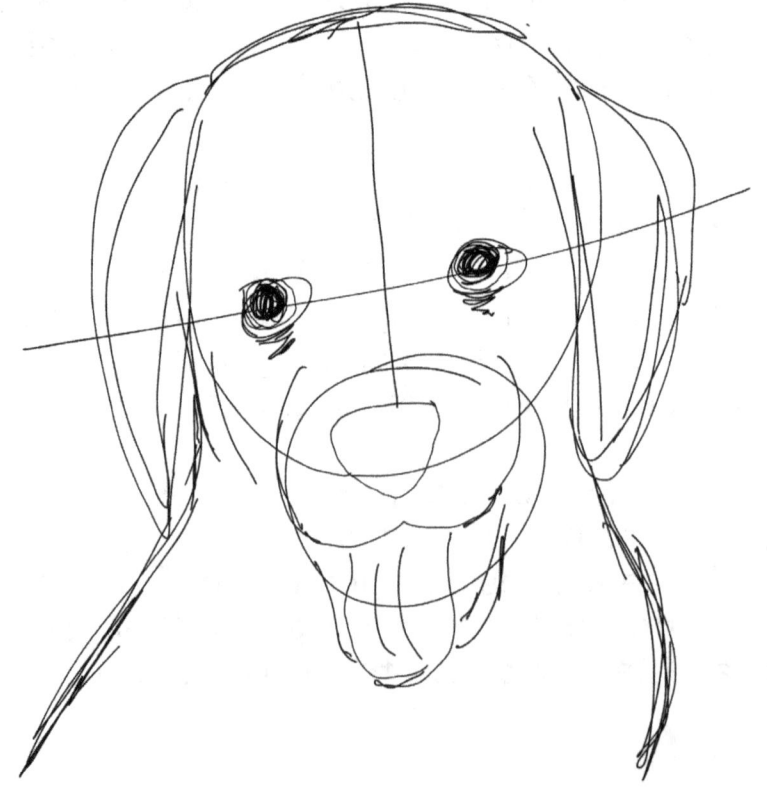

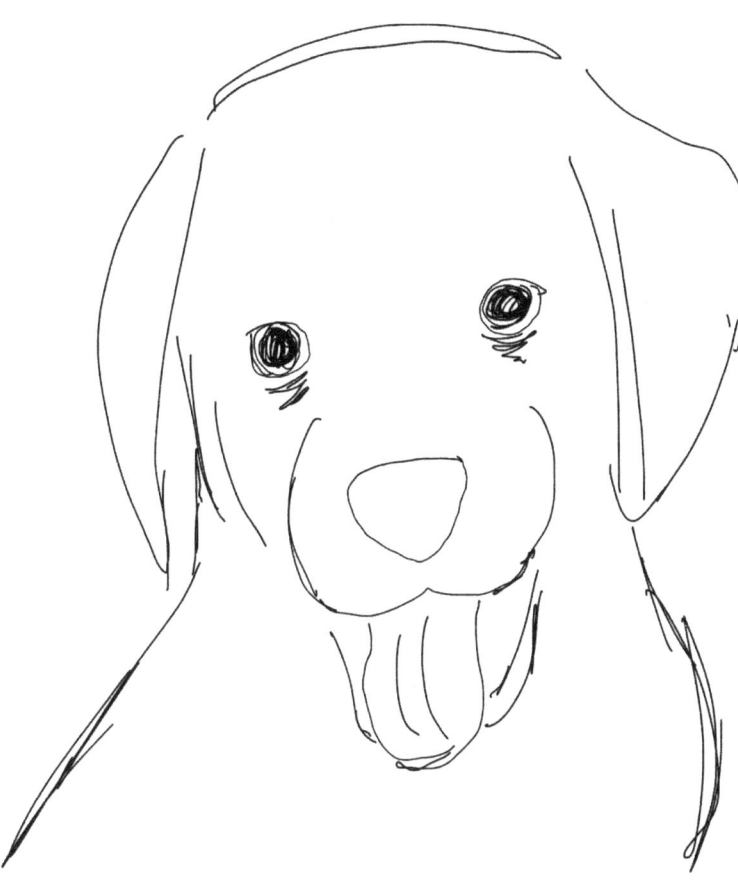

When the pencil art gets too dark, gently erase it so it is about half as dark and half as messy.

Here we keep adding detail to Barry's head.

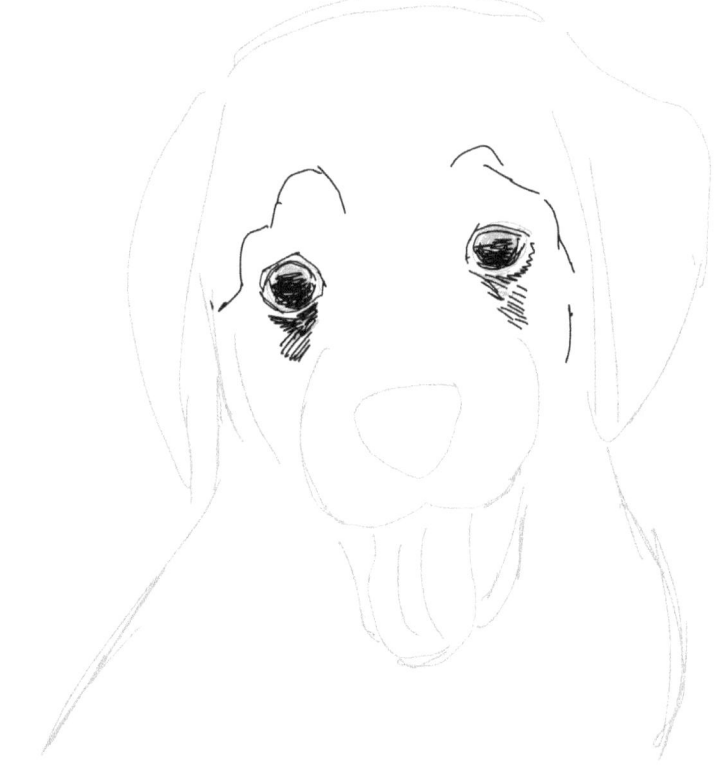

A little more
detail on the
nose and mouth.

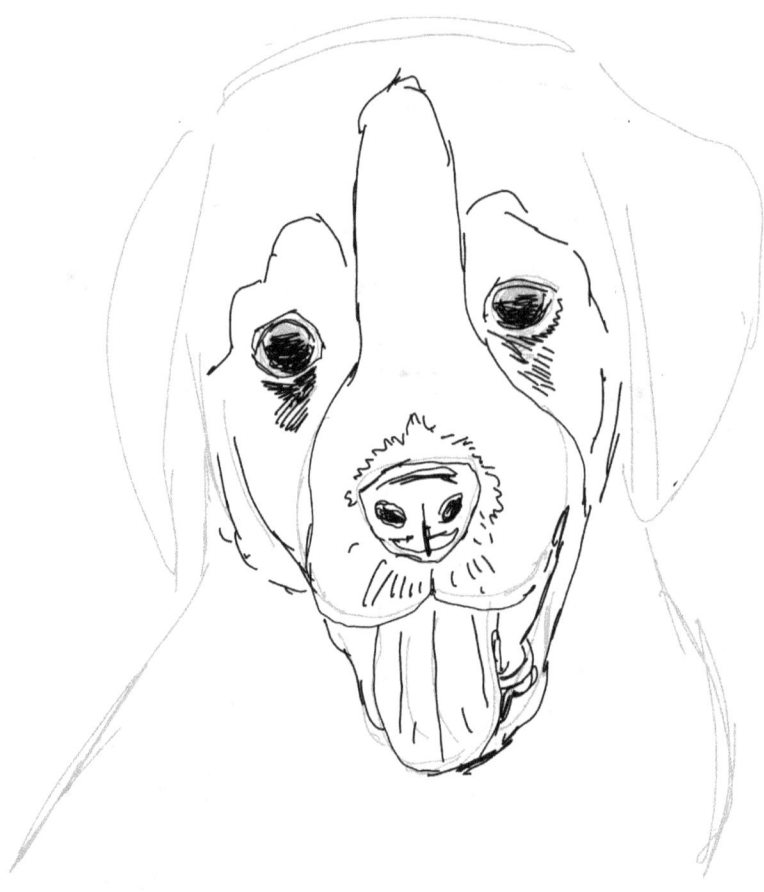

Now we work
on the eyes
and face so we
get an idea of
where the parts
of Barry are.

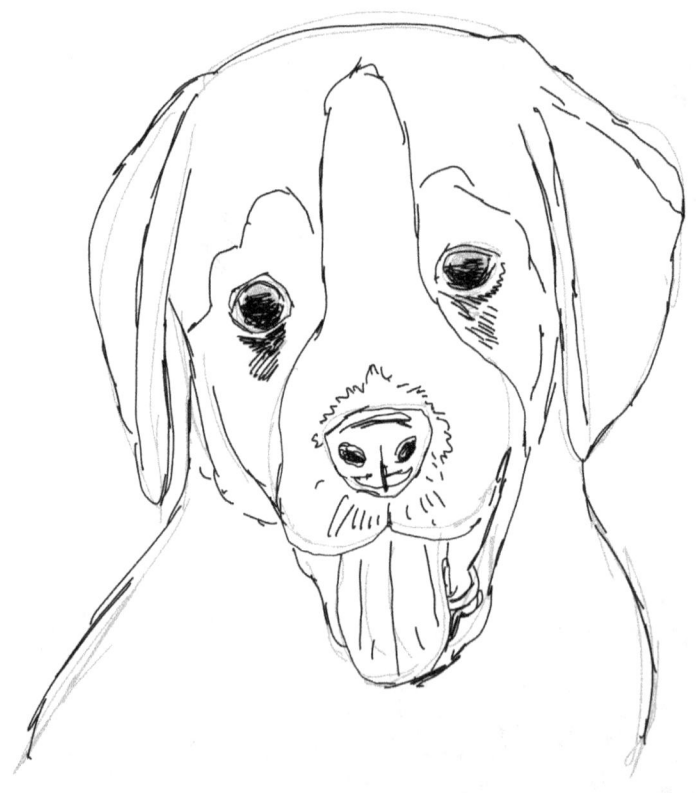

Barry's fur is short and coarse, so we have to draw lots of little lines that all come together and look like Barry's fur.

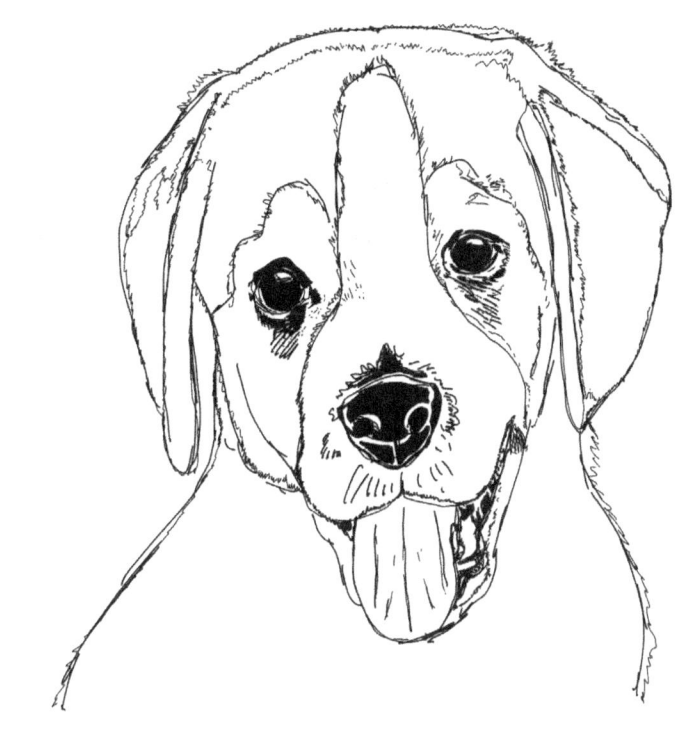

Carefully pen the lines you want to keep.

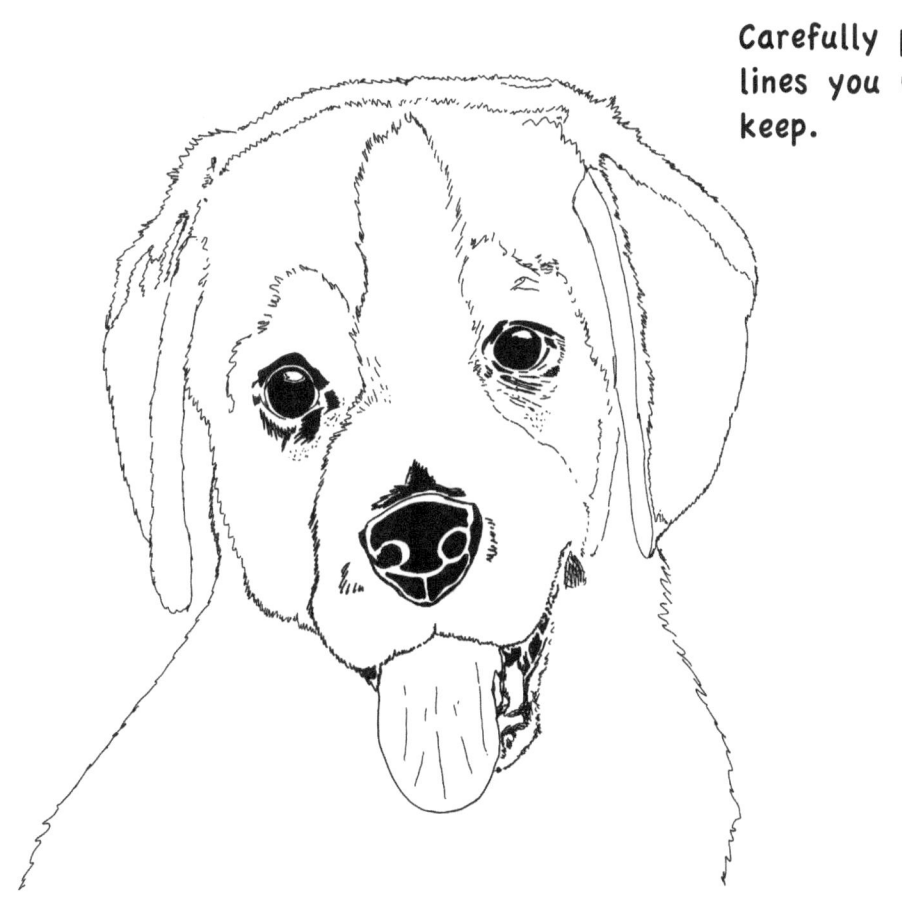

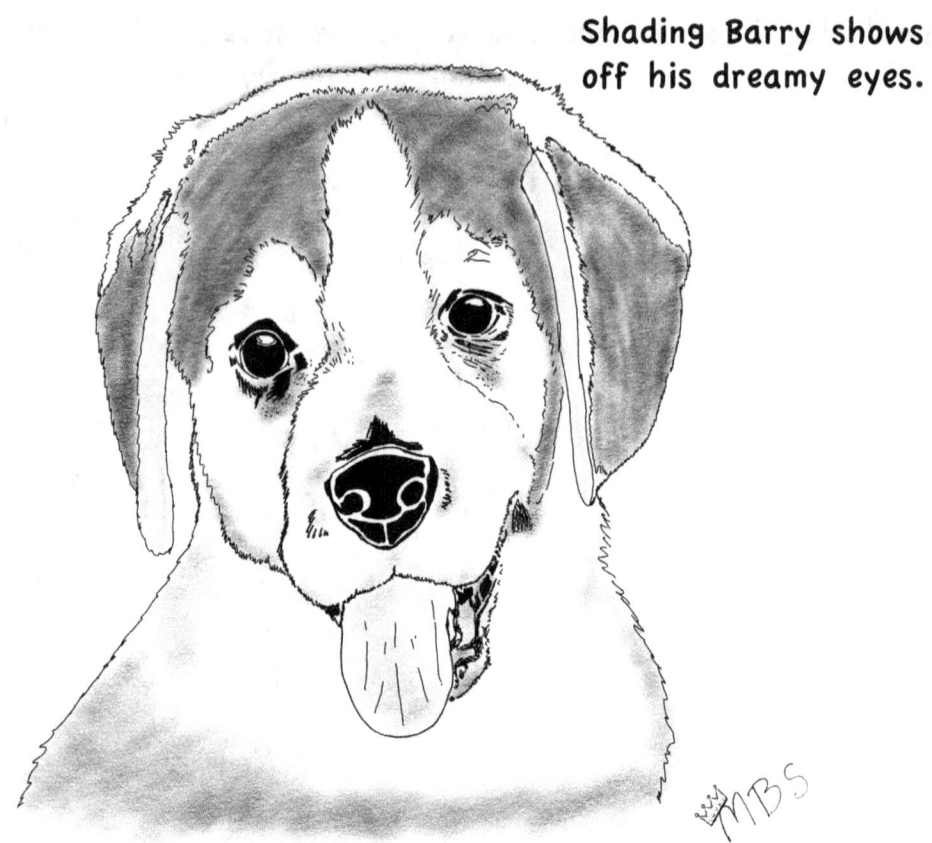

Shading Barry shows off his dreamy eyes.

A few hours later, Juanita paid Mary Beth $6.50 for her drawing of beautiful Barry. Both girls agreed it seemed like a funny and fair price.

Juanita told Barry, as they walked off towards home, "You're way better than any old county fair giant corn dog!"

Chapter 11
How to draw a cartoon dog

When it comes to a cartoon dog, you will know it when you see it. If it looks like a cartoon dog, it is. One nice thing about cartooning is you get to do it your way.

Mary Beth was looking forward to going down the street to keep growing her custom dog drawing business, but it was raining. It was raining hard. And even worse than that, Mom said that the stupid cousins were coming over for the day.

"But Mom! I don't want to spend time with the stupid cousins."

"Mary Beth, you know I don't like it when you use that word," Mom said.

"But they are stupid. They eat boogers and don't like hats!"

"That's enough! You are going to help Aunt Jenny by babysitting."

"But, they don't listen. They're glue eating, bath hating, boys!"

"Yes," Mom said, "they do avoid bathing, but you have to help. Play with them. It can't be that hard, I'm sure you can do it."

"Mom," Mary Beth whined. "How do you entertain caveman babies? Even Jazz thinks they are missing a few billion brain cells."

Jazz was watching all this drama unfold, but refused to be drawn into the bickering. She turned her head away, exhaled deeply, and pretended to fall into a deep sleep. Jazz was a smart dog.

Mom crossed her arms. Her face made it clear that the last words of this discussion were coming. "You will never hear me say that the cousins are about as useful as a box of hair, but <u>you will</u> watch them. Why don't you teach them how to draw? But," she raised her index finger, "<u>do not let them eat the crayons</u>."

Mary Beth's mind was racing. How was she going to get the cousins not to eat crayons? *Ah,* she thought. *I'll teach them how do draw a cartoon dog. I don't think that they have ever eaten a pencil, and anybody can draw a cartoon dog.*

As it turned out, the cousins liked the idea of drawing cartoon dogs. They listened as Mary Beth explained the basics and then tried their best. To Mary Beth's surprise, except for the farting incident, it was fun to draw with the cousins.

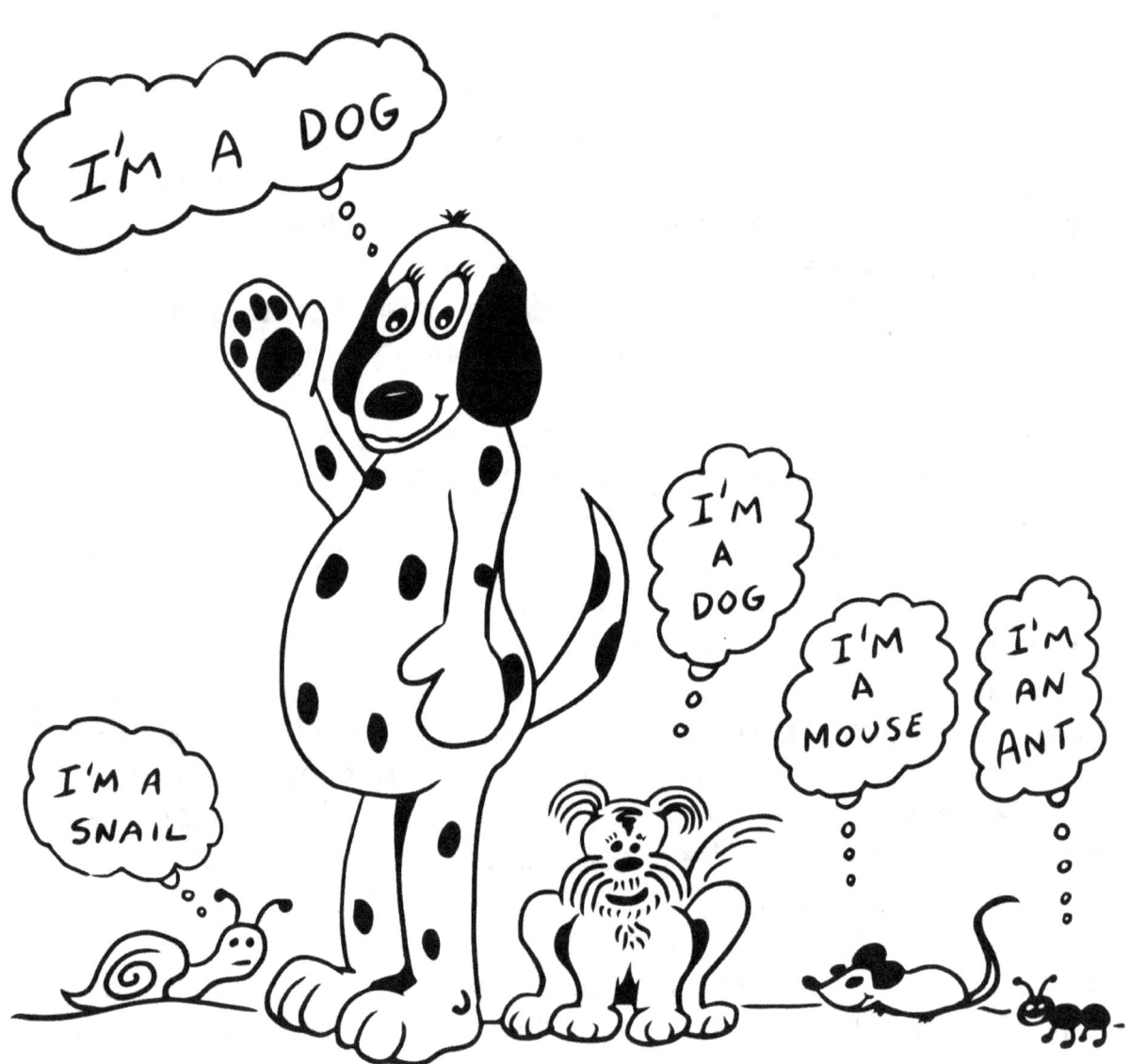

Mary Beth explained that when drawing cartoon dogs you get to be silly. By starting with the body shape, you get to play with the personality of your cartoon friend.

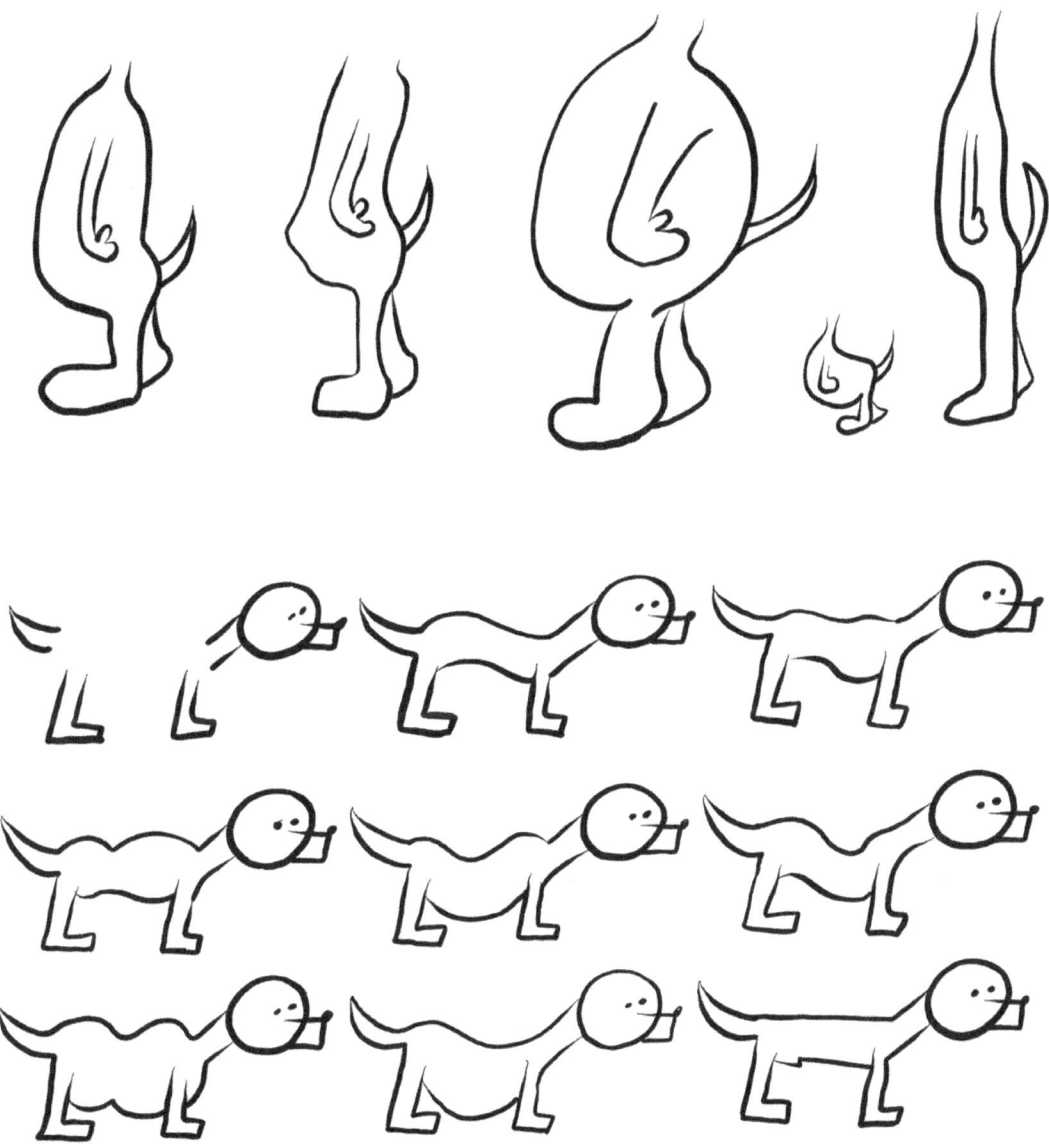

Mary Beth showed the cousins a trick she learned from her teacher in second grade. "If you start with the basic parts, like the head and the tail, you get to goof off with the other parts to see what you find. With just a few lines you can create lots of different cartoon personalities."

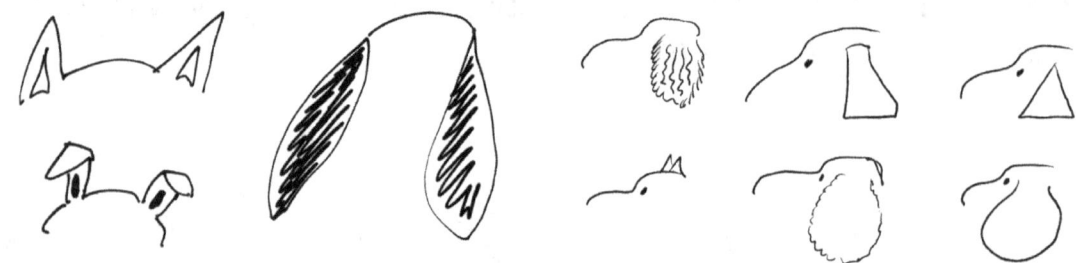

Mary Beth showed the cousins how different shapes make up a dog's ear.

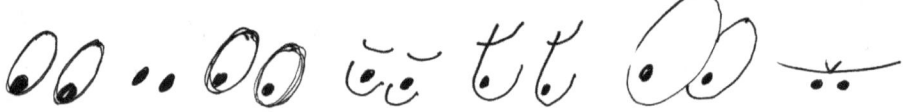

Eyes give information about what the cartoon dog is thinking. (One time, Mary Beth got into trouble in school for drawing cartoon eyes on her math paper.)

Dog noses tend to be funny. Mary Beth showed the cousins how to start with a dog snout and then add different shaped noses for different types of dogs. (Another time Mary Beth got into trouble for drawing 100s of dog noses on her math paper.)

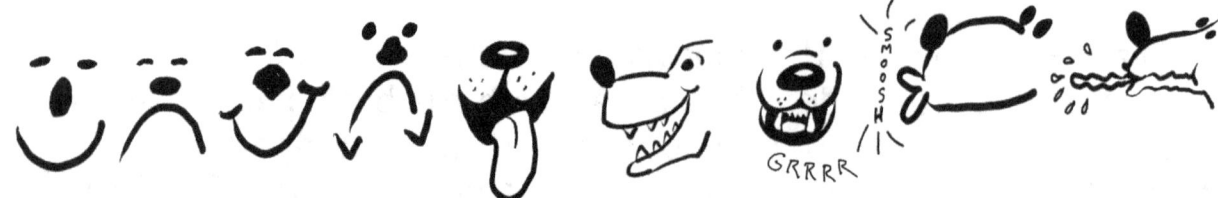

Dog mouths show feelings. Often the mouth shows who is talking in the cartoon.

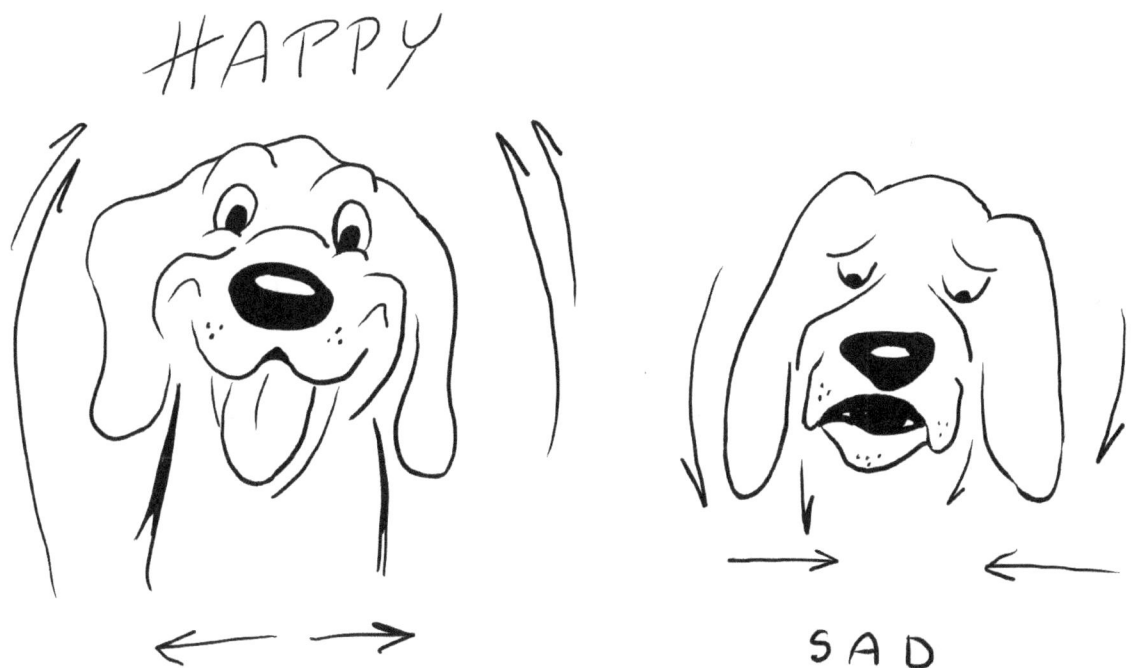

HAPPY

SAD

When cartooning feelings, the whole drawing takes on the feeling. Notice that the whole head is either happy or sad. Happy feelings are drawn up and out, while sad feelings are drawn down and together.

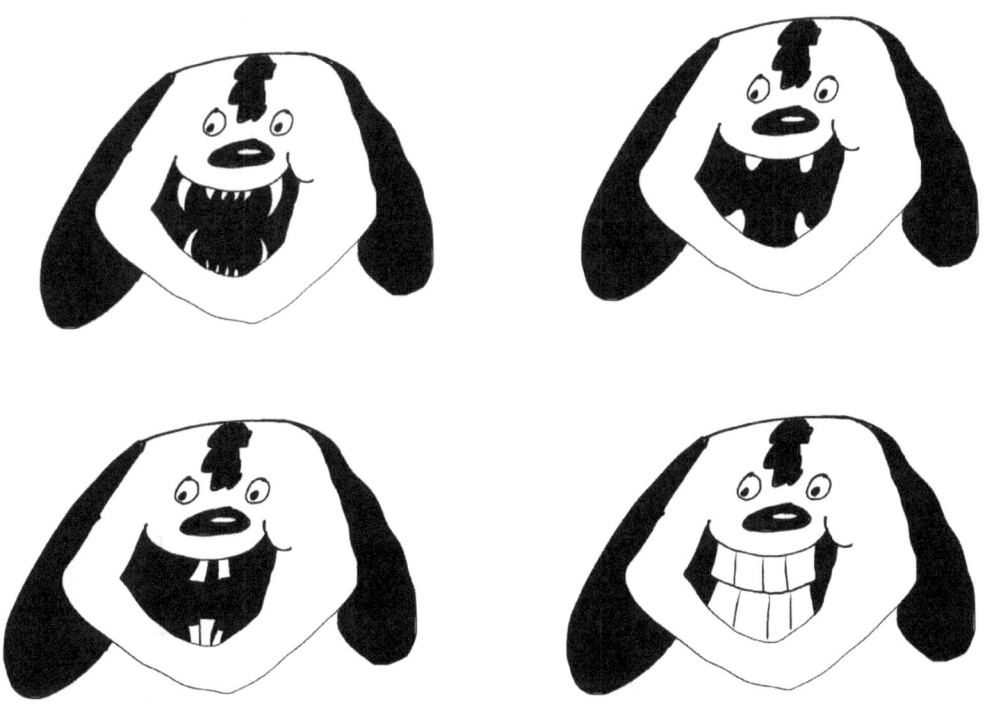

Dog teeth are lots of fun to draw. They can be sharp, smooth, or mostly missing. They can even look like human teeth which makes a cartoon dog look mischievous. The cousins liked drawing their cartoon teeth looking mean and sharp.

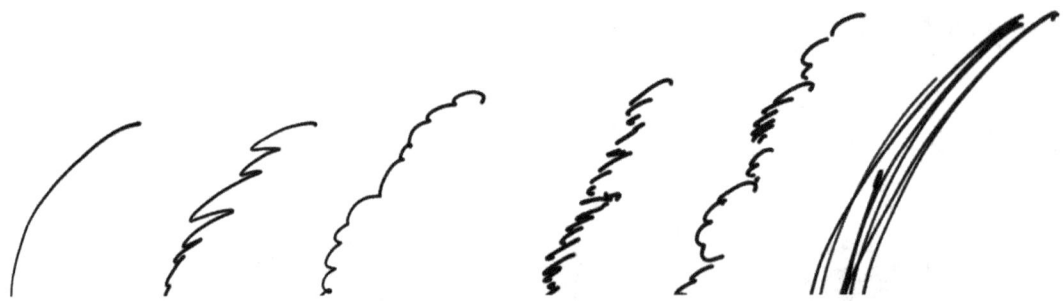

Mary Beth showed the cousins you can make the fur look fuzzy, rough, smooth, or long. It is a lot harder to do than it looks. But, with practice, you will get good at drawing lots of different types of fur.

Mary Beth told the cousins, "I'll tell you a secret, fur on a dog or leaves on a bush are really the same type of pencil line. Part of what cartoonists do is trick the eye of the reader."

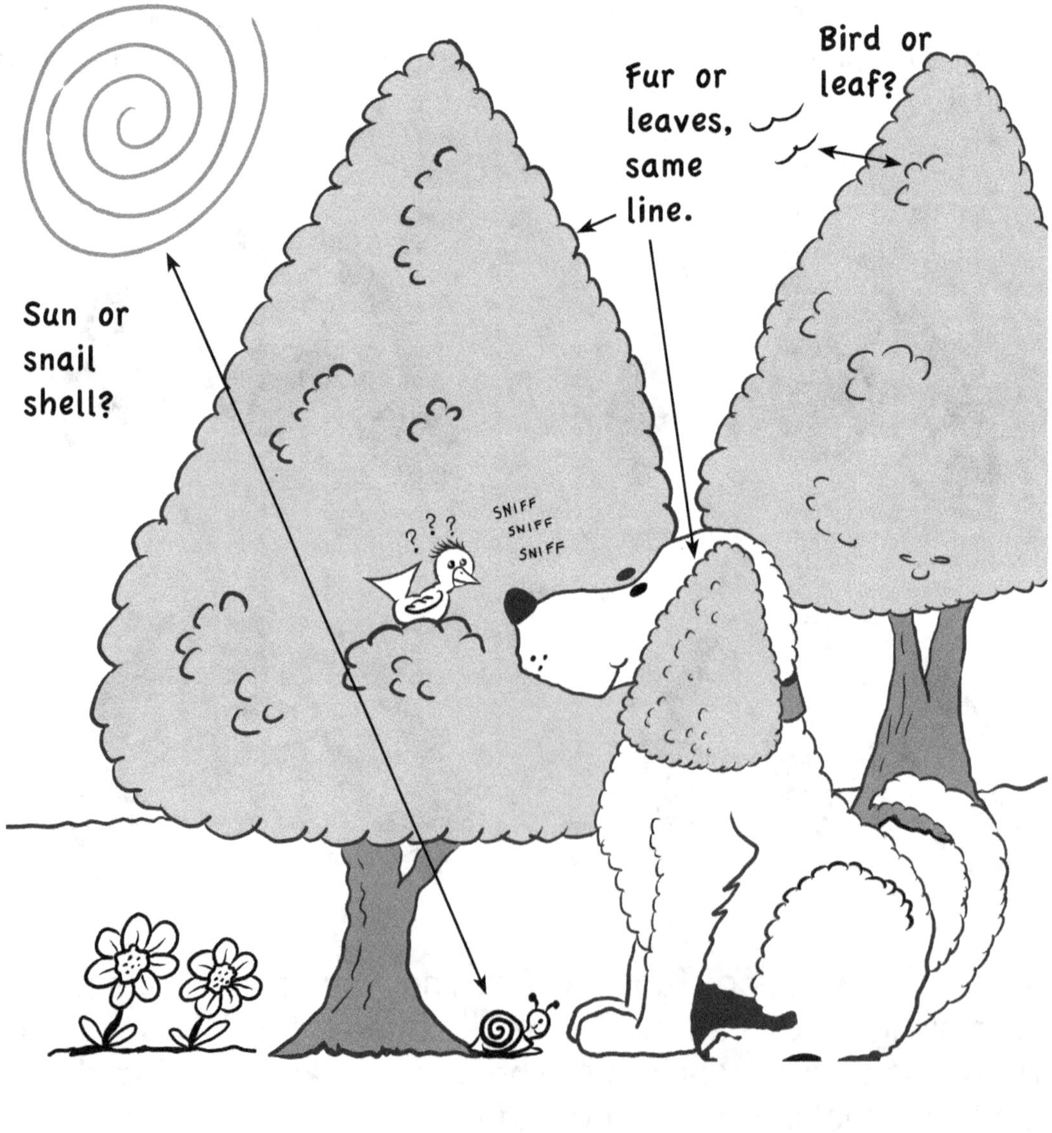

Bird or leaf?

Fur or leaves, same line.

Sun or snail shell?

SNIFF
SNIFF
SNIFF

A Happy Cartoon Dog

Advice from Mary Beth on how to draw cartoon dogs.

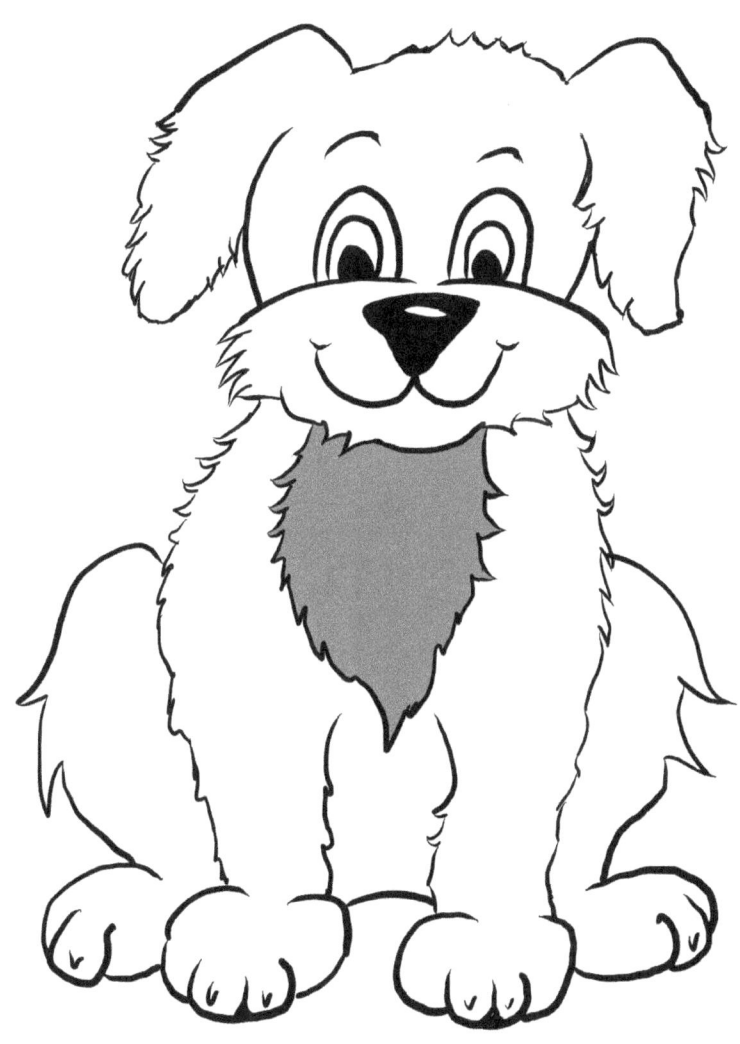

Use very light pencil lines to start.

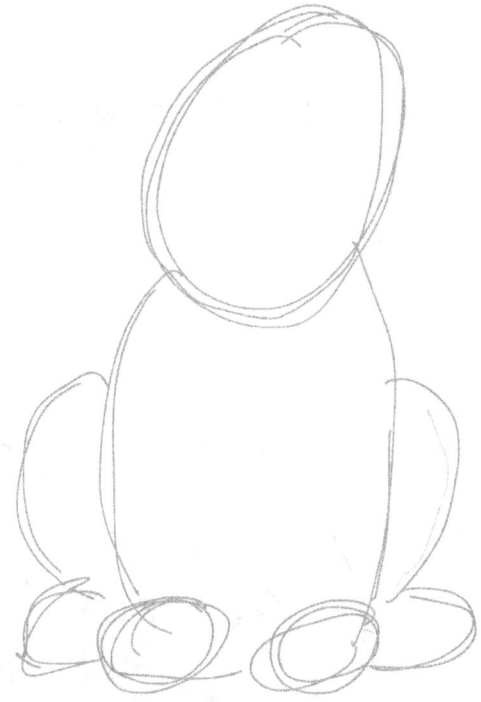

Find the puppy's face.

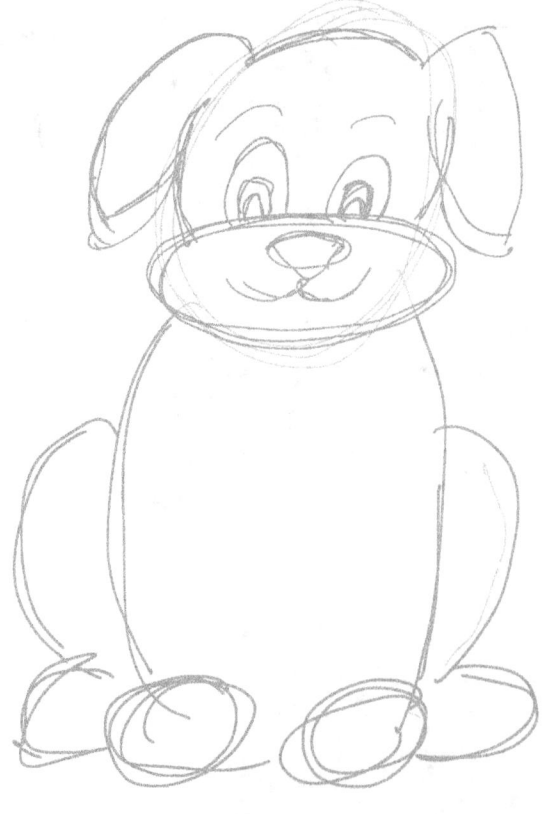

The oval of the snout lets you find where the eyes go.

Gently build up the
body with more
light lines. Erase
lines that get out
of control.

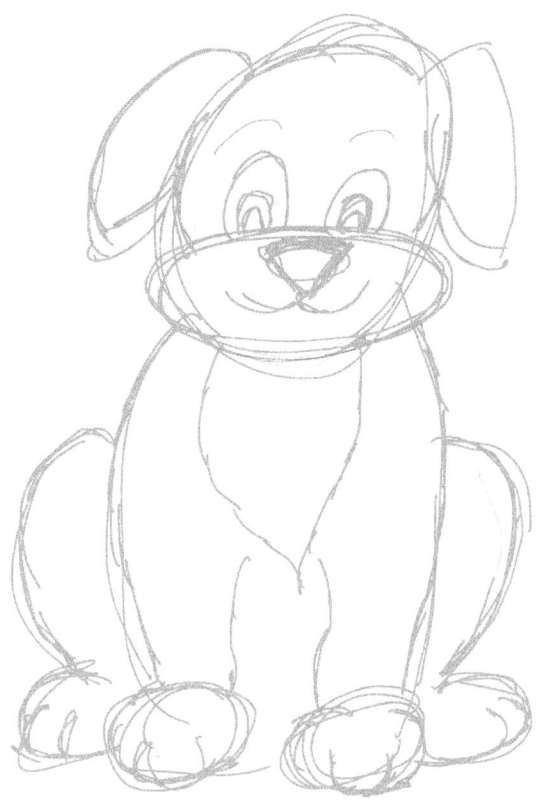

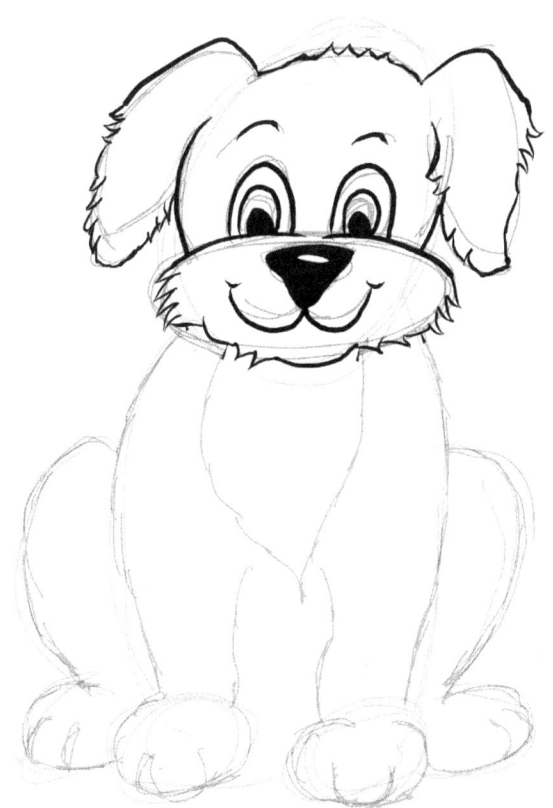

Draw in fur on top of your guidelines.

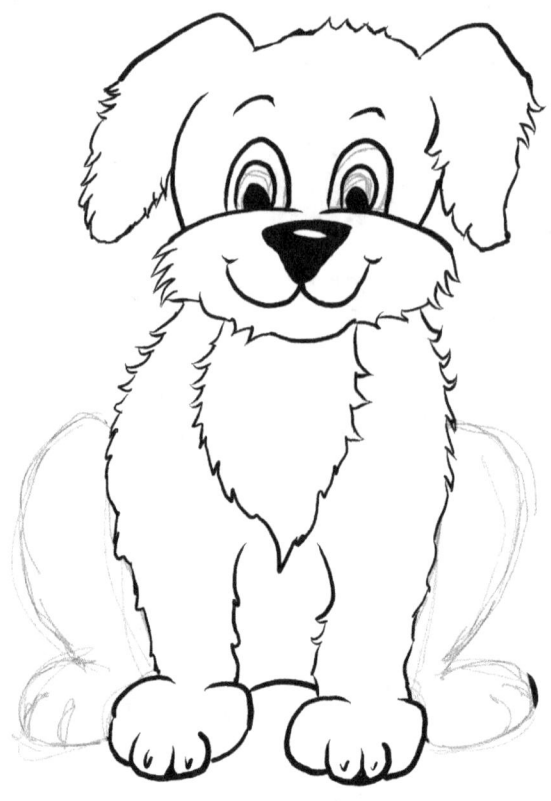

Happy cartoon
dog is starting
to come along
nicely.

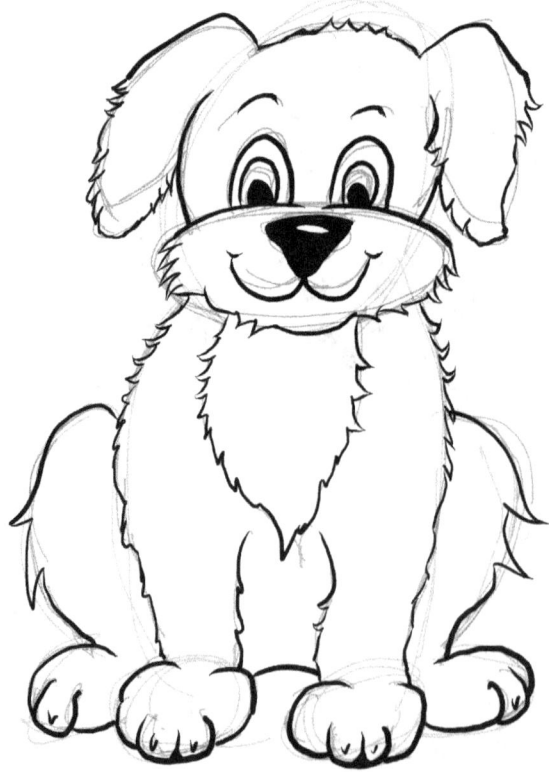

Pen the lines you like then erase all your pencil guidelines.

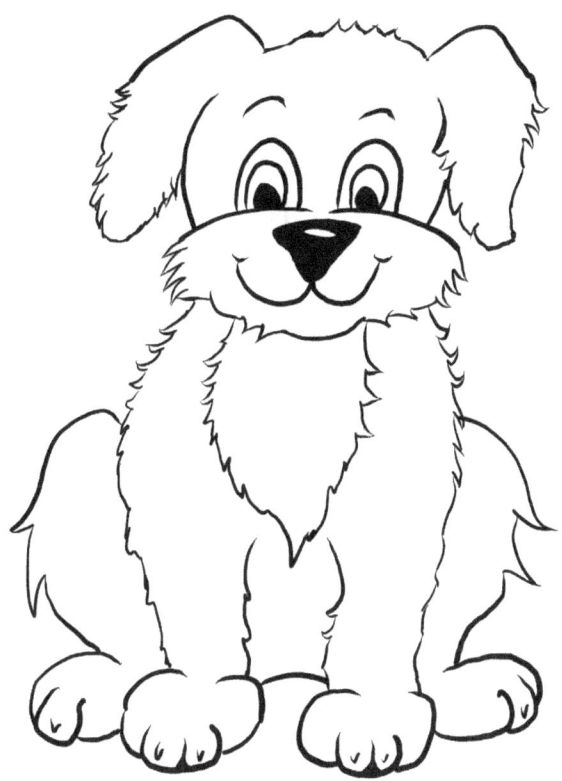

Shade or color if
you want to.

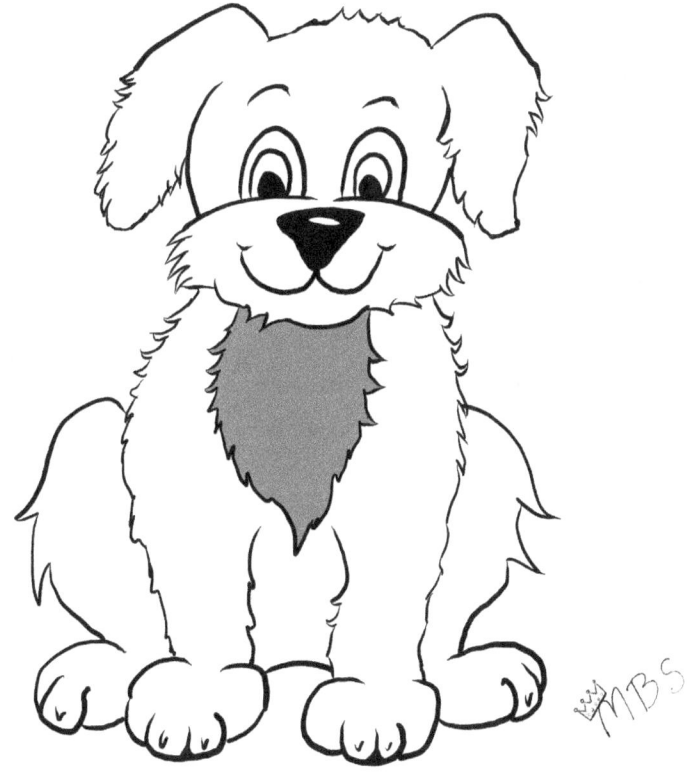

5 Tips To Better Drawing

While practicing drawing the Happy Cartoon Dog, the cousins got a little grumpy.

"It will take time to get better at drawing," Mary Beth told them. "But there are some tips I can share with you that will help you get better at drawing."

The cousins wanted to know. And to Mary Beth's surprise, they listened quietly.

1) Sketch lightly

There is a lot of erasing in drawing, so draw lightly making the erasing much easier to do. If you build up a heavy line because you drew lightly over and over, you can knock the line back by erasing it lightly. Gum erasers work best for this.

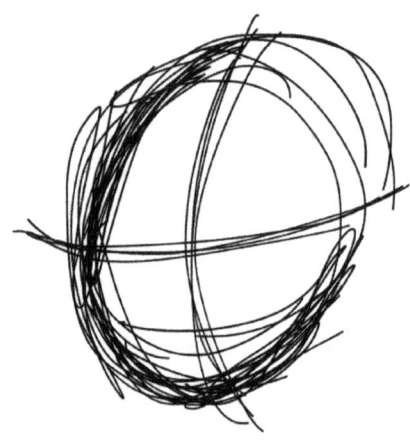

A heavily built up line.

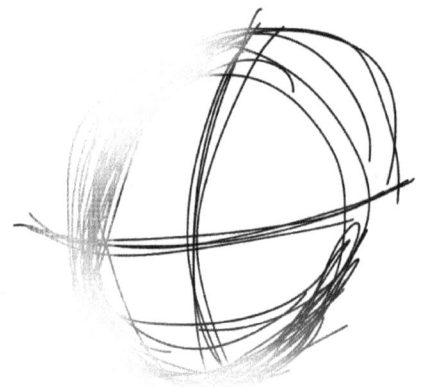

A heavily built up line knocked back with an gum eraser.

2) Draw real lines, not timid choppy lines

Even though you are drawing very lightly, you still want to draw a full line. It is usually best to make a sketch line longer, then erase the extra bit. This is called "pulling the line" and it helps you see the curves and end points better.

A timid line gets messy and lost easier than a full line.

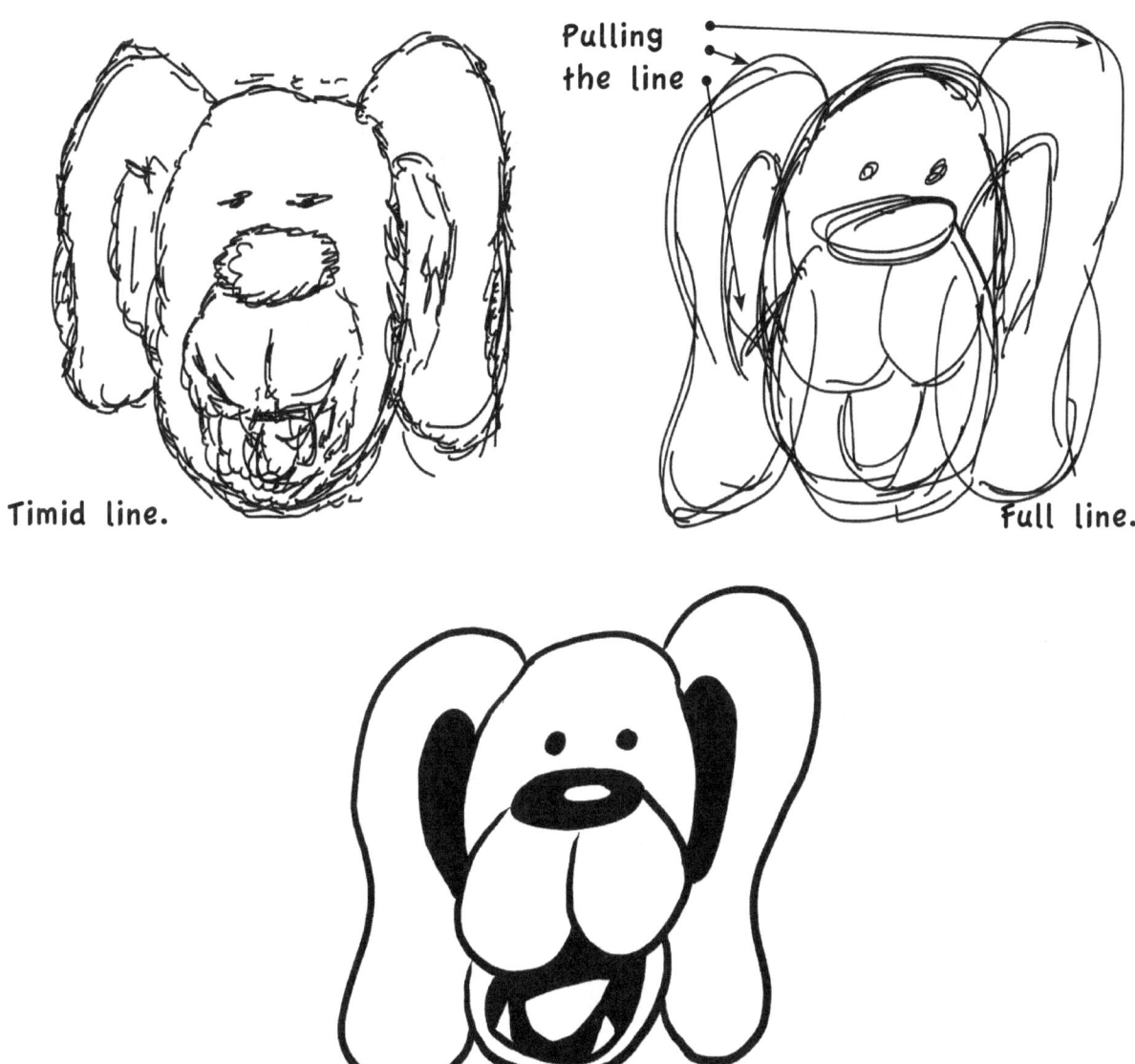

Pulling the line

Timid line.

Full line.

3) Draw towards yourself

To get the cleanest line, draw the line towards your center. On longer lines it is best to draw from your elbow, moving your whole lower arm. Drawing from the elbow will also protect your wrist from getting hurt while drawing for hours and hours.

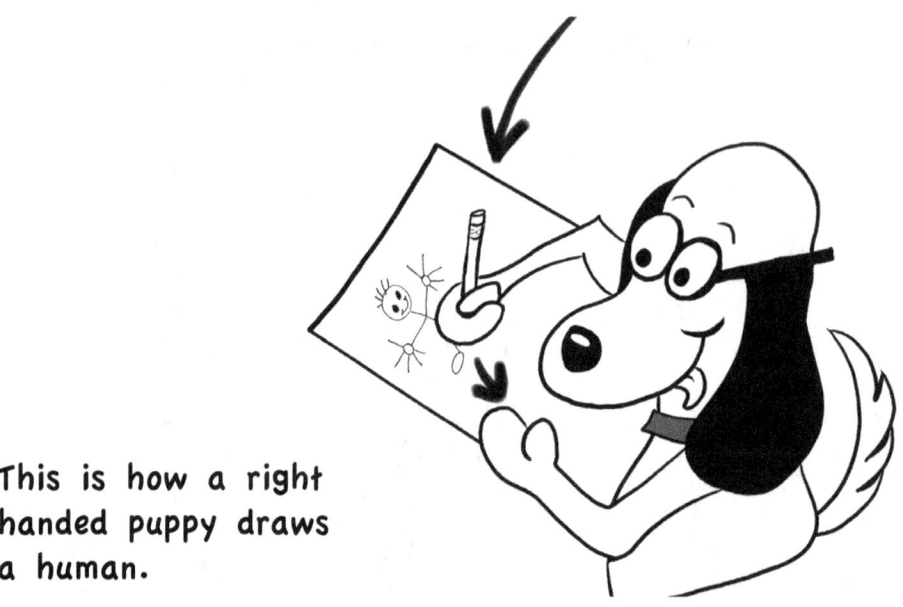

This is how a right handed puppy draws a human.

4) Turn the paper

To make your line flow well in any direction, turn your paper. Your paper is your work area. Place your work area where it is easiest for you to draw the line you want.

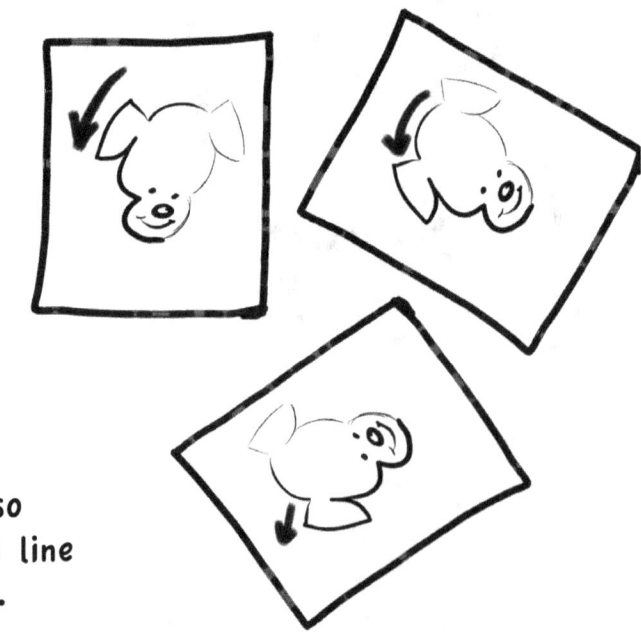

Turn the paper so you can pull the line towards yourself.

5) Vary line thickness

If your pen lines are all the same thickness your cartoon will look boring. You can get different thicknesses of lines by changing the pressure you put on your pen's tip. There are also pens made with angled nibs that make changing pen strokes a whole lot easier. Brushes are also used to paint lines using India ink.

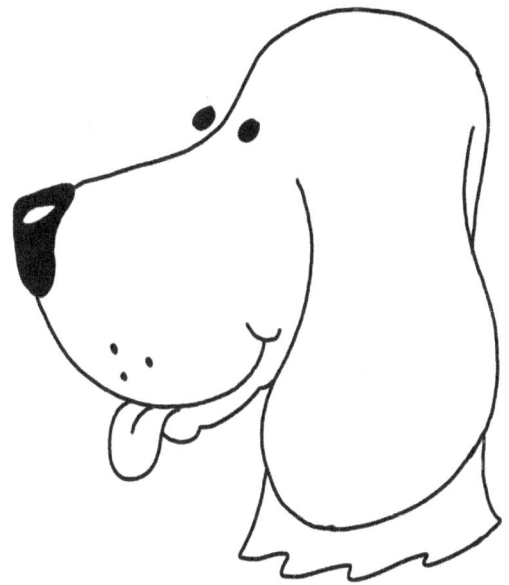

One consistent line.

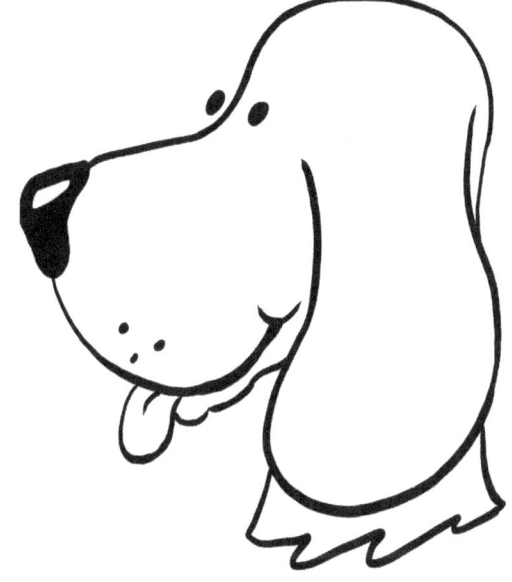

Varying line thickness makes for more interesting cartooning.

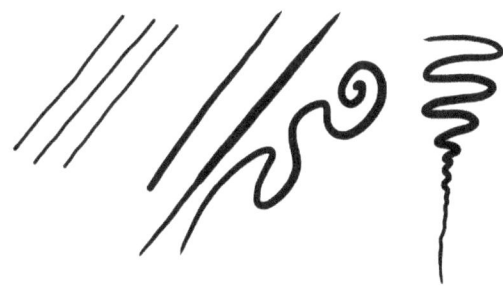

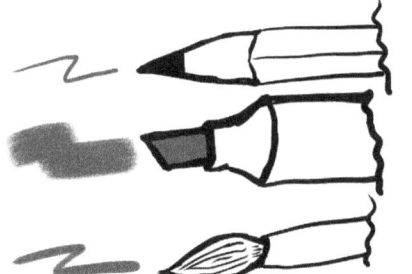

Artists end up with lots of pens, brushes, and erasers. They are always looking for their favorite one for the art they are working on.

Drawing A Cartoon Wiener Dog

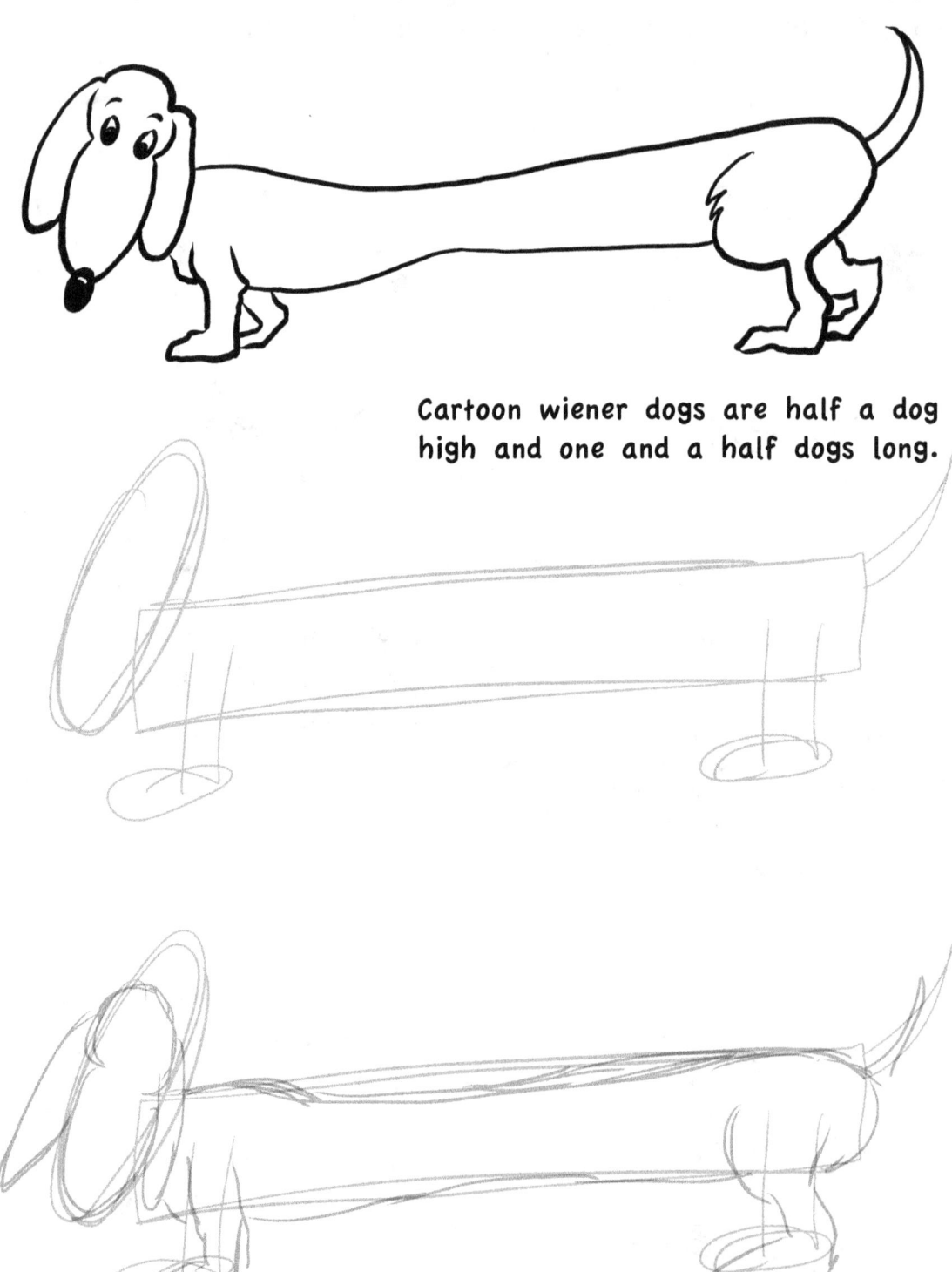

Cartoon wiener dogs are half a dog high and one and a half dogs long.

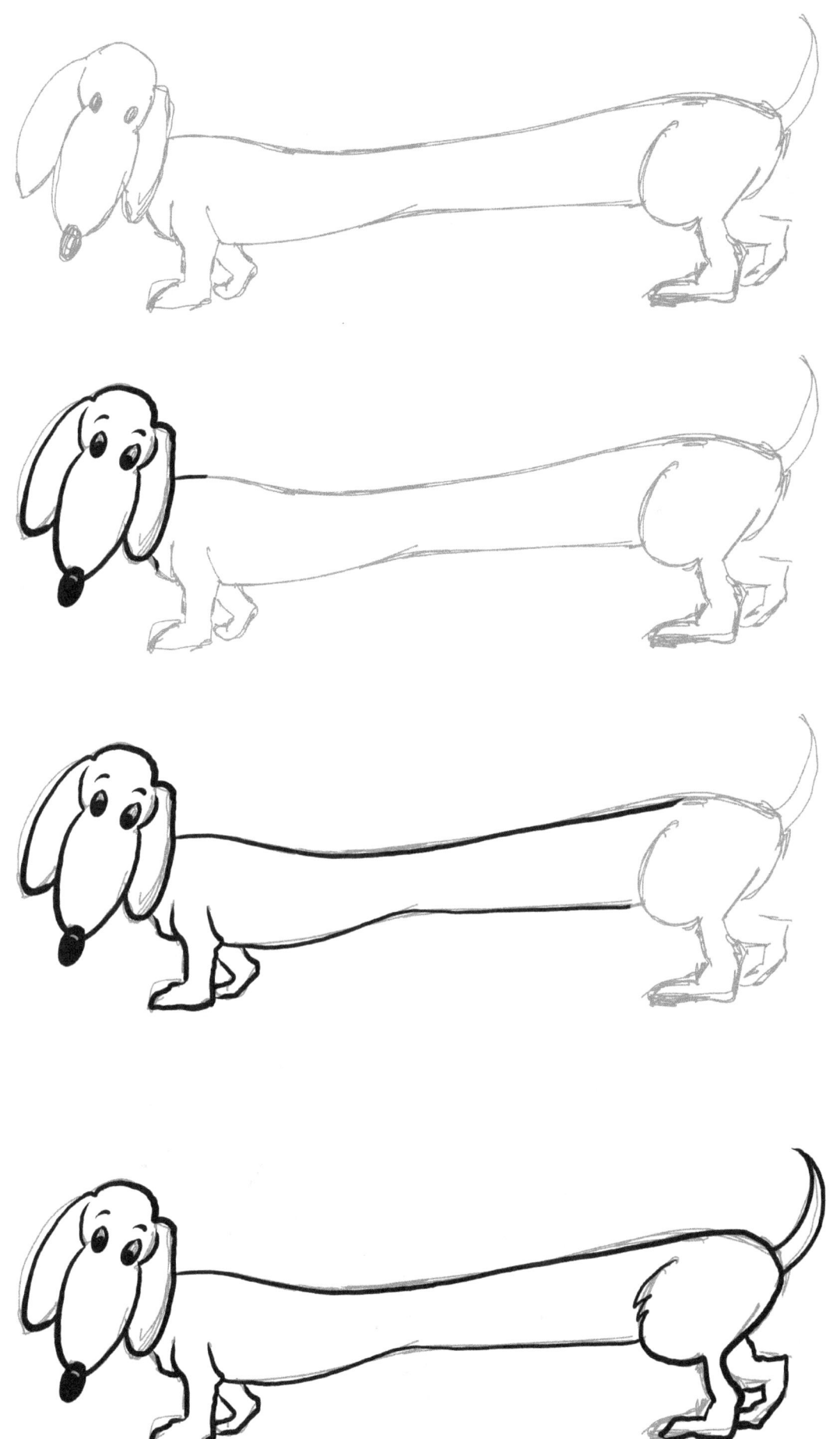

Pen the lines you like then erase all your pencil guidelines.

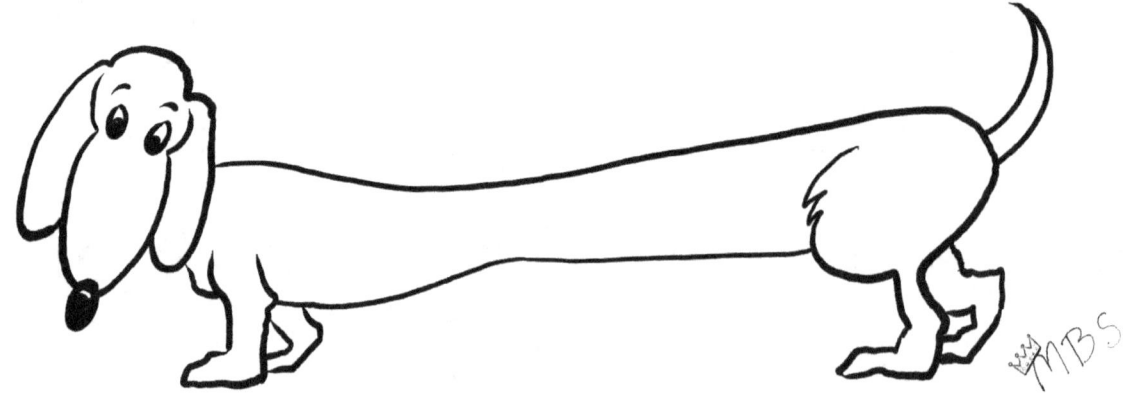

For their next cartoon dog the cousins wanted to practice drawing a silly dog.

Silly Cartoon Dog

Everyone enjoyed some laughs while drawing this happy go lucky four pawed fellow.

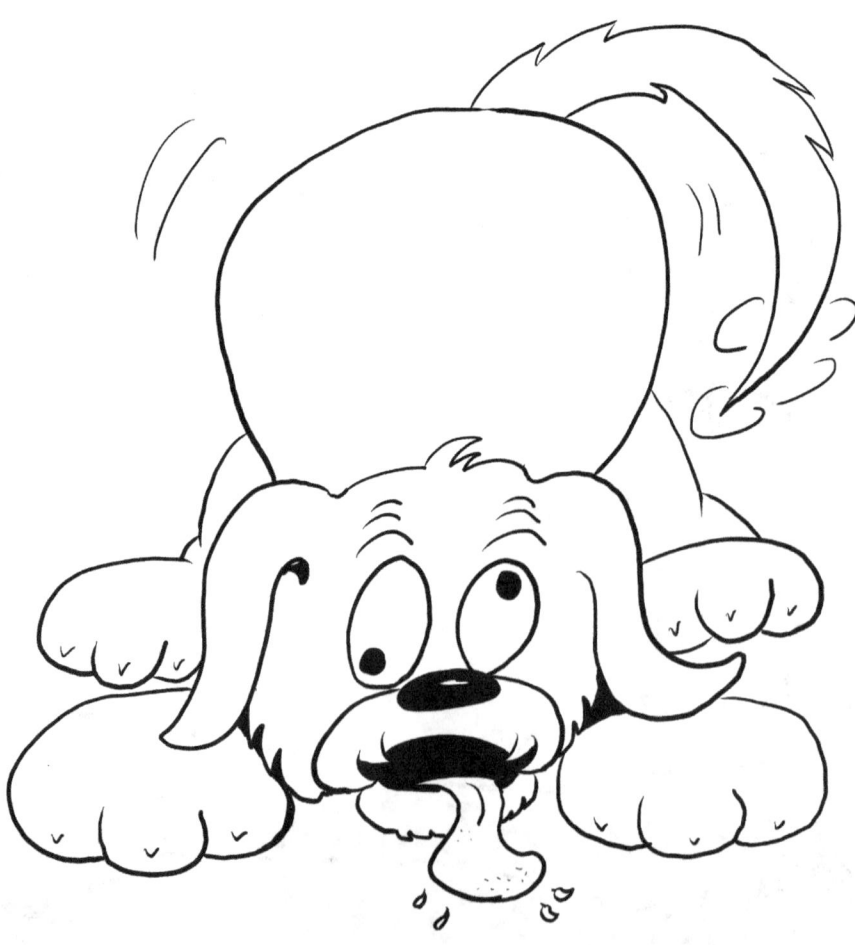

Drawing motion
in a cartoon is a
little hard. But
cartoon dogs are
emotional and
active beings. So
in this cartoon we
go butt up and
silly face down.

By using soft
guidelines, we can
find the silly face
of this puppy.

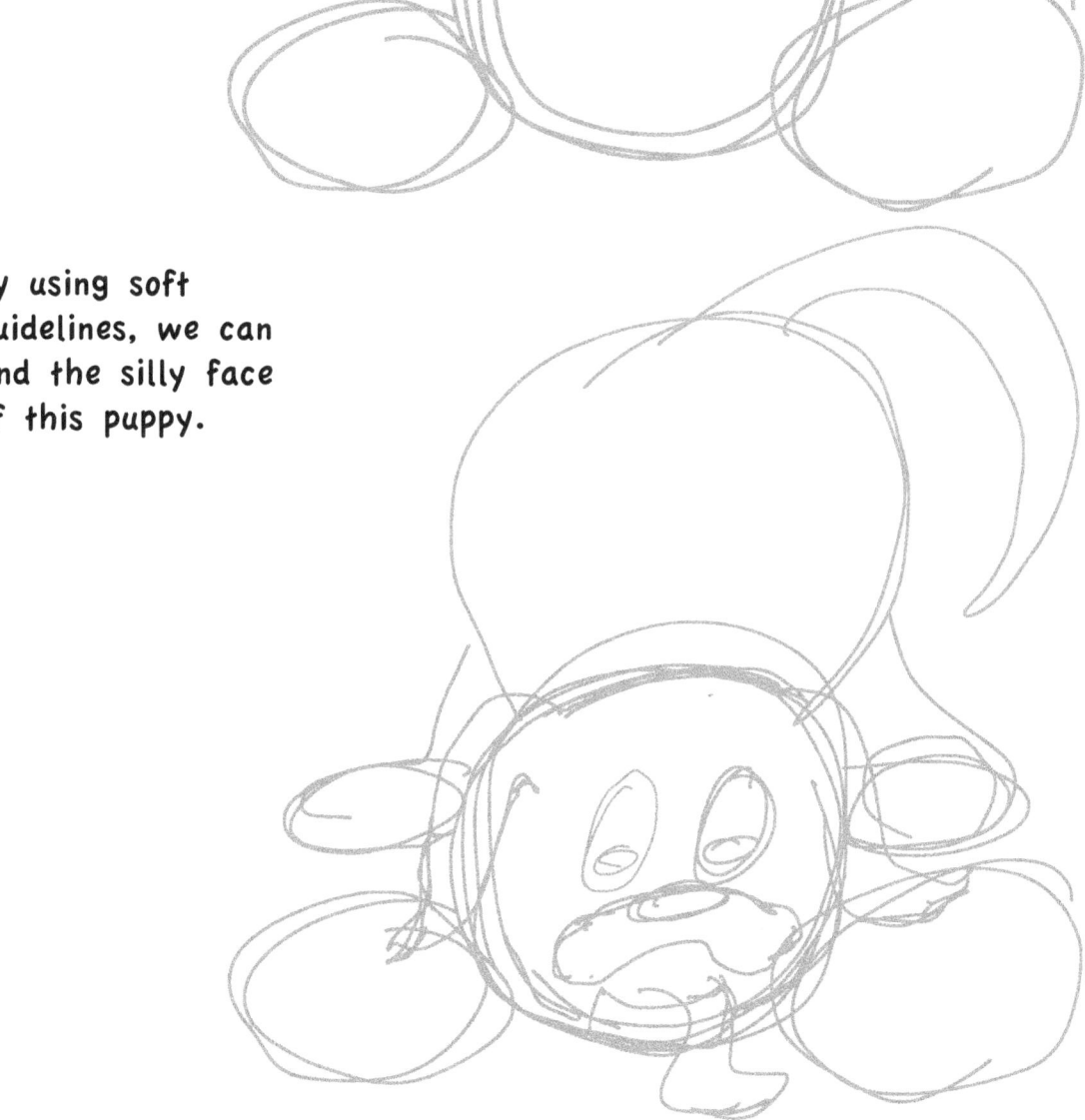

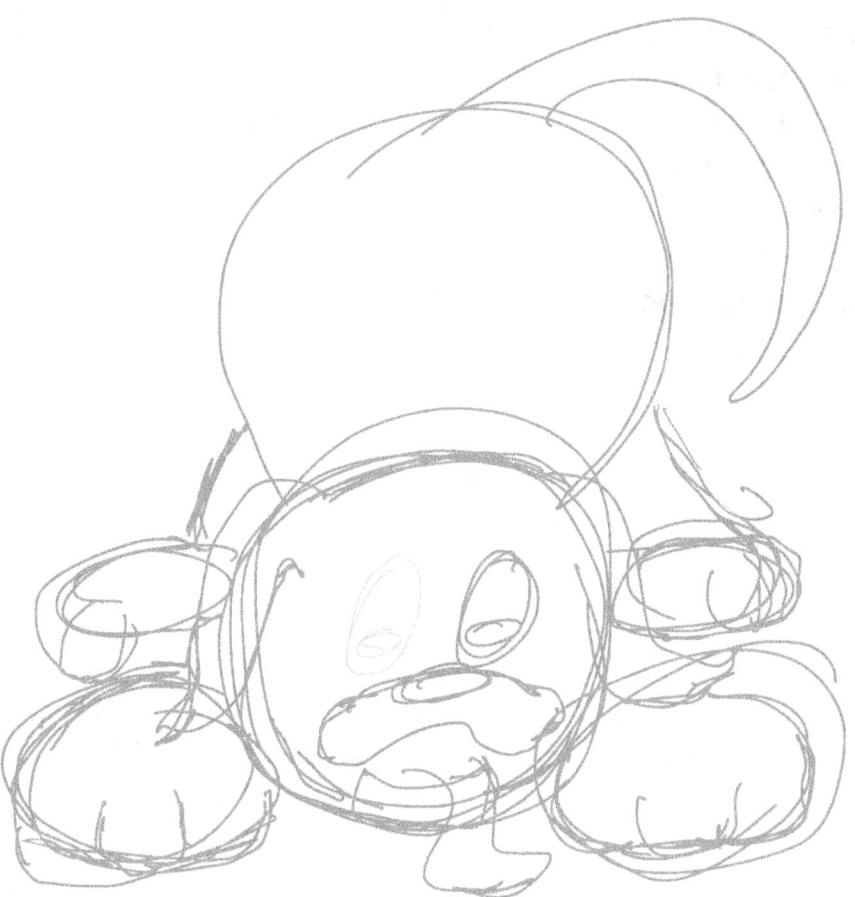

More light lines.
Erase lines that
you don't like.

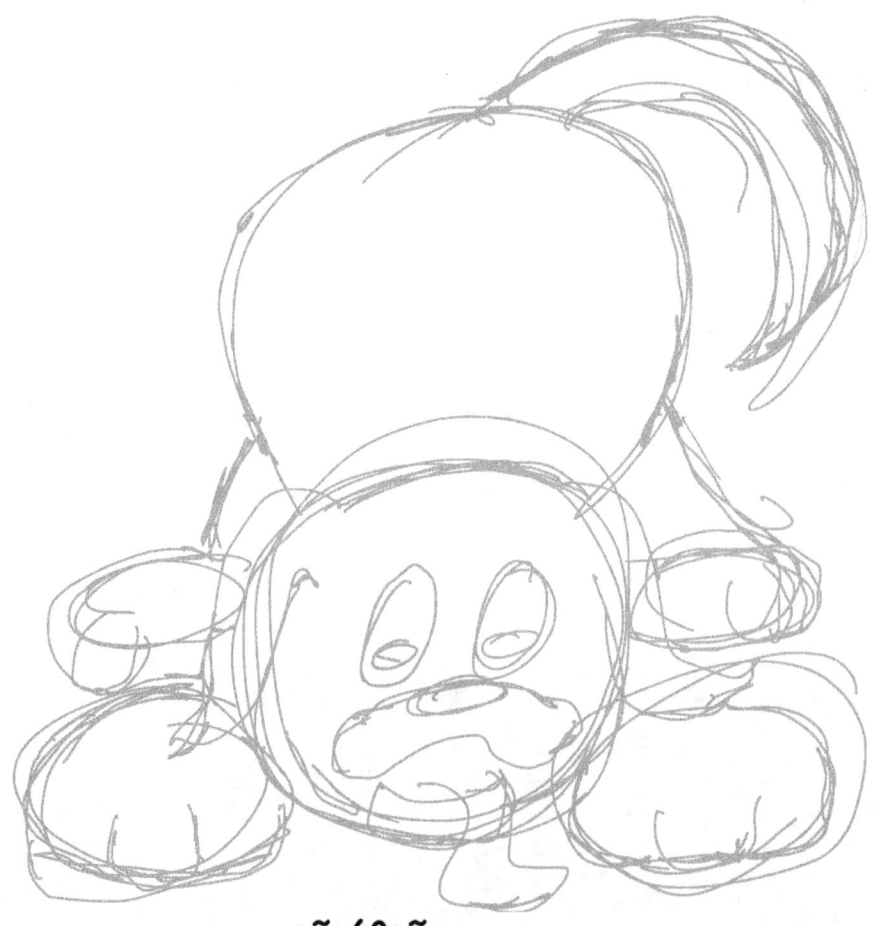

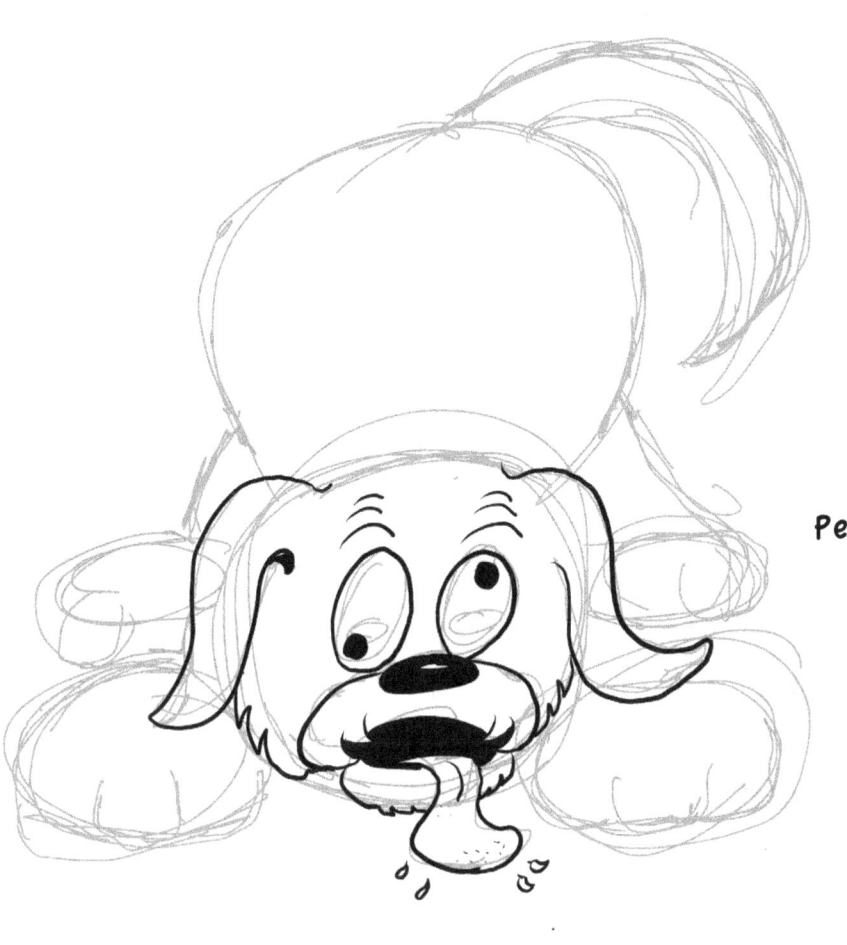

Pen the lines you like.

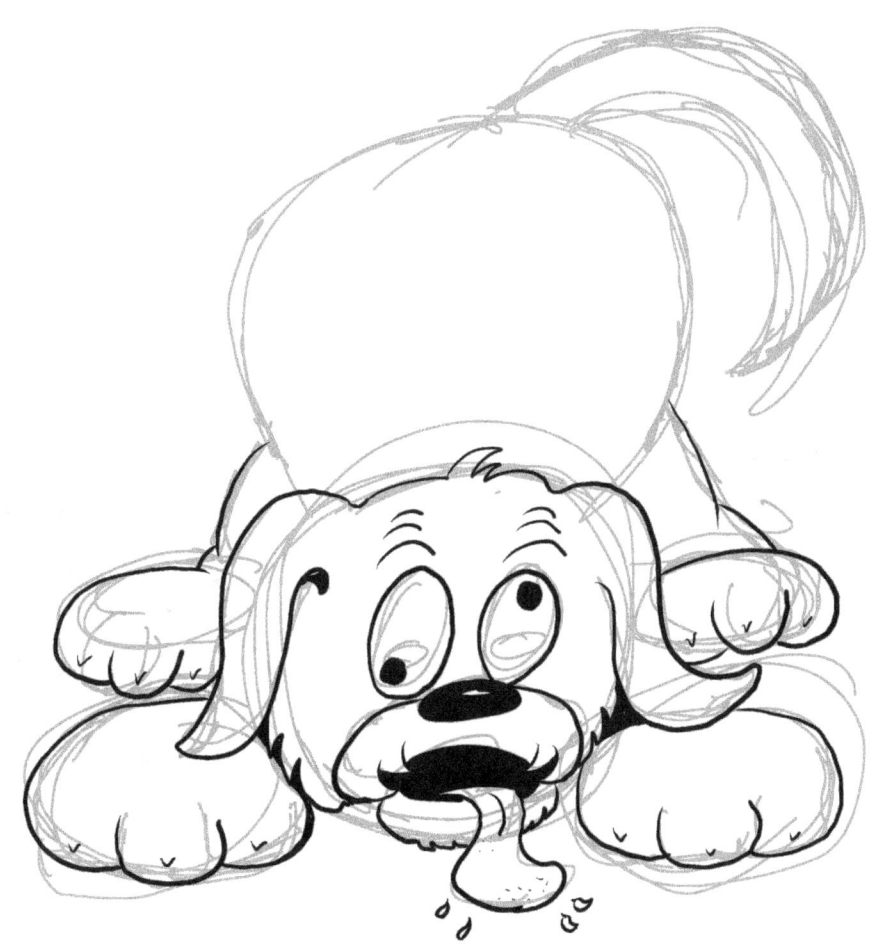

Movement lines

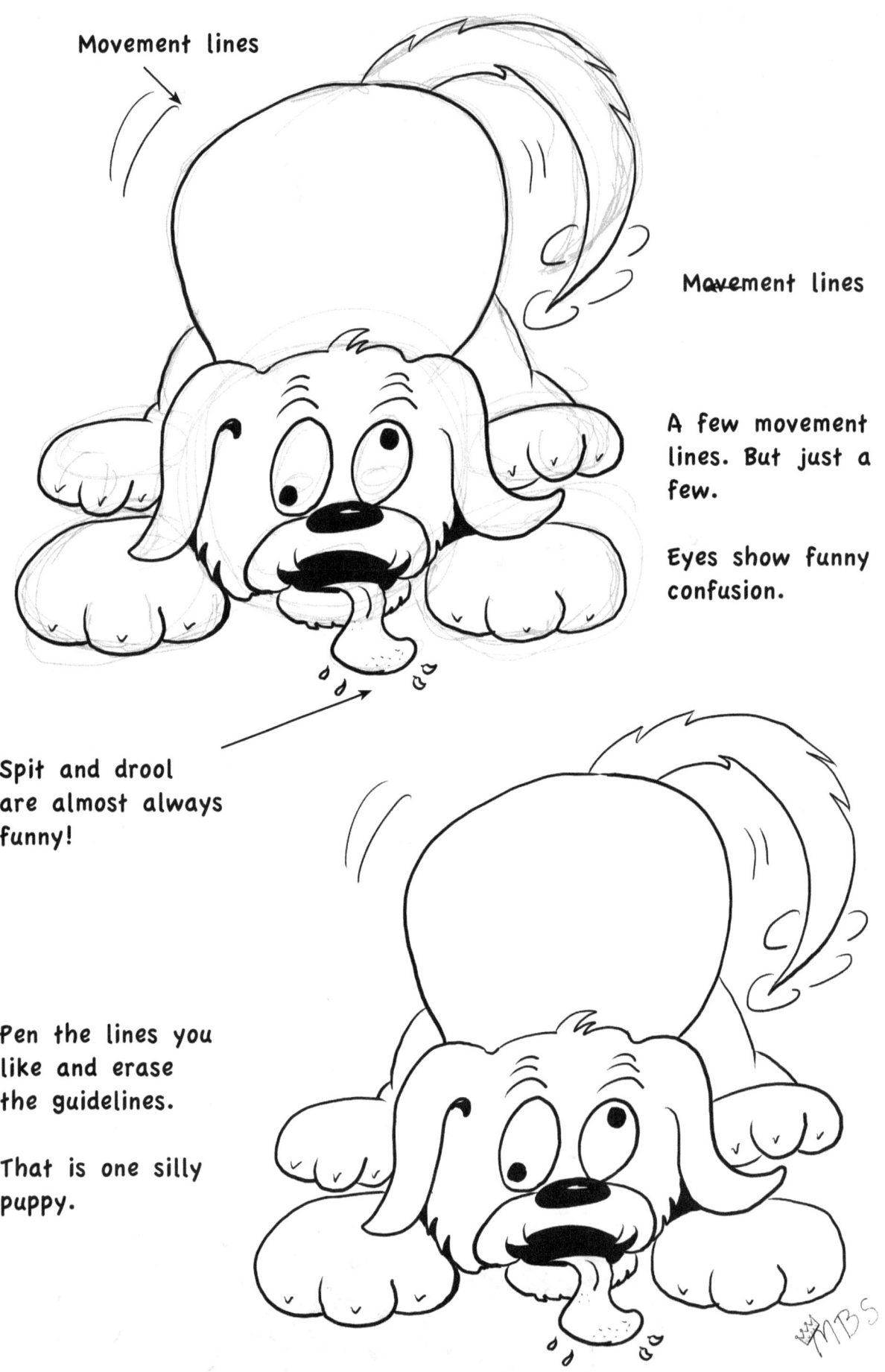

Movement lines

A few movement lines. But just a few.

Eyes show funny confusion.

Spit and drool are almost always funny!

Pen the lines you like and erase the guidelines.

That is one silly puppy.

The moms came home and ruined everything. They said it was time to go, but everyone was having so much fun they begged for just one more cartoon dog. Finally, after lots of whining, the moms decided they really wanted a cup of coffee, so they said the kids could draw for, "Just 15 more minutes!"

Mary Beth showed the cousins how to draw a small active cartoon dog.

Small Active Cartoon Dog

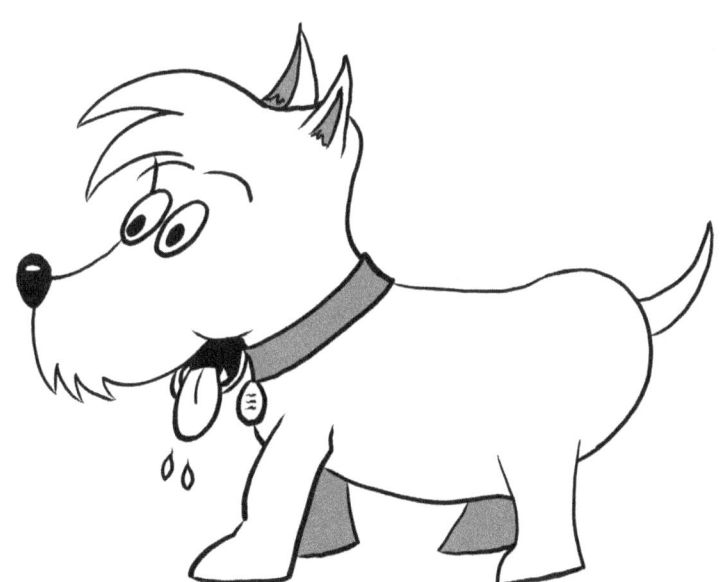

For this pup they started with an oval for the head and a box for the body and legs.

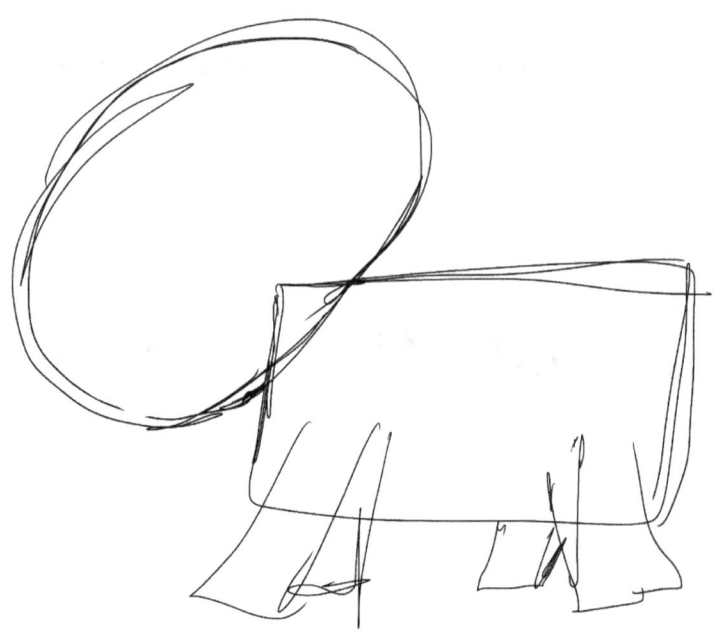

The oval is just a general guide. Draw a boxy head inside the oval. (Since Mary Beth was in a hurry, she didn't tell the cousins that she once got into trouble in math class for drawing boxy heads inside of ovals in her math book.)

Now carefully erase the first guidelines.

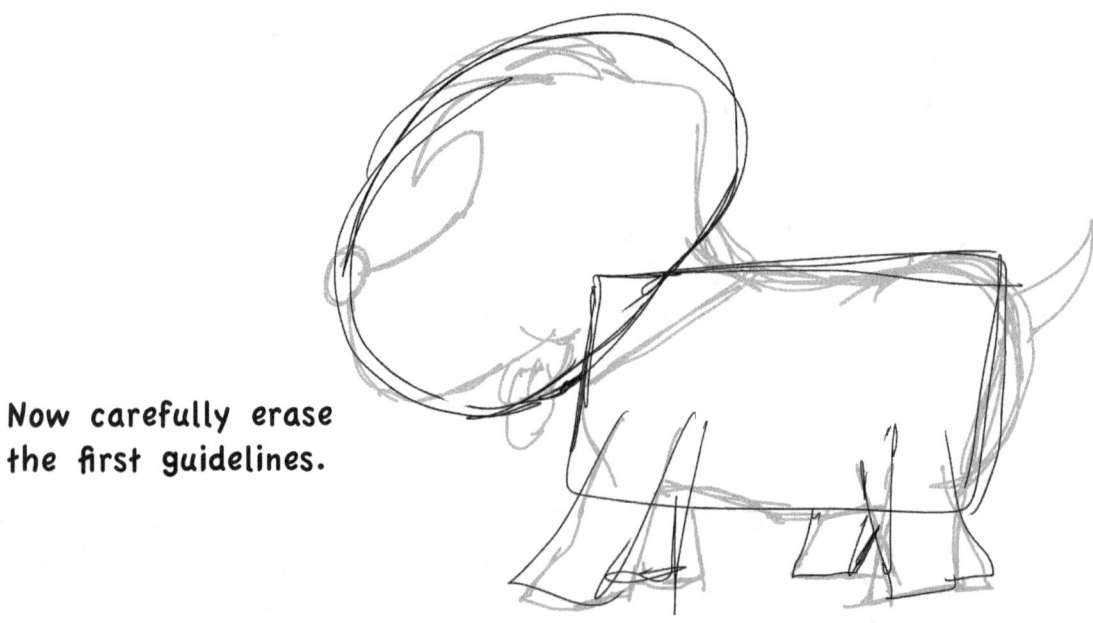

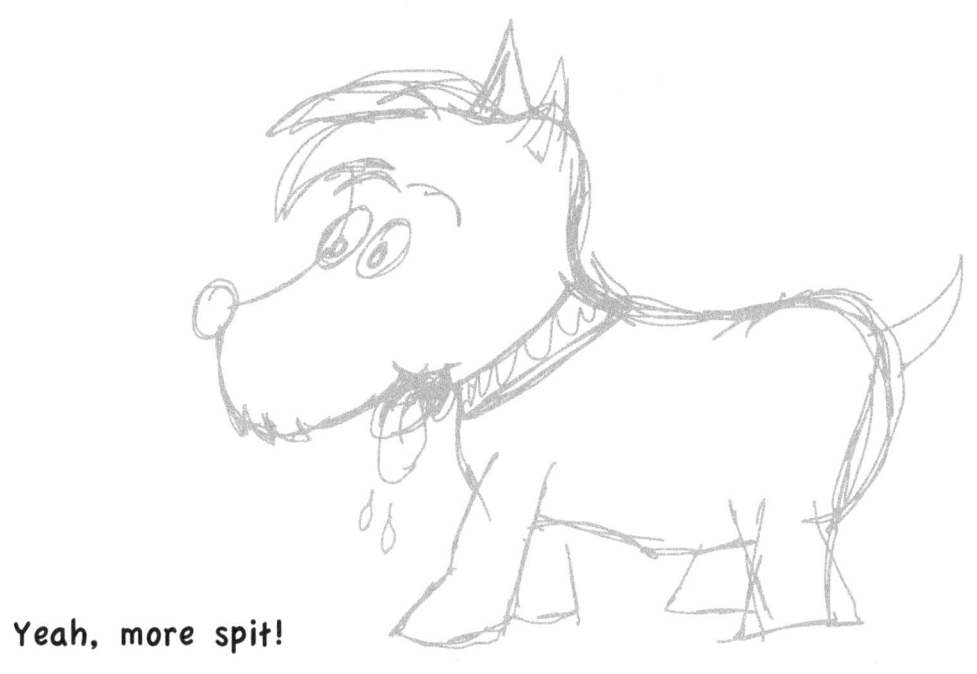

Yeah, more spit!

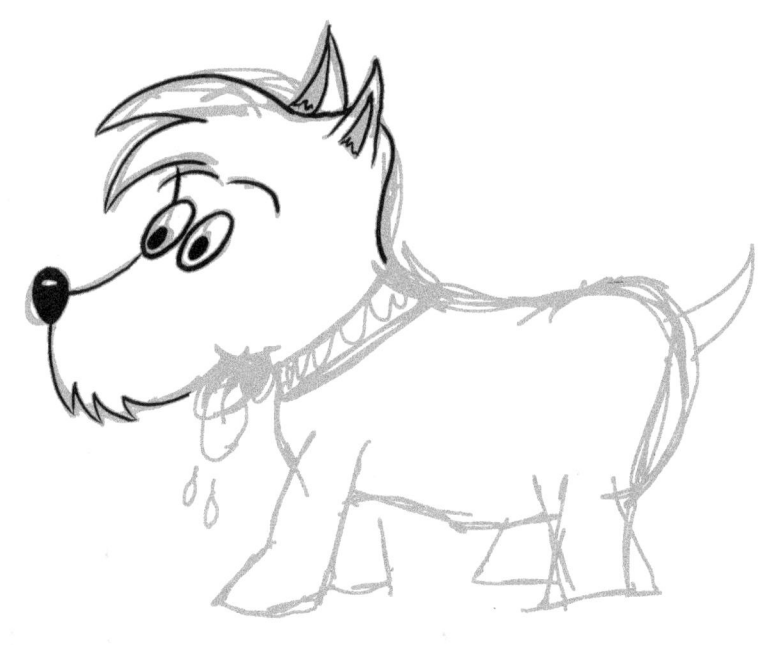

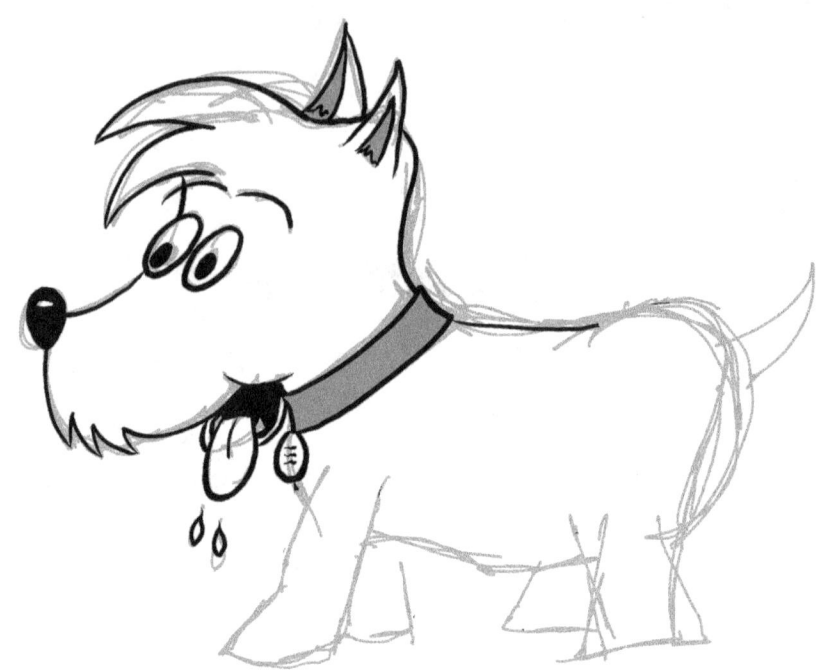

Pen and erase.
It was time for
the cousins to go
home.

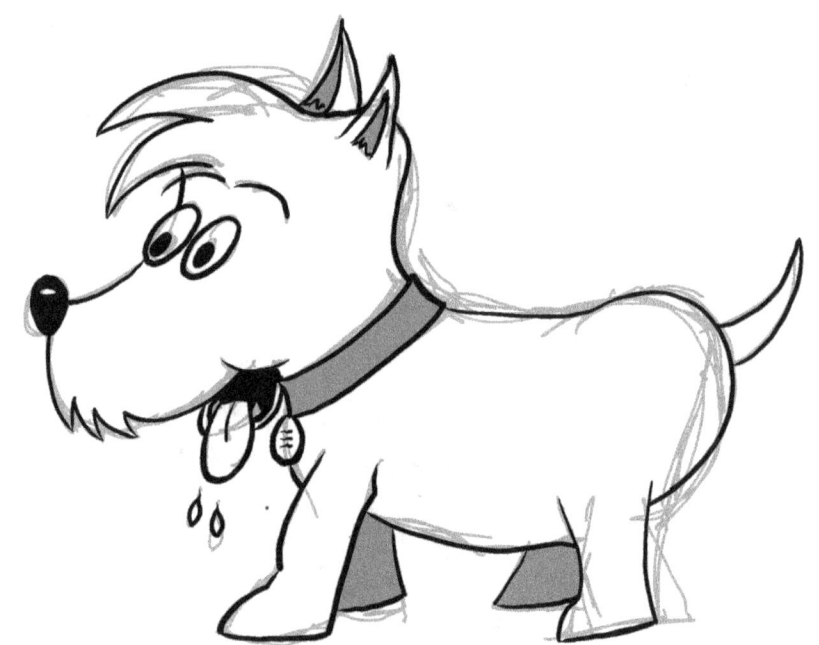

Even though Mary Beth enjoyed drawing with the cousins she didn't let on to her mom.

"Thanks for watching the boys. It was a great help," her mom said.

"It's not fair," Mary Beth grumped. "All they did was talk about farting, butts, and spit."

"Sorry honey, but that is what boys at this age do."

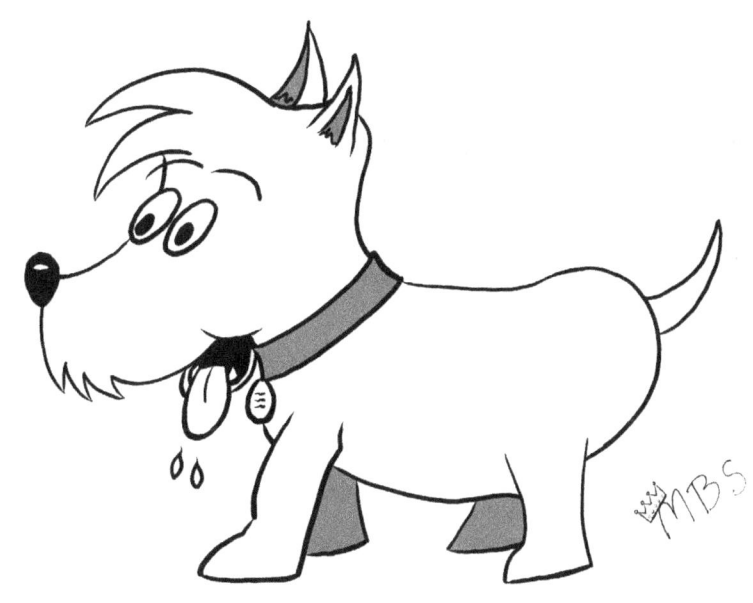

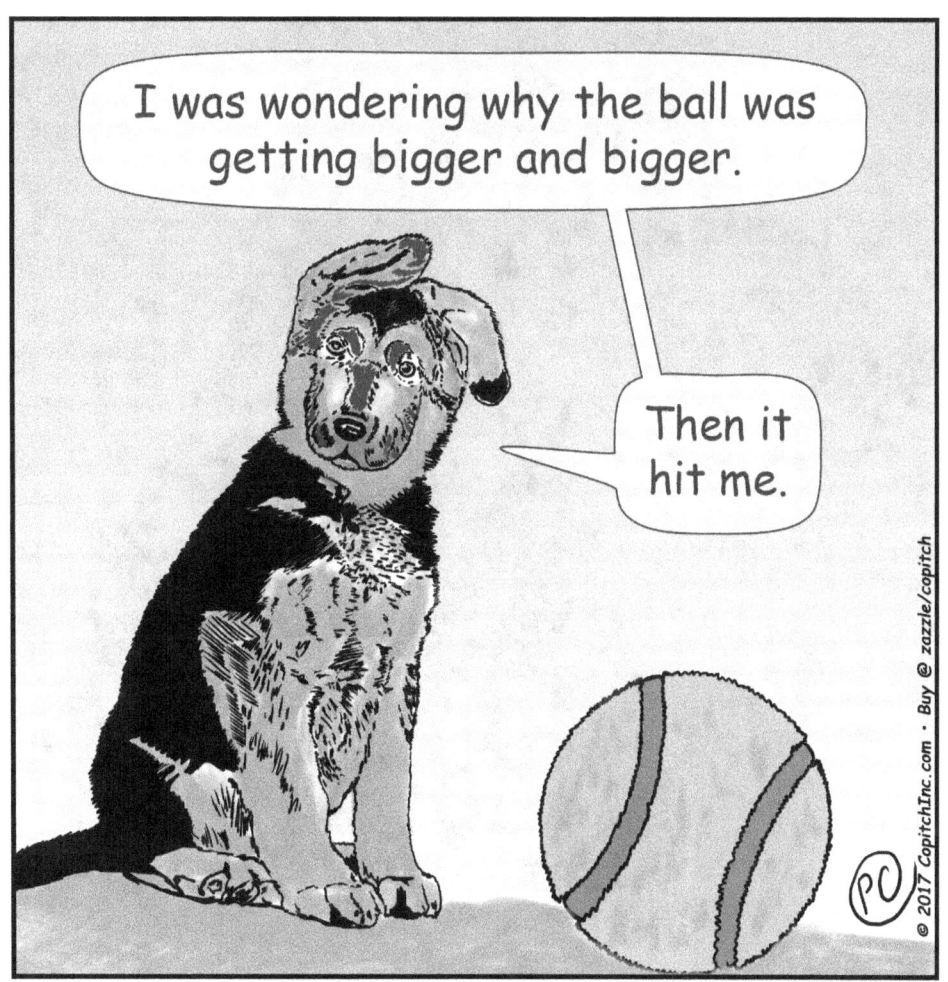

Baby Jazz started out small.

Chapter 12
How to draw a Doberman named Debbie

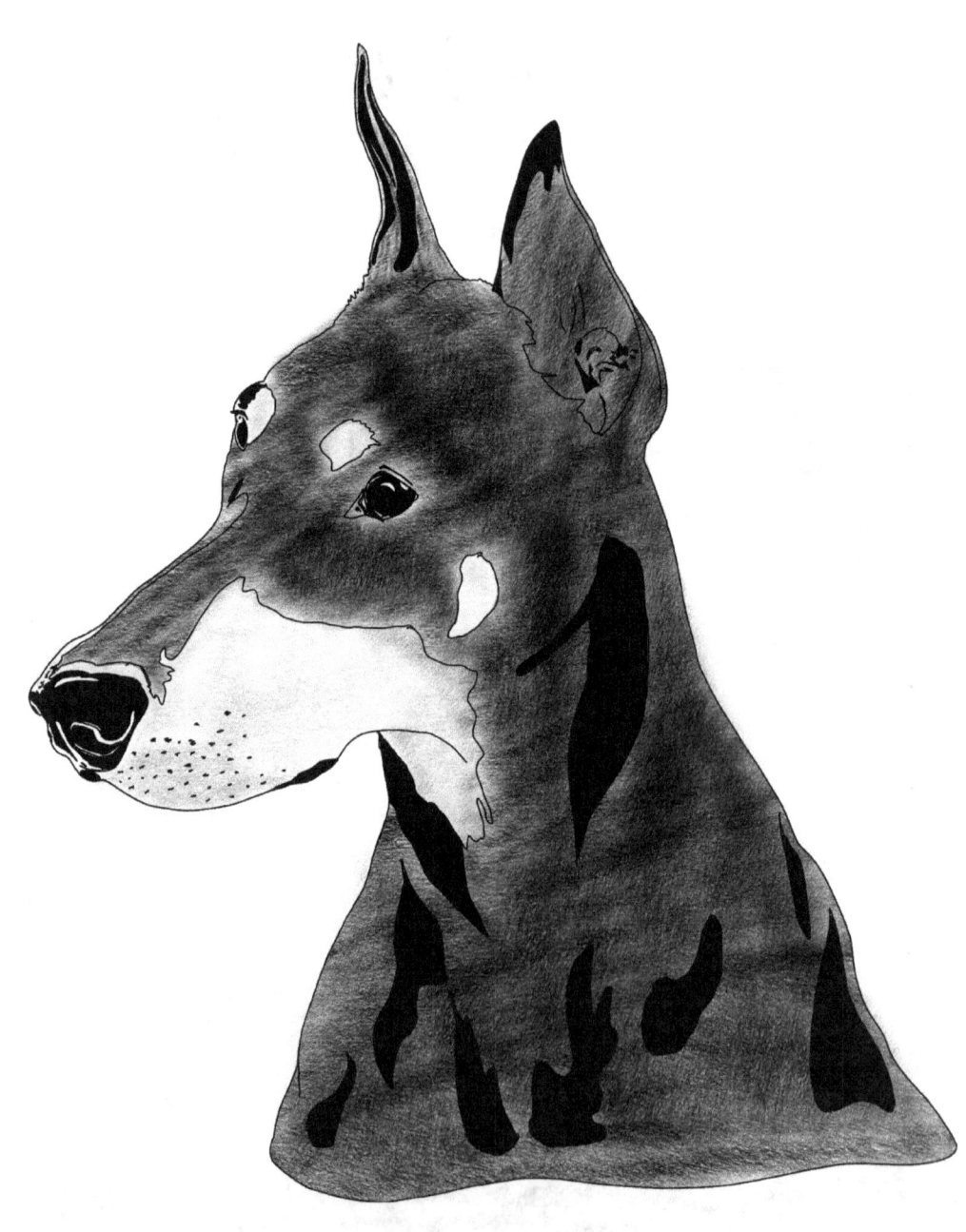

General Fenwick comes to visit Mary Beth's dad about once a month. Even though she has known the general her whole life, Mary Beth is a little afraid of him. He is very loud and large, with wide shoulders and a chest full of medals. It isn't his size that scares her, it's that he always has other soldiers around him. One soldier drives the large black truck. He opens the general's door and snaps to attention as the general gets out. The driver never comes in, he stands like a stone figure by the truck. A second soldier is a captain, named Ross. She follows the general around and is often on the phone. Mary Beth knows that Captain Ross is really smart because she used to be her dad's student at the university.

"General Fenwick is coming to the lab after lunch," Dad said, as he put the tuna sandwiches on the table. "I'm sure he would love to see you. He always says he misses you, now that you are usually in school when he visits."

"OK, I'll wear an army hat after lunch."

At one o'clock exactly, the general's vehicle pulled up in front of the house.

Mary Beth met the visitors with her dad at the lab door.

"Hi, Mary Beth," the general boomed. "Boy, have you grown. Pretty soon you'll fit into your helmet."

"Thank you, sir," Mary Beth said, as she held the helmet up off her nose.

"What are you doing this summer? Anything fun?" asked the general.

"I've started a business, I draw dogs for money."

"Really, are you any good?" said the general.

"Yes sir," said Mary Beth, as she snapped to attention and saluted. As she did this, she wondered why she did. Then she felt silly.

"Very good," said the general.

"I'll take care of this, sir," said Captain Ross, "You have a meeting with Dr. Schmendrick."

"Yes, yes," said the general, as he walked into the lab.

Captain Ross walked over to the driver and said, "Sergeant, bring Debbie into the house, she is going to have her portrait done."

"Yes ma'am," said the sergeant.

Debbie was a magnificent Doberman Pinscher, and the best trained dog Mary Beth had ever met. Jazz and Debbie seemed to know each other and that made Mary Beth think that stuff happened at her house when she was at school.

Advice from Mary Beth
on how to draw Debbie.

For Debbie the
Doberman we
start off using
triangles and
oblongs as our
guides,

Remember, very
light at first.

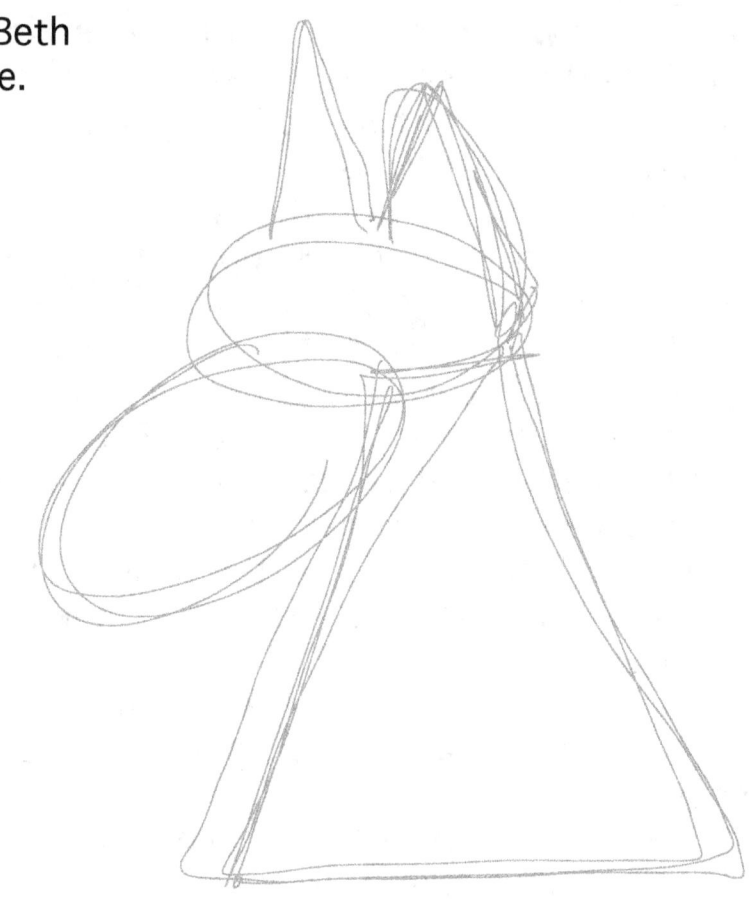

Now we find the
forehead, eyes, and
the top of the snout.

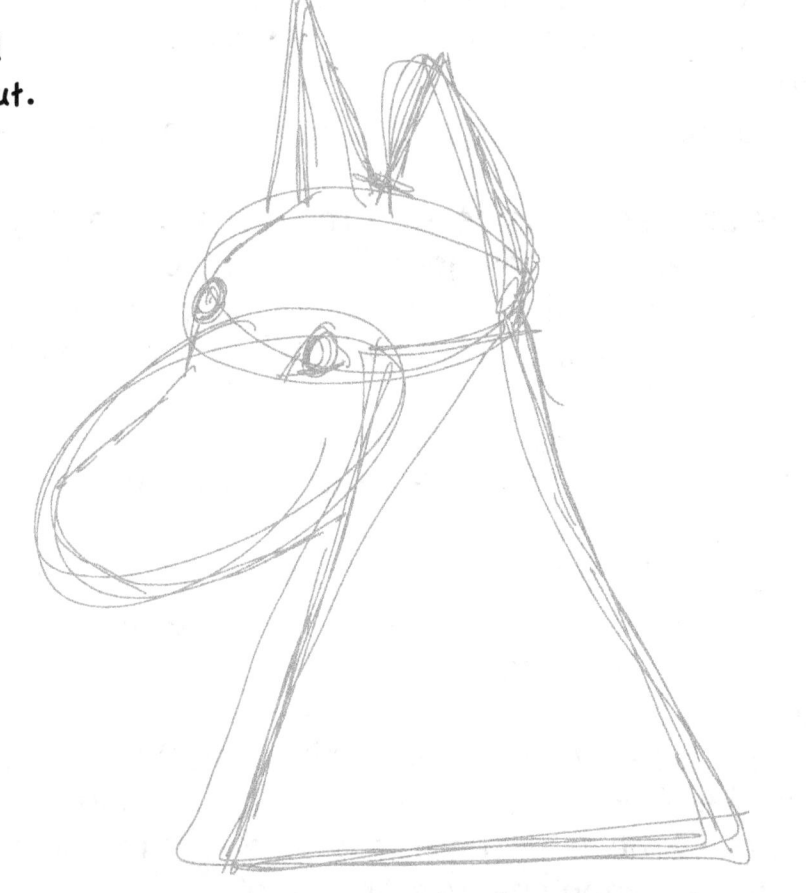

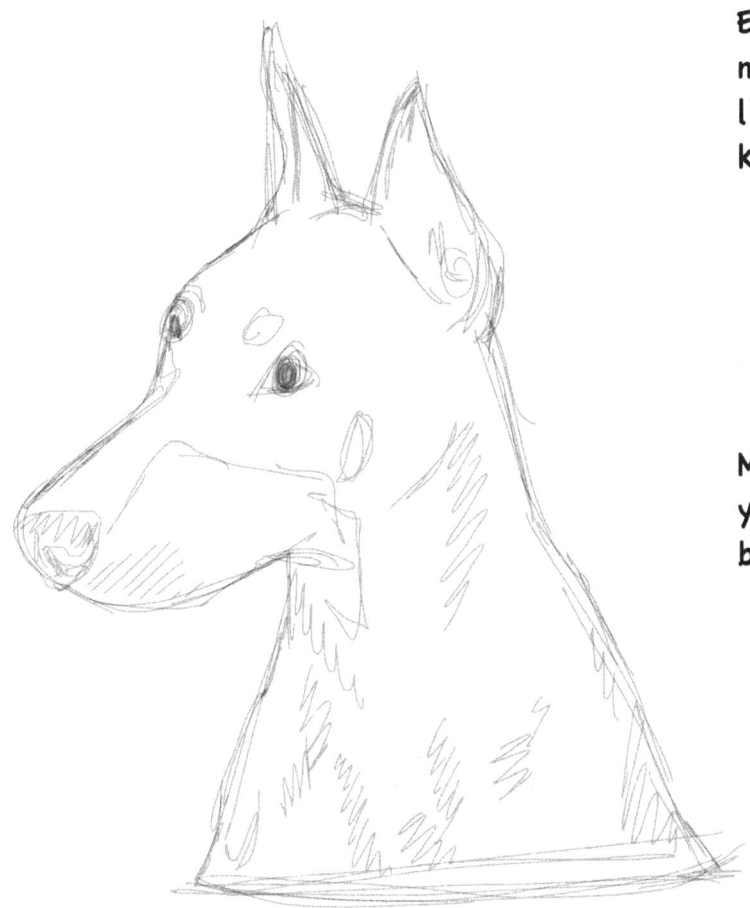

Erase lines you don't need and strengthen lines you want to keep.

Mark off the areas you want to be all black.

Pen the black areas. This is tricky because Debbie has a lot of black fur. We will use dark and light gray to show contrast.

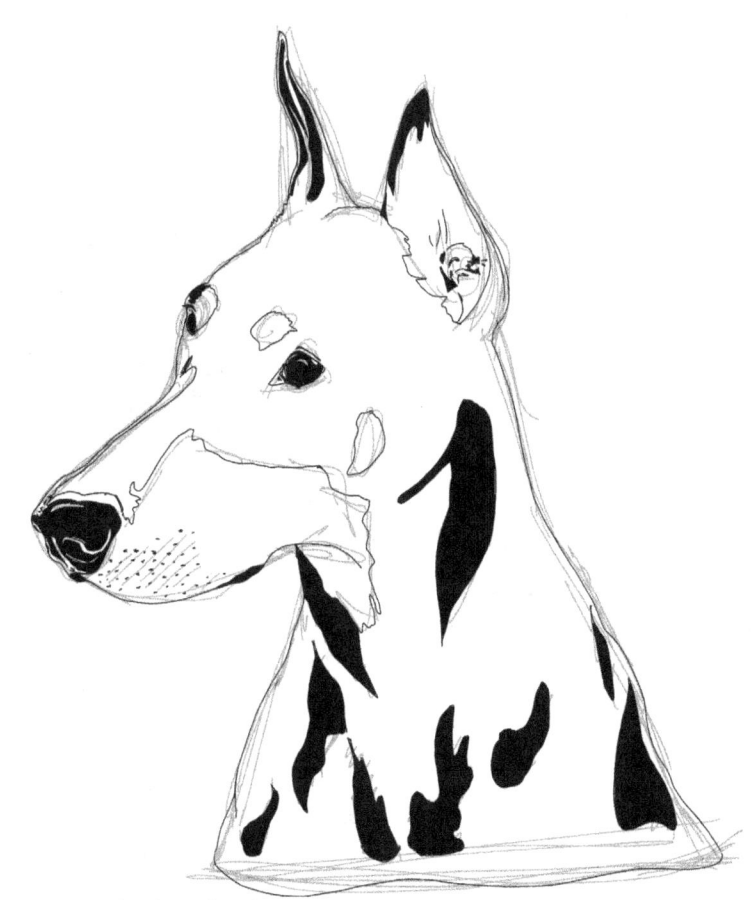

Debbie's nose is almost all black, so we will trick the eye by using white lines (not penned) and black blotches.

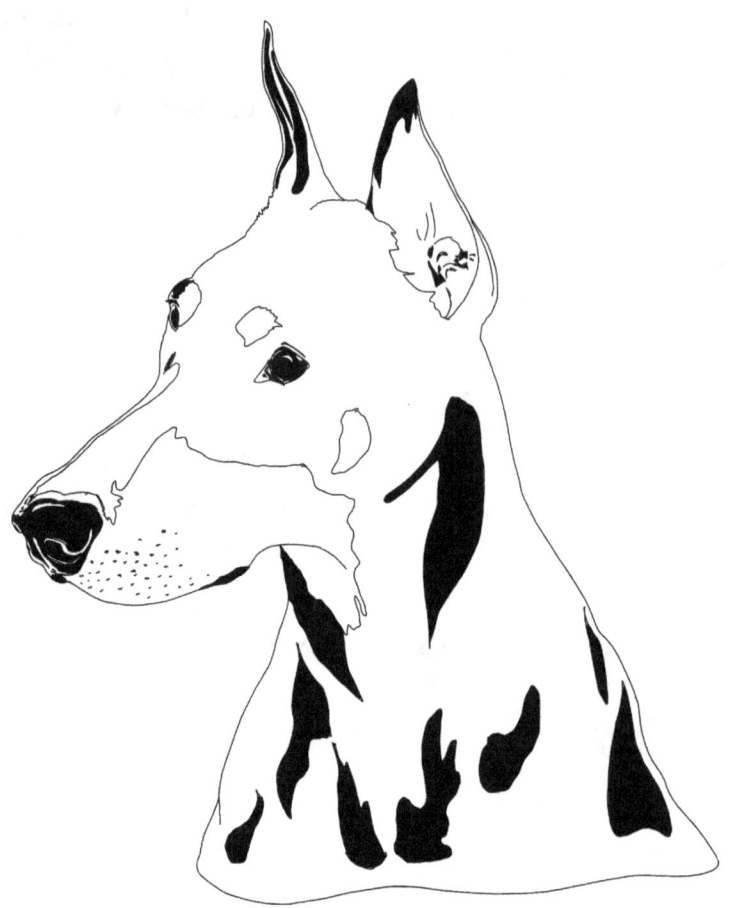

Removing the pencil lines shows you where you need to shade.

Build up shading to show the contrast of Debbie's coat.

If an area of shading gets too dark, knock it back with a gum eraser.

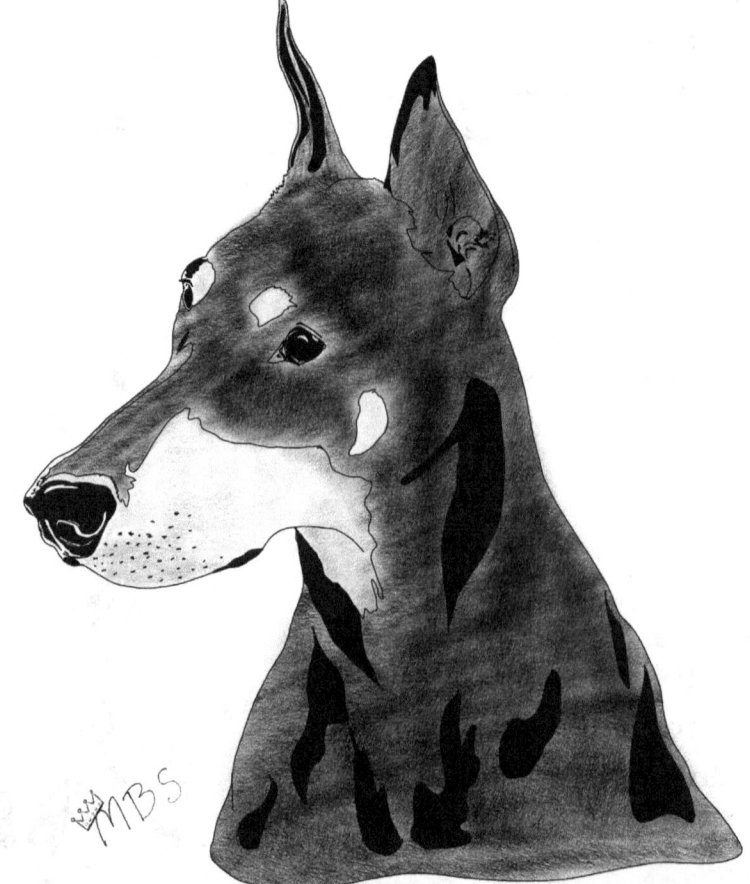

~ 72 ~

Chapter 13
How to draw a Goldendoodle

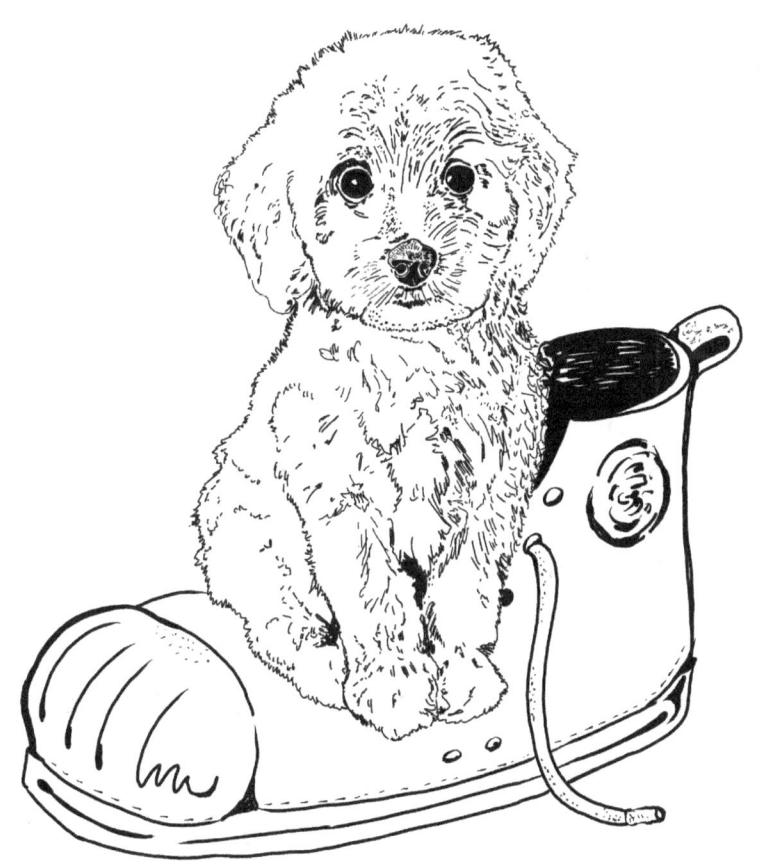

Light colored dogs are tricky, you have to show the definition of the pup without really drawing that many lines.

Mary Beth and her dad were at the tire store getting new tires for the family car. On the drive over, Dad told Mary Beth, "Before we go camping I want to get the tires replaced and the brakes checked. It's best to be able to stop if you need to."

Mary Beth was only half listening. She was still angry that her dad didn't let her bring Jazz along.

"The tire store parking lot is not a safe place for you and Jazz to walk around," Dad said.

"But, Jazz and I want to stay in the car when it goes up on the lift," Mary Beth explained.

"Dogs and children aren't allowed in the work area," Dad said.

Mary Beth hated it when parents made up rules to win arguments. So, before she left the house she put on a big white sun hat, and pulled it down low over her eyes, so she wouldn't even have to look at her dad.

At the tire store, Mary Beth noticed the smell. It was yucky. The tires smelled like melting boy cousin socks on a hot summer day.

"Nice hat," a soft voice said.

Mary Beth looked up and saw a plump grandma lady wearing a green dress covered with a daisy flower print.

"Thanks," Mary Beth said, "I got it last summer just in case I ever get to go to a fancy dress luncheon like in the movies."

"Are you a fancy lady?" the plump grandma lady asked.

"No, I'm a business woman. I draw dogs for money," Mary Beth said, and she patted her old satchel. Her cookie tin filled with art supplies made a pleasing thud, thud; proof she was an artist.

"My dog is in the RV. I'd love you to draw her," the plump grandma lady said.

As it turned out, the plump grandma lady had a Goldendoodle puppy named Daisy. Daisy was happy to prance around and sometimes sit on the wooden picnic table just outside the door to the tire shop. Daisy had an old high top sneaker that was her favorite toy. She and the sneaker were about the same size.

Mary Beth chitchatted with Daisy's mom as she drew Daisy. When she was done, Daisy's mom said, "How about $3 for the drawing?" and handed her three crisp dollar bills.

"OK," Mary Beth said, as Daisy and her mom went off towards the parking lot.

Mary Beth was thinking about the $3 when she realized she was being rude. "Bye, and thanks for the job!" she yelled.

Mary Beth explains how to draw Daisy.

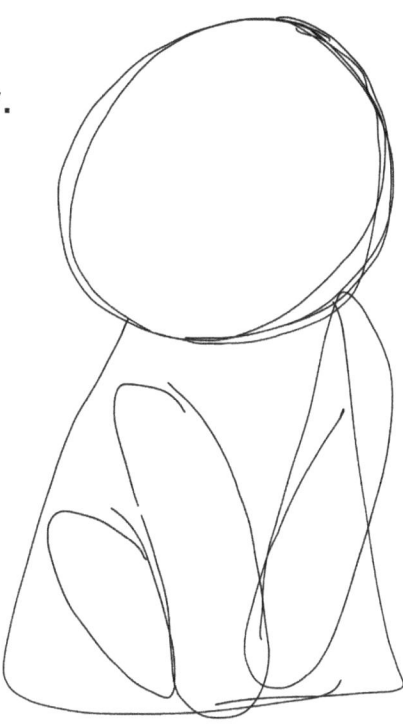

We start with a frame of our cute little friend. I am leaving space under her for her shoe. Since I can get the shoe to sit still, I will add it after Daisy has lost interest in being a model.

The large shoe will help show how small and cute Daisy is.

Start by finding the head shape. Then the body shape.

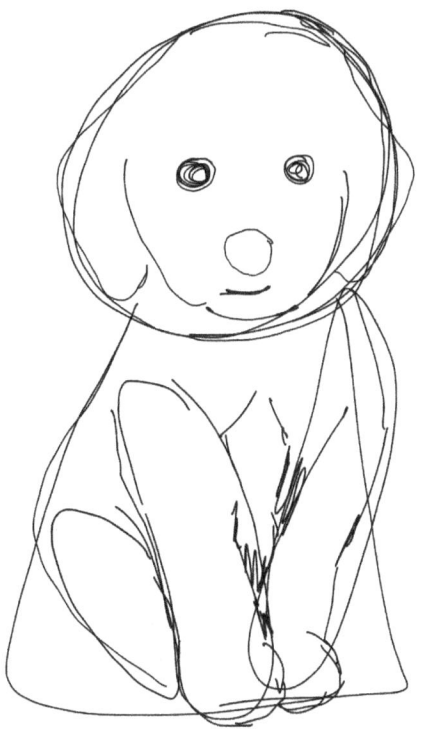

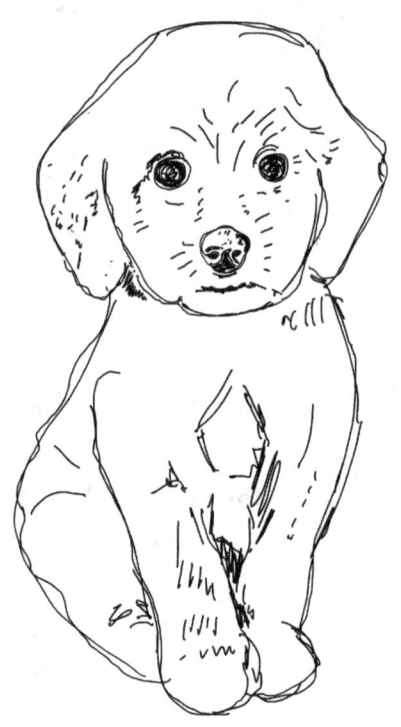

Erase lines you don't like. Gently build up lines you do like.

At this point, the puppy laid down and took a nap. She was completely bored with being a model. Now I worked on the shoe. Sneakers are known to be patient models.

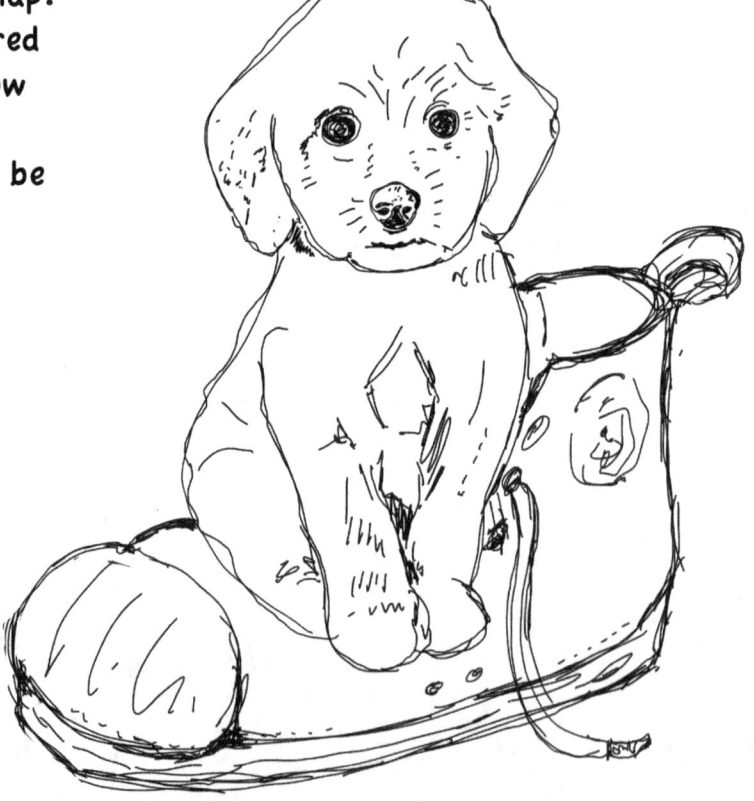

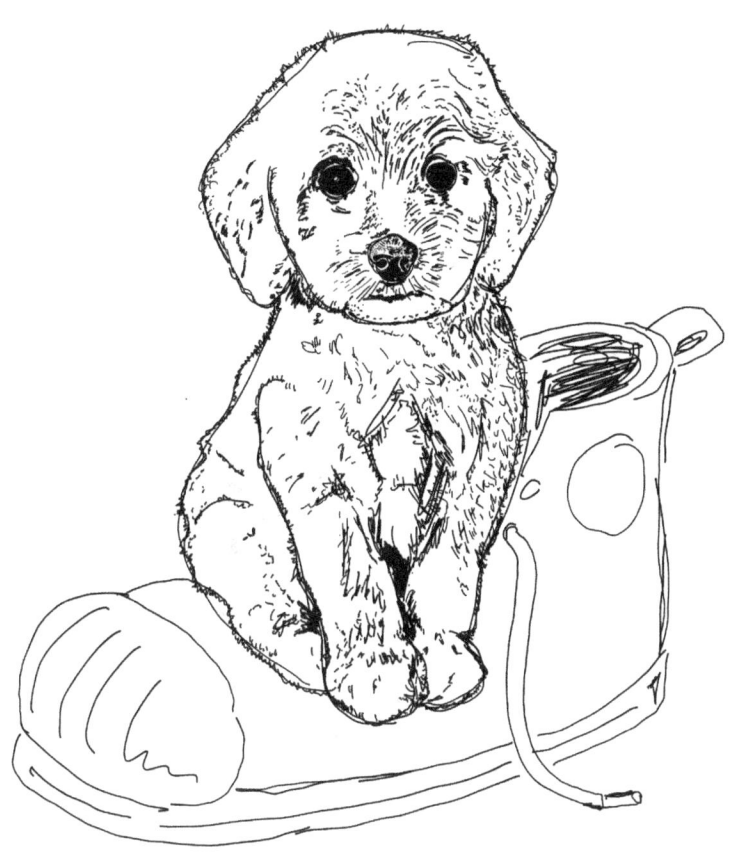

Even when she's napping
we get glimpses of Daisy's
supreme cuteness,

Because Goldendoodles are
pretty much one light color,
we have to be very careful,
making each line count.

I used the .07 pen on the
outside and the .05 pen for
the face and chest fur.

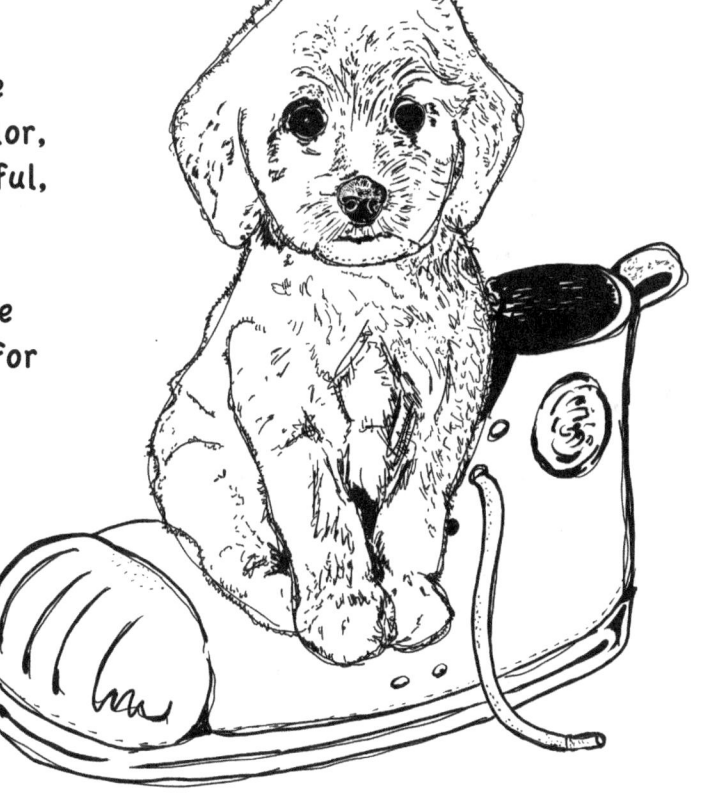

Erase the rest of your guild
lines so that your pen lines
can jump out.

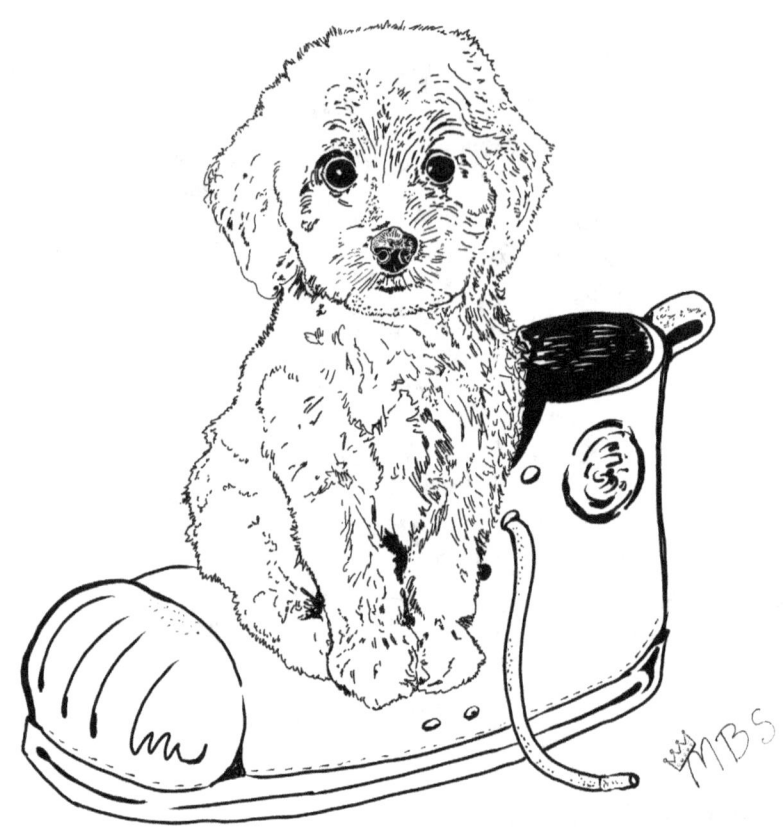

On the drive home, Mary Beth told her dad about the
Goldendoodle and the $3.

"Daisy's mom just kind of forced me to take $3 as payment. I
don't understand this selling stuff," Mary Beth said.

"I don't know about the money part, MB, but it seems as a
business woman you need to know the real names of the people you
are working for," Dad said.

"Yeah, that too," Mary Beth said. "At first I thought her name
was... ah... never mind. It's hard to ask someone their name."

"It makes sense that it's hard," Dad said, "but no one gets mad
if you ask their name. In fact, I think it's important to keep track of
your customers' names. It's part of business."

The rest of the ride home Mary Beth pulled her white sun hat
down and thought about how much fun drawing was and how hard
business was.

Chapter 14
How to draw a Lhasa Apso

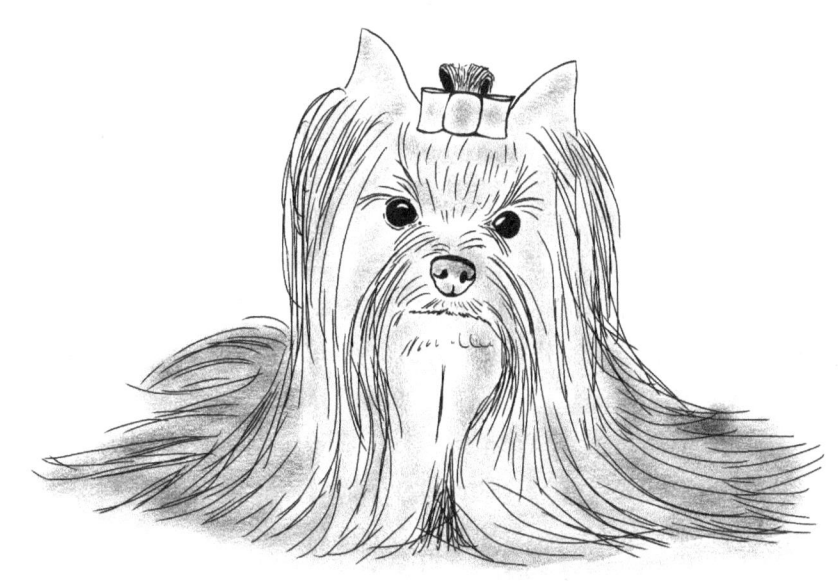

About ten houses away, and just around the corner, there was a fancy house. A company came once a week to mow the lawn and trim the hedges. A different company came to take care of the pool in the backyard that no one ever used.

The kids in the neighborhood called the quiet older couple that lived in the house, the "Mean Ones." But, everyone really knew their name was Monroe. Mary Beth heard that if your ball or Frisbee landed in the Mean One's backyard you would never get it back. Sparky Thompson said that Mr. Mean One once yelled at him for doing nothing, but Sparky says that every adult yells at him for doing nothing. Mary Beth thought this was stupid, like Sparky, because he was always in trouble for doing dumb stuff.

The Monroe house had a large picture window. In this picture window was a long haired little dog. The dog looked very pretty, but a little angry, kind of like Mr. and Mrs. Monroe. Every day, the tiny dog had a colorful bow in her hair between her itty-bitty ears.

"Mom, I want to draw the long haired tiny dog that lives in the picture window, but I never see her people," Mary Beth said, at breakfast.

"Oh yes, the Monroes are quiet people, but they work across town and spend a lot of time in their cars."

"How do I get to talk to them about buying a drawing of their dog?" asked Mary Beth.

"I once read a book that had different ways to get sales. One was called the Puppy Dog Sale," Mom said.

"They already own a dog ..."

"No, no, the Puppy Dog Sale is named after the way people sell puppies outside of stores. If they ask, 'do you want a puppy?' people will just say no, but if you hand someone a cute warm puppy to hold, you have a chance to make a sale. It's an easier sale once they have the puppy in their hands."

"Is that how we got the cousins?" Mary Beth smiled.

"Noooooo, the cousins were a gift from God."

"OK, so I need to get my drawing into Mr. and Mrs. Monroe's hands. That can't be too hard," Mary Beth said, and she started out of the kitchen.

"Don't forget your plate. Please put it on the counter," Mom said.

Mary Beth pretended that she hadn't forgotten. "I was just about to do it!" But for reals, she was thinking about how to do a Puppy Dog Sale on Mr. and Mrs. Monroe.

Mary Beth drew the long haired dog by standing outside the big picture window. Below is Mary Beth's advice on how to draw this tiny pooch.

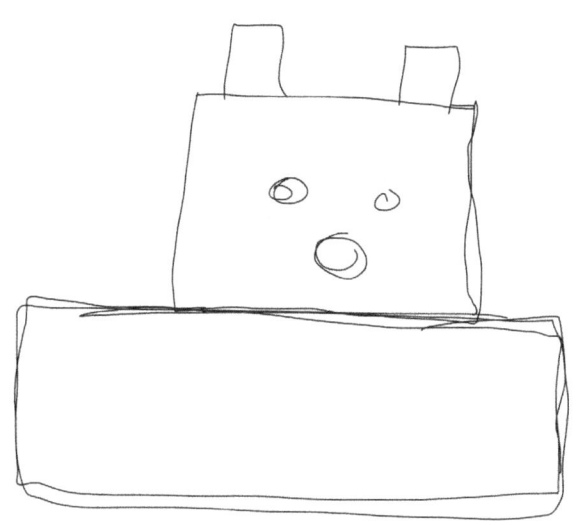

Let's start with box shapes to help define the body.

Circles for the nose and eyes.

Because this pup is mostly hair, we will have to show individual hair as lines. This can be a problem. Lots of lines can quickly become a mess of lines that look like a blotch of lines or just one really fat black line.

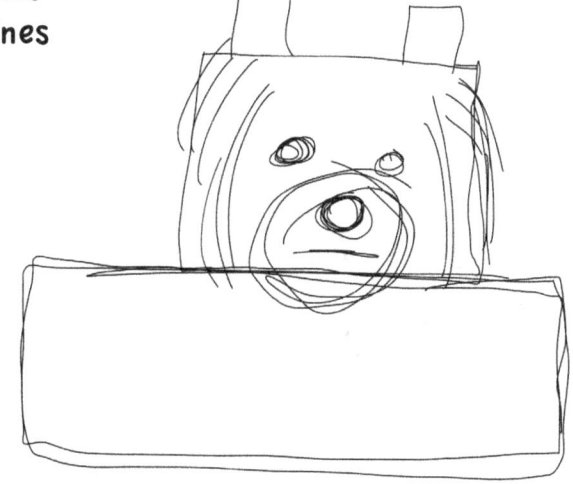

Here is where the artist has
to trick the eye into seeing
lots of hairs without really
drawing lots of hairs.

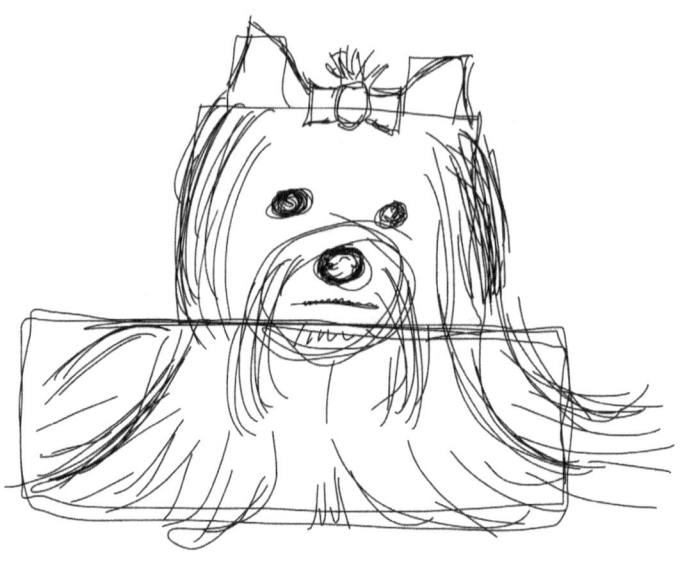

The white space between lines tricks the eye
into thinking there are many more lines.

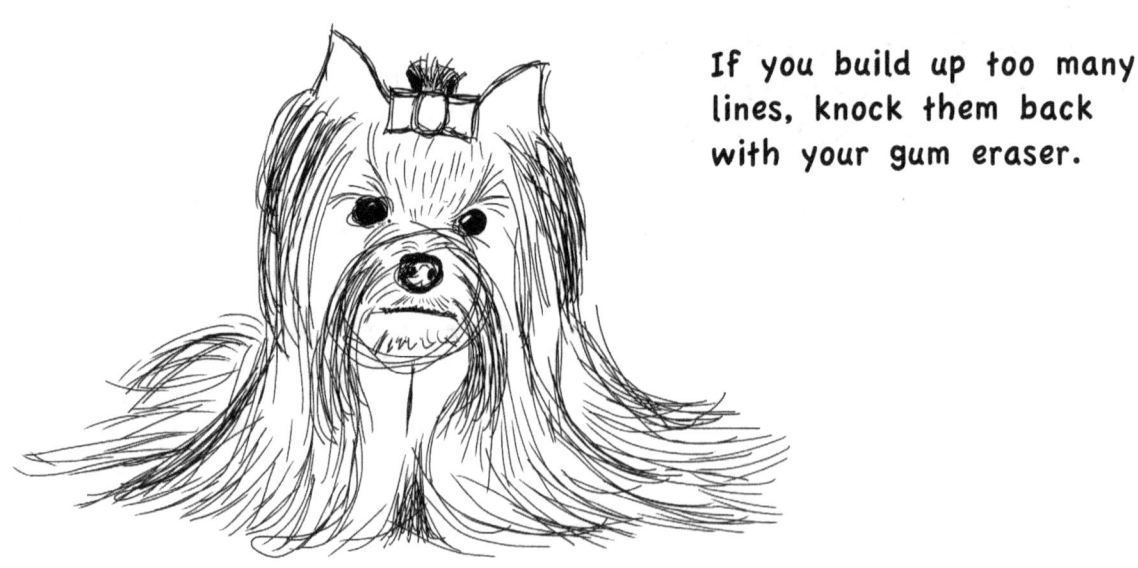

If you build up too many
lines, knock them back
with your gum eraser.

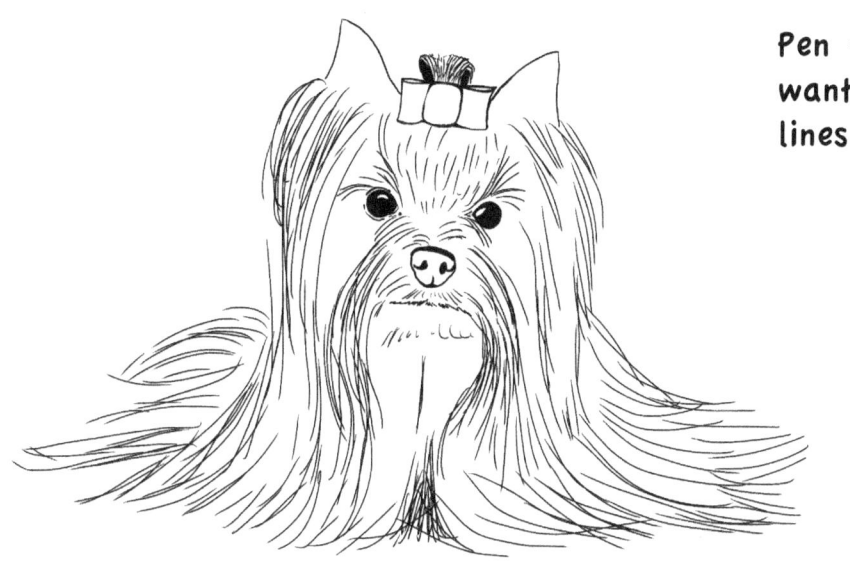

Pen the hairs you want to keep with thin lines.

Build up shade with the side of your pencil.

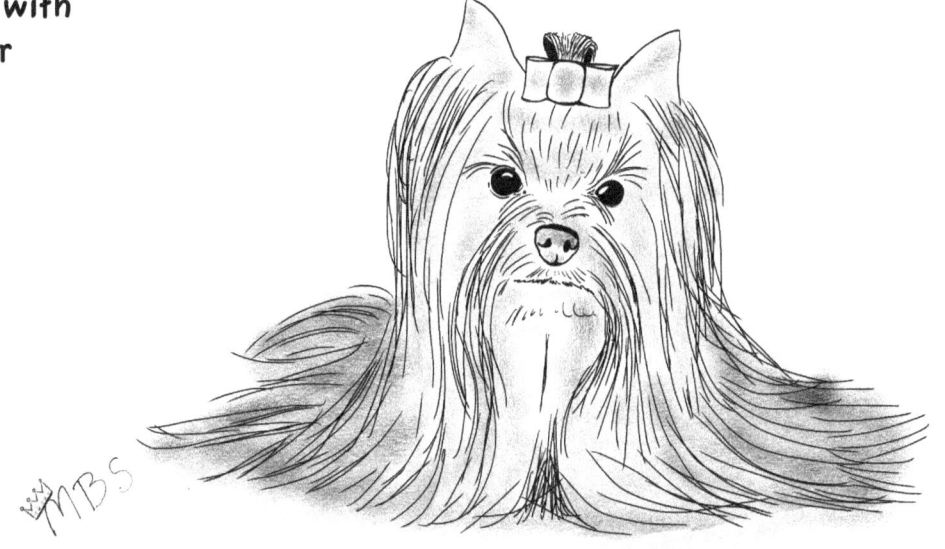

When Mary Beth was done with the drawing she went to her dad's lab in the garage and got a big envelope from the third drawer of his desk. Even though her dad always said, "YOU CAN'T GO IN MY LAB IF I'M NOT THERE," Mary Beth was pretty sure that he didn't really mean it.

Mary Beth wrote 'Mr. and Mrs. Monroe' in her best cursive, even though she knew she wasn't as good at cursive as the Amortiss twins. She figured that the Monroes didn't know the twins, so they would think she was the best at cursive in her class.

The envelope had a large red band across the middle that read TOP SECRET. Mary Beth decided to cross it out because she wanted the Monroes to open the envelope.

Mary Beth put her art and a letter into the envelope.

The letter read:

Dear Mr. and Mrs. Monroe,

I am Mary Beth. I have a company that draws dogs for people in the neighborhood. I have not gotten to meet you yet, so I hope you do not mind me looking in the window and drawing your dog.

She is very pretty and the perfect model. She didn't move a muscle the whole time I drew her. Not even when I had to run home to pee.

The day I drew her, she had a yellow bow in her hair. I had to draw it white because I don't have a yellow pen.

I hope you like my drawing. If not, please give it back to Mr. Villa. He is the postman. He goes to every house delivering mail. I think that is his job. He also was my first customer. He has a picture of Jazz taped to his dashboard.

If you like my drawing and want to keep it, please give Mr. Villa the money. He is nice. He won't steal it.

Mr. Peterson paid $5 for his dog's drawing, and Mr. King paid 3 pizzas.

Thank you,
Mary Beth

P.S. I would never throw balls or Frisbees into your backyard.

The next morning, Mary Beth asked Mr. Villa if he would deliver the large envelope to Mr. and Mrs. Monroe. He laughed at her and said he would be happy to, even without a stamp. Mary Beth was never sure why adults laughed at her, but this day she figured it might be because she was wearing a huge football helmet with a bulldog on the side.

A week later, Mr. Villa brought her a fancy envelope from Monroe Financial Service. There was a large green check inside printed by a computer. It was for "Twenty-Five and 00/00 dollars."

When Mary Beth showed it to her mom she said, "Interesting. No note. But what a nice Puppy Dog Sale you made."

Mary Beth was not sure what she could do with a check, but she was pretty sure it was kind of like money.

Chapter 15
How to draw a Papillon

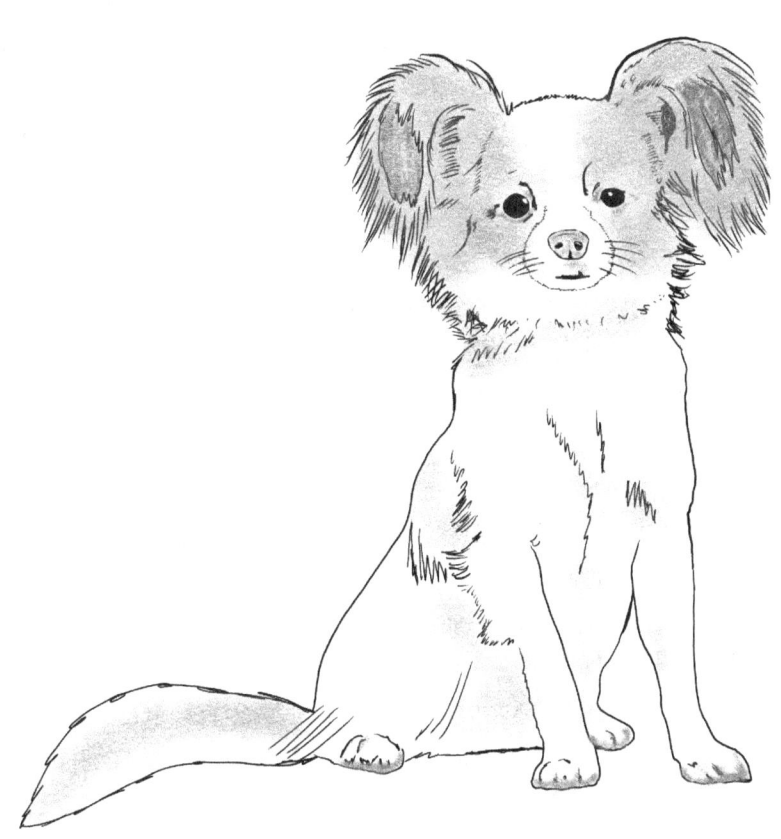

Mary Beth and her mom went to the Sisterhood Thrift Shop in the old building behind the church. Mary Beth got most of her hats there.

Mrs. Harriet Chapin ran the shop with her dog Sergeant. She was a kind lady with a lot of energy. When she organized stuff, she often hummed a tune to herself. Mrs. Chapin would sneak away prized hats when they were donated, knowing that Mary Beth was nuts about hats.

Sergeant was an old dog. He laid by the cash register and supervised. Often he would sleep.

"Hi Harry," Mary Beth's mom said, as she came through the door.

"Oh, it's so good to see you two," Mrs. Chapin smiled. "I have a few hats for you to look at, Mary Beth."

Mary Beth told her friend about her dog drawing business.

"How's business going, are you gaining market share? Getting ready to franchise?" Mrs. Chapin laughed. Mary Beth also laughed, even though she had no idea what was so funny. Mary Beth often didn't understand what adults were laughing about.

"I think business is going well. But, I am going to run out of dogs in the neighborhood to draw," Mary Beth said.

"Before I started running our thrift shop I ran a business for over 40 years," Mrs. Chapin said. "One thing I learned is that in business you have to pivot constantly or you won't be in business for long."

"Pivot?" Mary Beth said.

"Sure, you know, grow and change with the times. If you don't give the customer what they want, someone else will. Business is a dog eat dog world, ya know."

"How can I pivot? I'm not allowed to go out of the neighborhood," Mary Beth said.

"Every business has regulations and problems to solve. Your job as the business owner is to figure out how to get things done." Mrs. Chapin started to talk to Sergeant in baby talk. "Isn't that right Sargy-poo, we have to keep growing, or our business is going to be left in the dust."

"I want to pivot, any ideas? I'm pretty sure I would be good at pivoting." Mary Beth said, not knowing if 'pivoting' was a real word.

"Sure, let's see. Can you draw a dog from a photo? If you can, you can advertise and have people send you photos of their dog."

"Advertise?"

"You know, make signs and put them up. You could put one up over there on the Community Board. Loads of people look at that board every week.

Mrs. Chapin pulled open a drawer behind the counter. After a little scrounging, she handed Mary Beth a photograph of Sergeant. "I would like to hire you to draw a picture of Sargy-poo," she said.

"Sergeant is sitting up?" Mary Beth asked.

"Sure. He used to sit up all the time, But, now that he is retired, he just lies around making mommy do all the work," she said, as she scratched his head. "Isn't that right Sargy-poo?"

Mary Beth had never drawn from a photo before. At first, she was nervous. But then she thought about the dog in the picture, *It's nice that they don't walk away, lick themselves, or try to eat your pencil.*

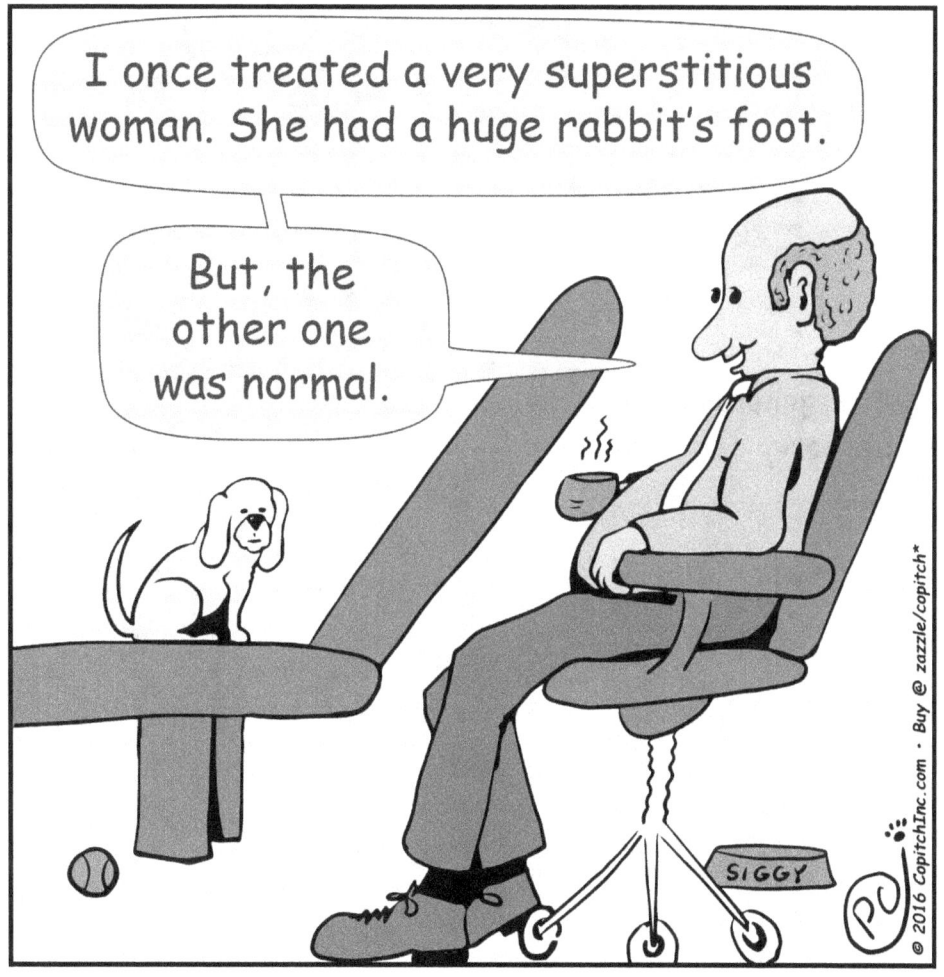

Advice from Mary Beth on how to draw Sergeant.

We start with the general
shape of boxes topped with
circles.

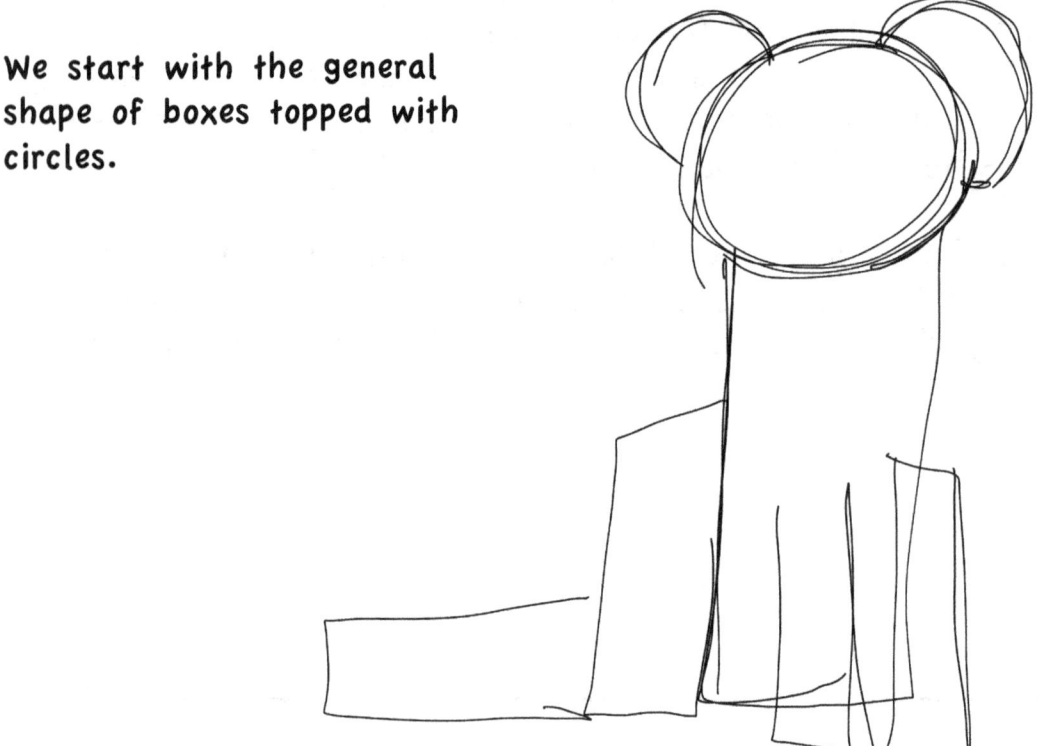

Here we get a general idea
of where the nose, snout and
eyes would go.

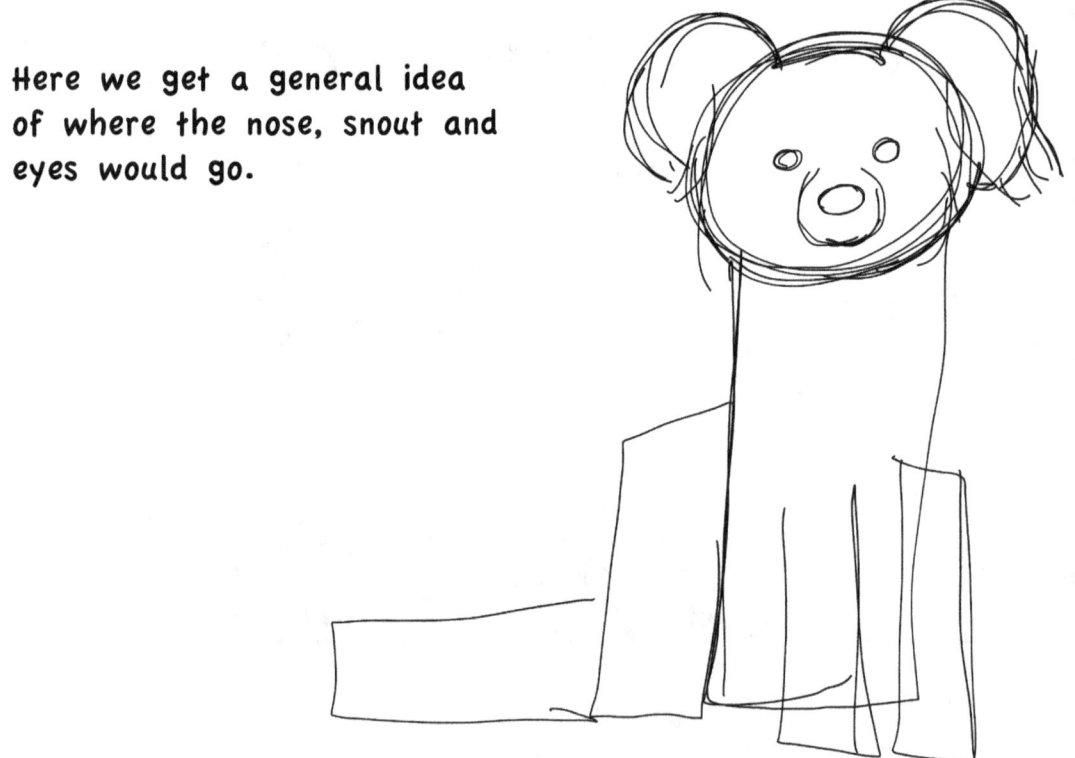

Build up gentle lines for the
back, tail, and legs.

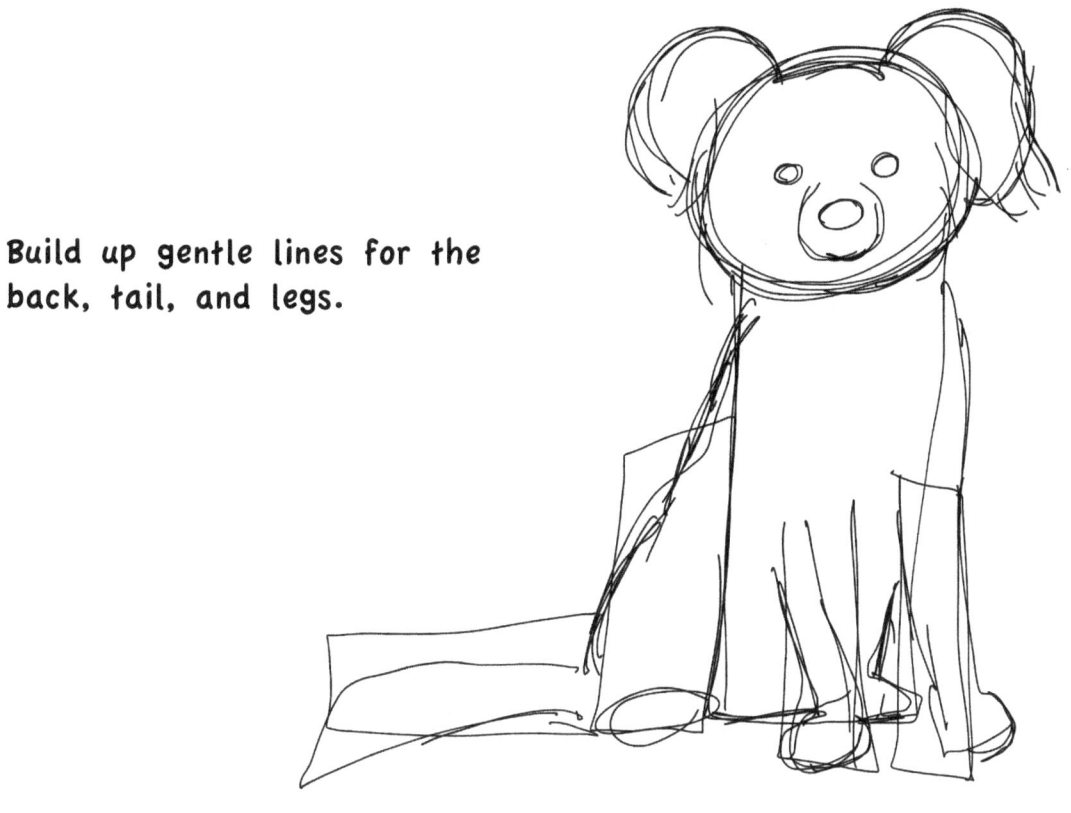

It helps to remove the box
guides so we can see what
we are doing.

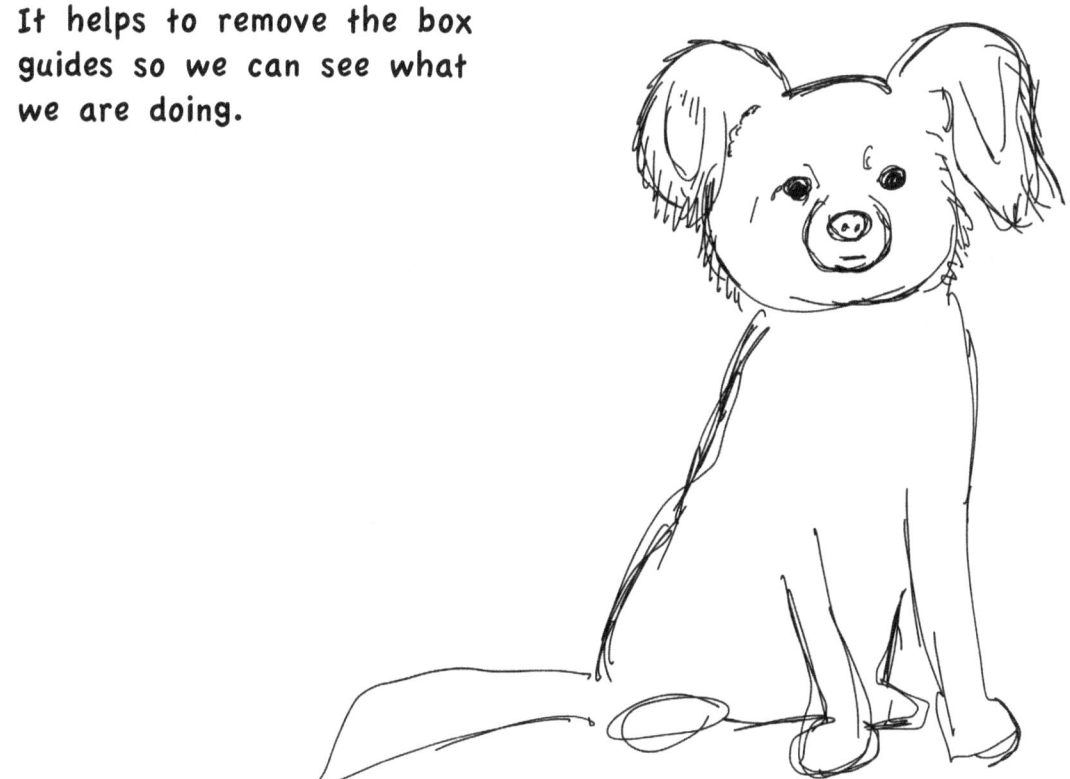

We should build up lines of
fur. If you overdo it, knock
down the pencil lines with a
gum eraser.

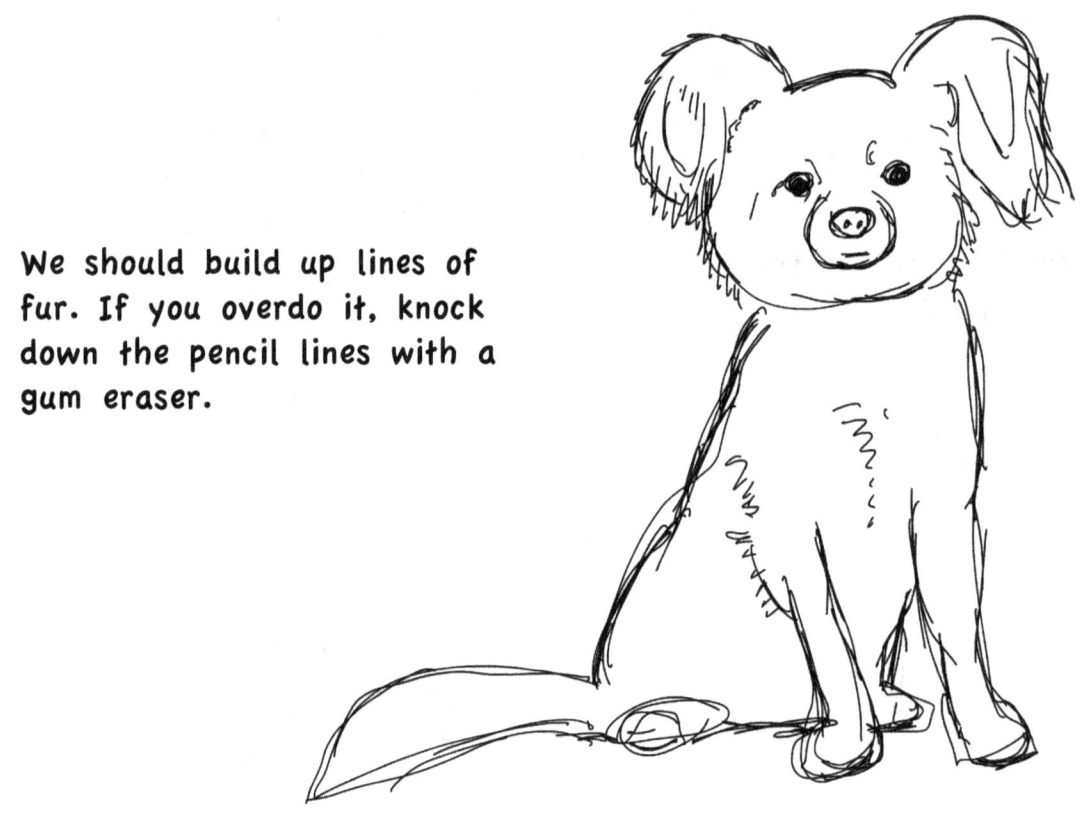

By keeping the lines we like,
we are starting to see our
Sargy-poo friend.

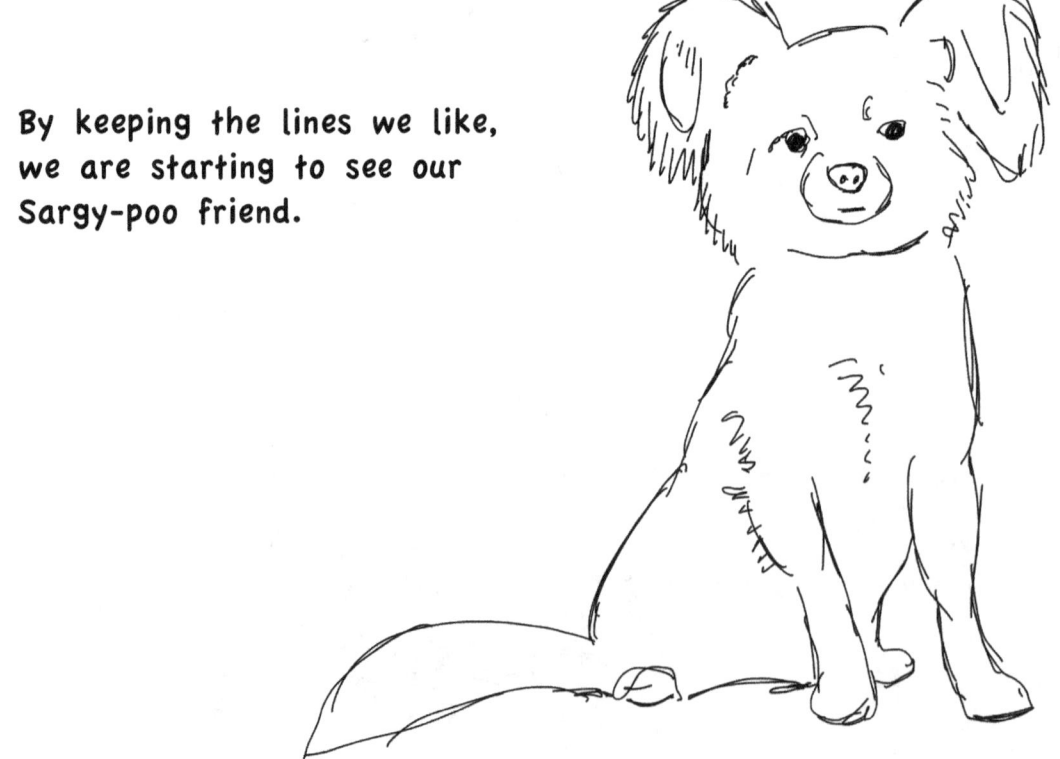

Pen the lines you like the best.

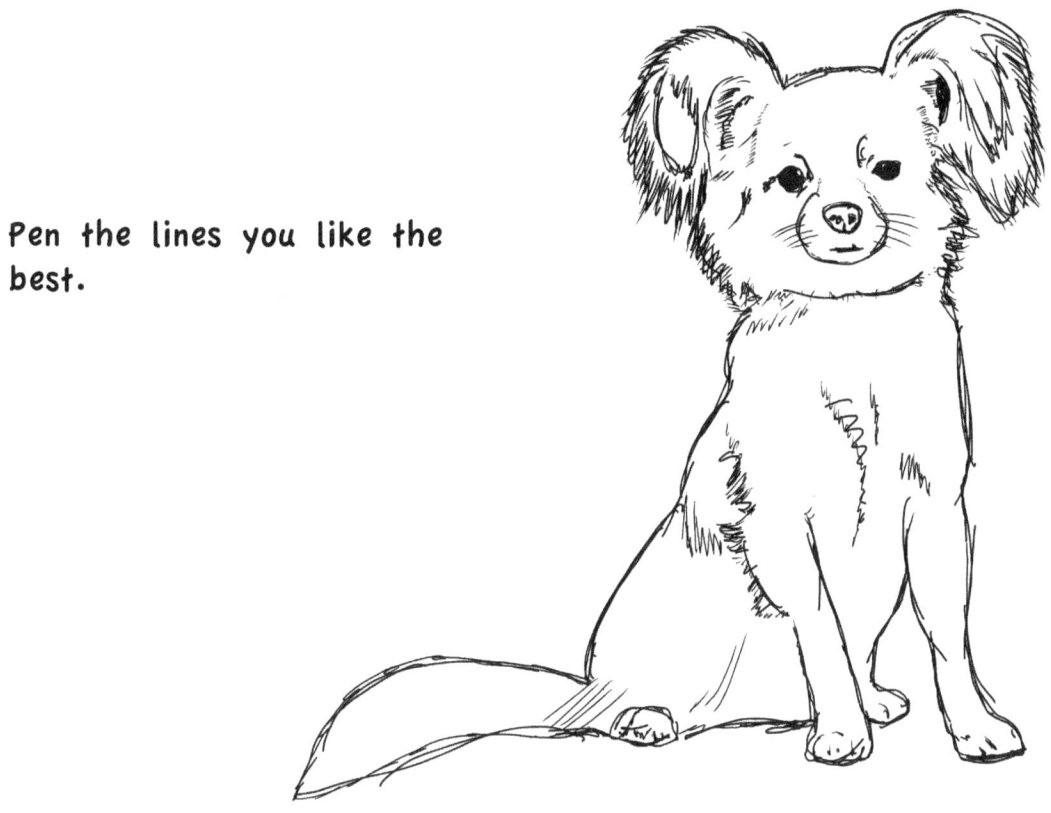

Erase the pencil lines. Looking good!

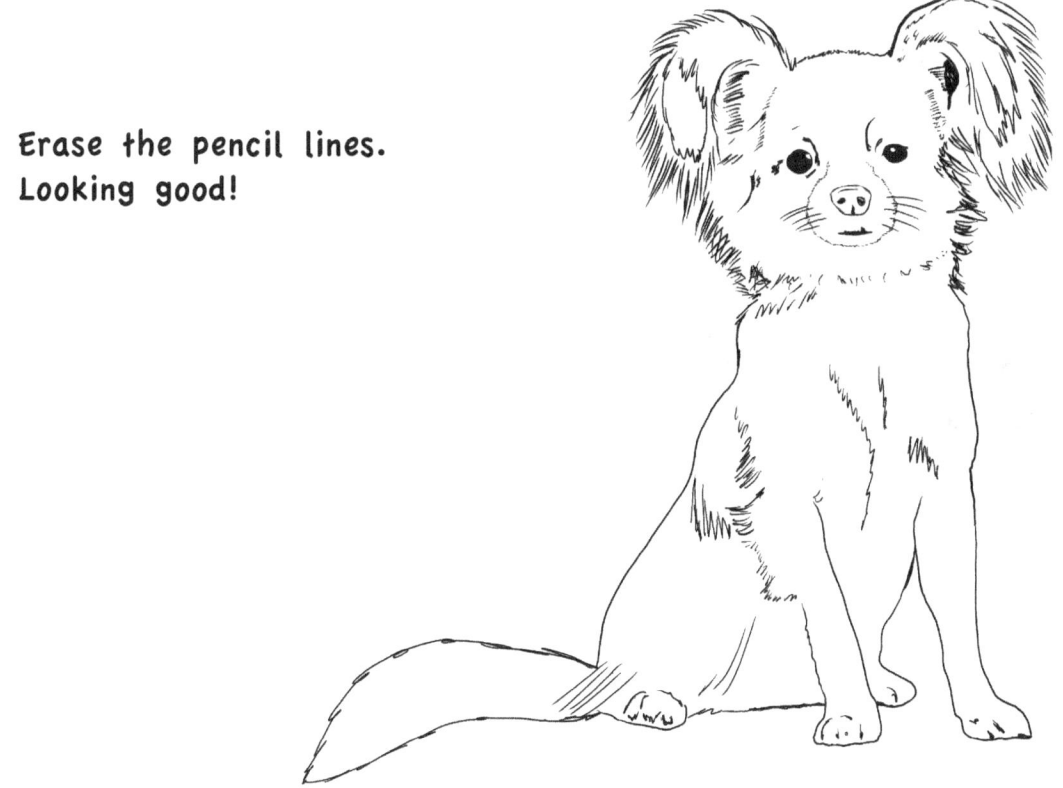

Shade with the side
of your pencil.

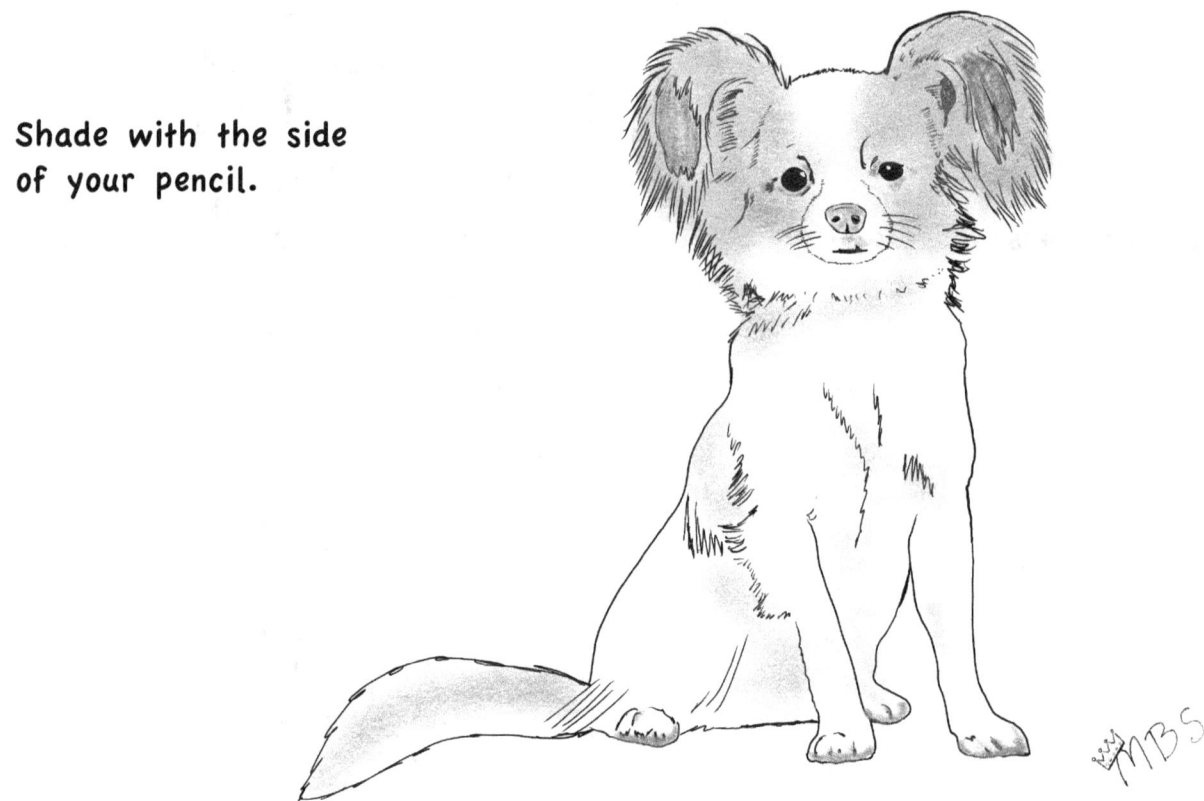

Mary Beth and her mom finished buying a few things, Mrs. Chapin said, "I've been thinking, if you can't leave the neighborhood, it's going to be hard to get your fliers out to people. You could ask your mom and dad to post a few at work, or better yet, your mom could put it on her Facebook page."

"Thanks for the good ideas," Mary Beth said. "Loads of people read my mom's Facebook page."

Mary Beth and her mom walked to the car. Mary Beth thought that posting a flier in her dad's lab in the garage probably wouldn't get seen, but maybe he would put one on his office door at the university next to the old yellowed cartoons and the picture of his favorite scientist, Albert Einstein.

Chapter 16
How to draw Cool Connie the Corgi

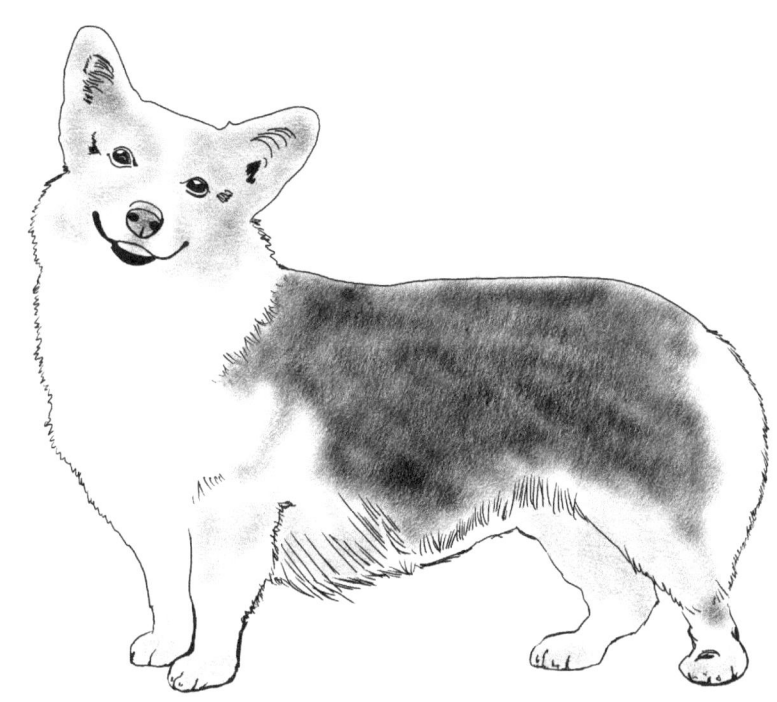

Mom posted a note about Mary Beth's dog drawing business on her Facebook page. A teacher friend, Mrs. Treadwell, was very excited by the offer. She sent 32 photos and 3 videos of her Corgi, Cool Connie. Mary Beth's mom said she wasn't upset by the large email, but Mary Beth knew she really was, because the photo files were huge, and the video files were huger. "This eats up the limited gigawiggles we get from the overcharging weasels at SkyNet," Mary Beth's mom was prone to say.

Mary Beth picked out the picture of Cool Connie the Corgi that she liked, and drew it.

Advice from Mary
Beth on how to draw
Cool Connie.

Corgis are kind of boxy, so
we start with box shapes
for our guides.

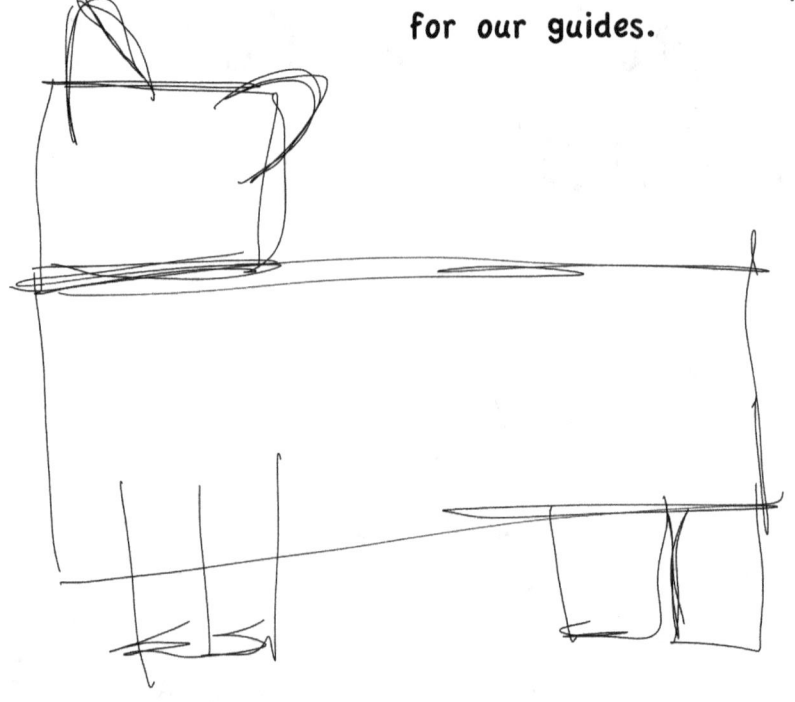

Find the head and ears in
the head box.

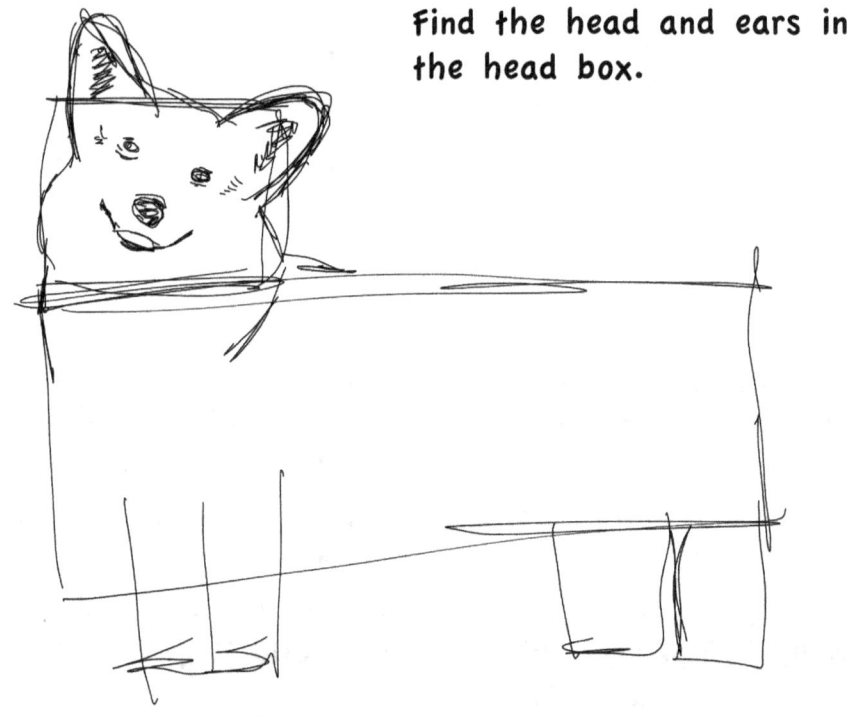

Add chest and legs with a
little of the upper back.
Remember, draw gently, all
this will need to be erased.

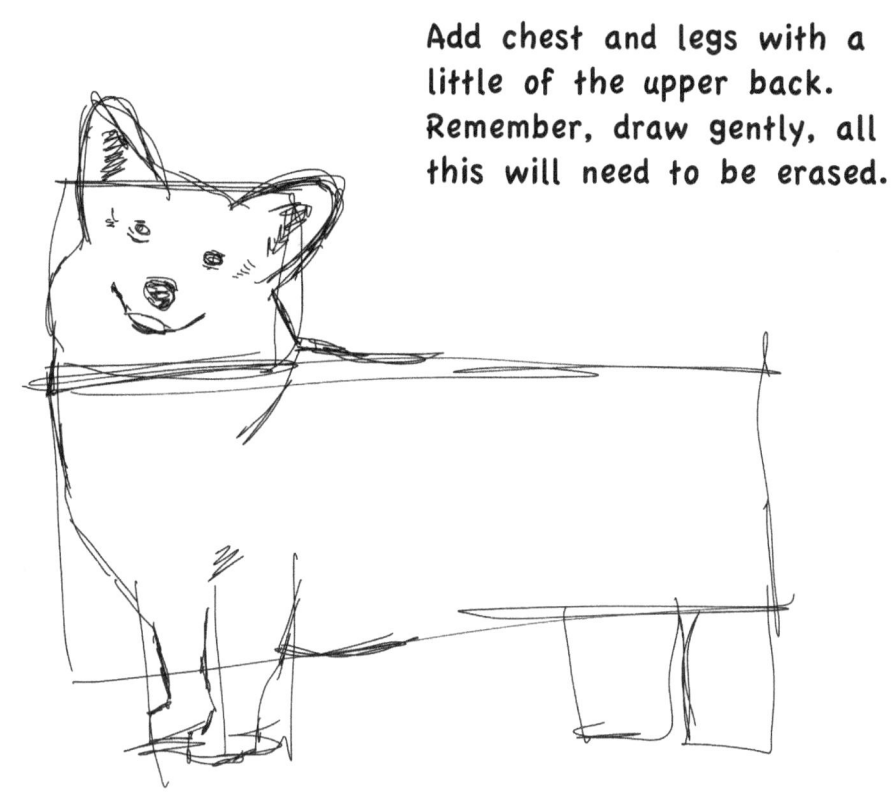

Lower back, tummy and back
legs. Cool Connie is starting
to take shape.

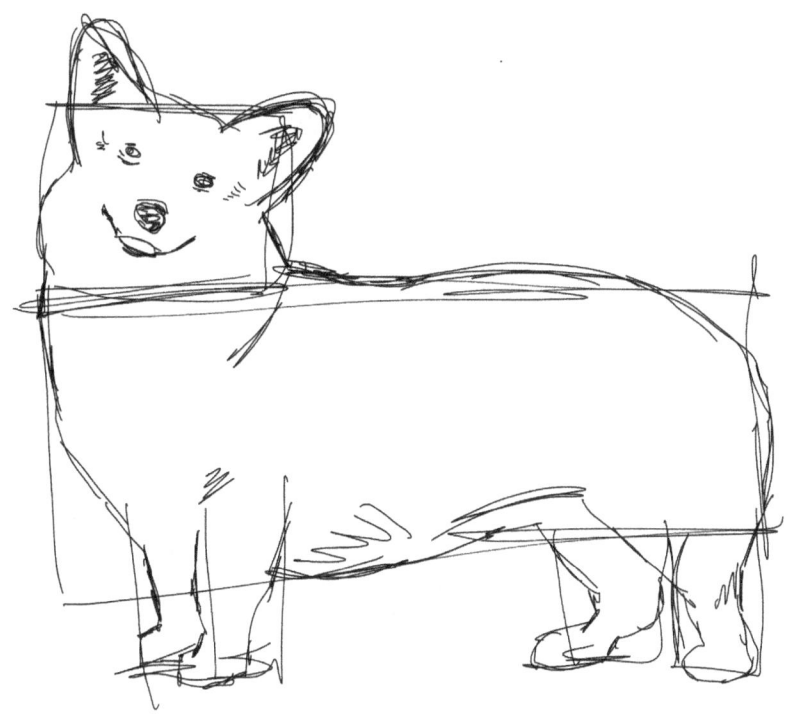

Erase the lines you don't need, building up the pencil lines you do need.

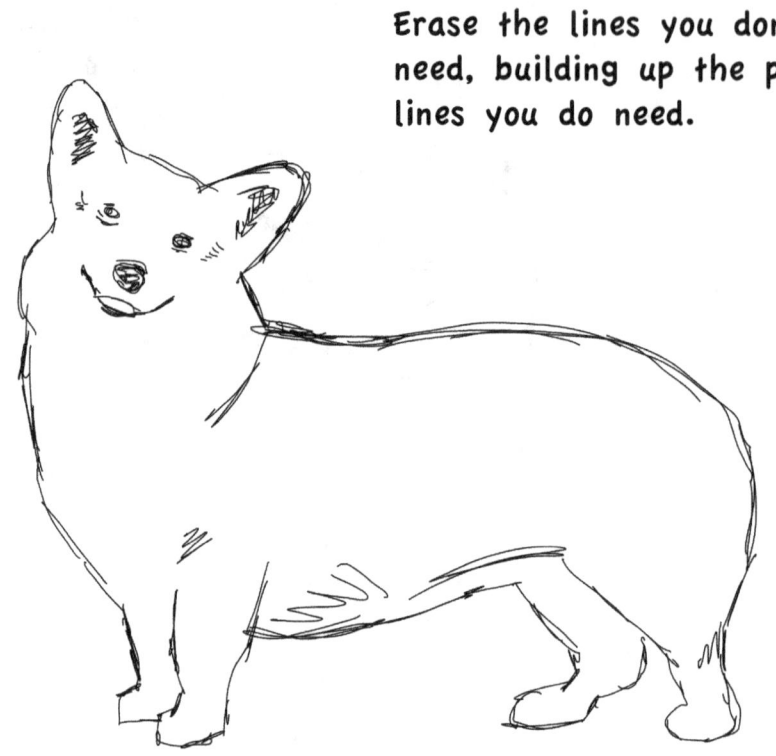

Pen the lines you want to keep. By using lots of small lines for fur you show the coarse fur of the Corgi.

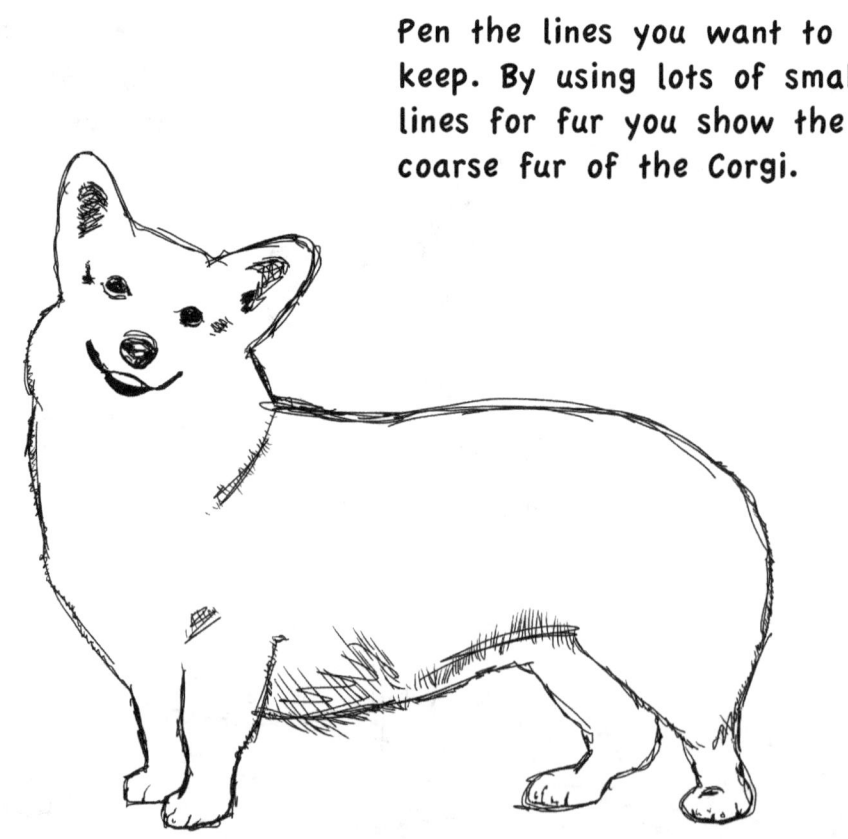

Erase all the pencil lines.

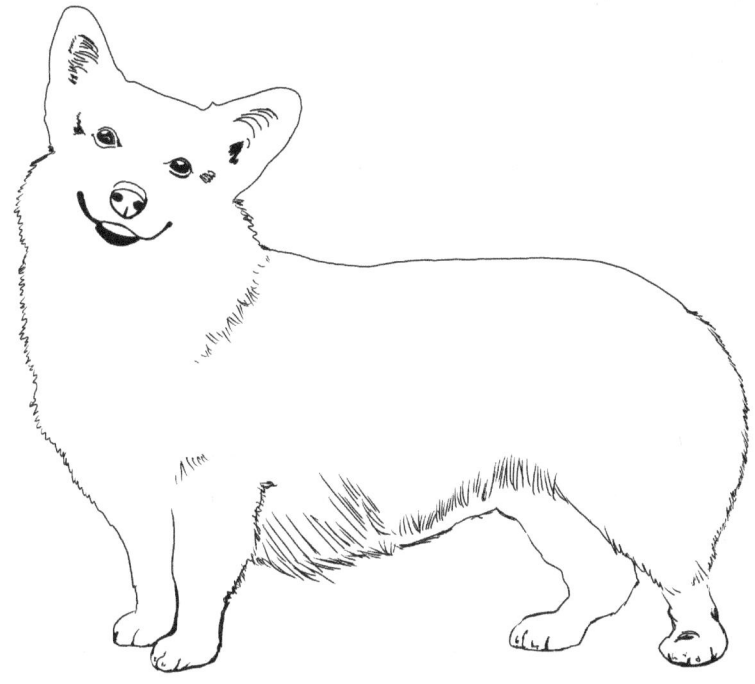

It is a little known fact that dog drawings really like it when you erase pencil lines from around their ears.

Use the side of the pencil to build up the shaded areas of the fur. Nice!

After she was done drawing Cool Connie, her dad showed her how to use the scanner in the lab.

"Now remember, don't come in here without my permission. It is not safe for you or Jazz to be in here. Plus, I don't want to have to explain to the general how a little girl broke some of their expensive equipment," Dad said, for the millionth time. But, Mary Beth was pretty sure that he didn't really mean it.

"We can take this digital copy of your art and send it to Cool Connie's mommy," Dad said. "How much do you charge for your doggie art?"

"I don't really know, people just seem to pay me," Mary Beth said.

"Interesting," Dad said, as he stopped to clean his glasses. "When Mrs. Chapin is over for dinner next week you should ask her about pricing your art. You know, she got rich in the music business."

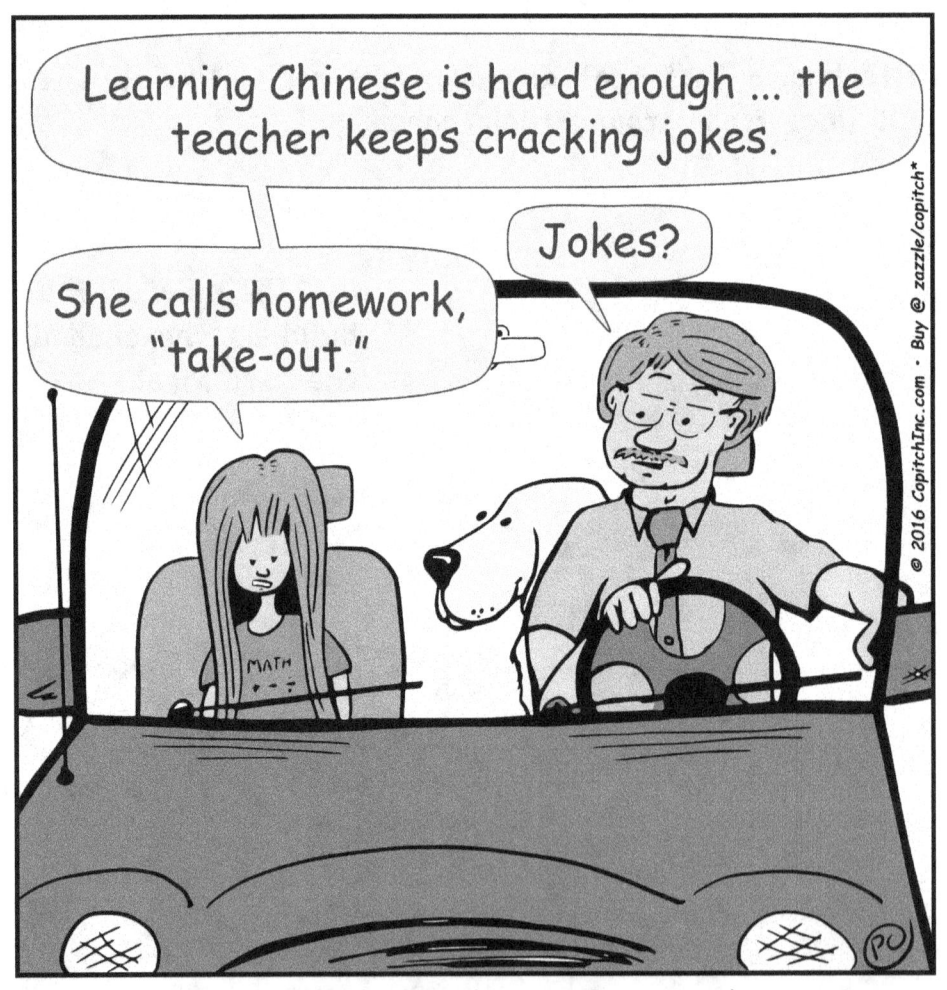

Here are Mary Beth and her dad, Dr. Schmendrick, driving home from school.

Chapter 17
Pet toys and stuff

Draw pet toys to add to your dog drawings. Mary Beth's dog, Jazz, thinks everything is her toy, even Mary Beth's homework and best shoes. A few examples of toys Jazz is allowed to have:

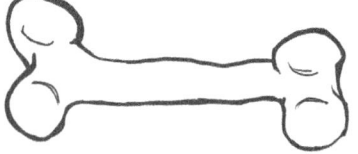

Jazz thinks this bone is a dinosaur bone. But it's a cow bone.

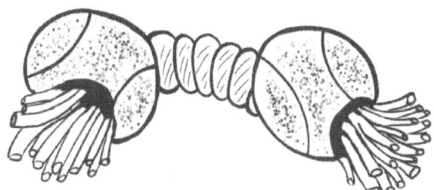

Ball and rope toy.

This is Swimmer, a plastic bath toy Mary Beth got when she was a little girl. Jazz fell in love with it when she was a puppy, so now it is her toy.

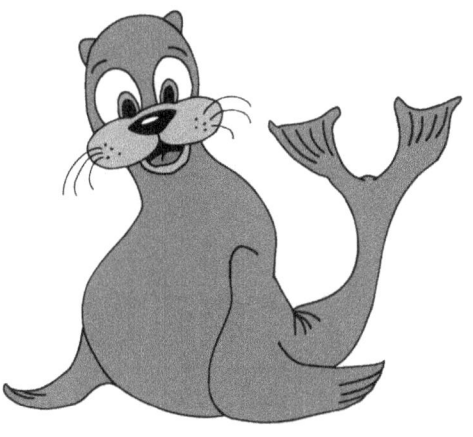

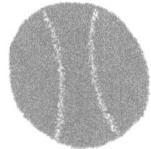

This is Jazz's tennis ball. It is drawn with the side of the pencil to make it look fuzzy. To make the lines, use your eraser to trim back the fuzz.

Jazz thinks of this toy as her square ball.

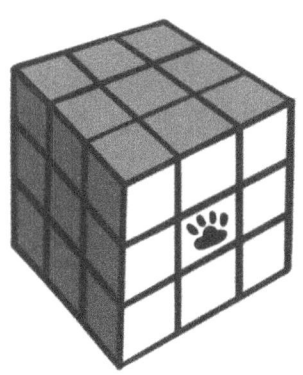

Toy hot dog

Draw the bun in pencil

Add hot dog

Add puppy eyes and ears

Ketchup

Mustard

Relish

Onions

Warm to make yummy!

Pen the lines you like, erase the pencil guides.

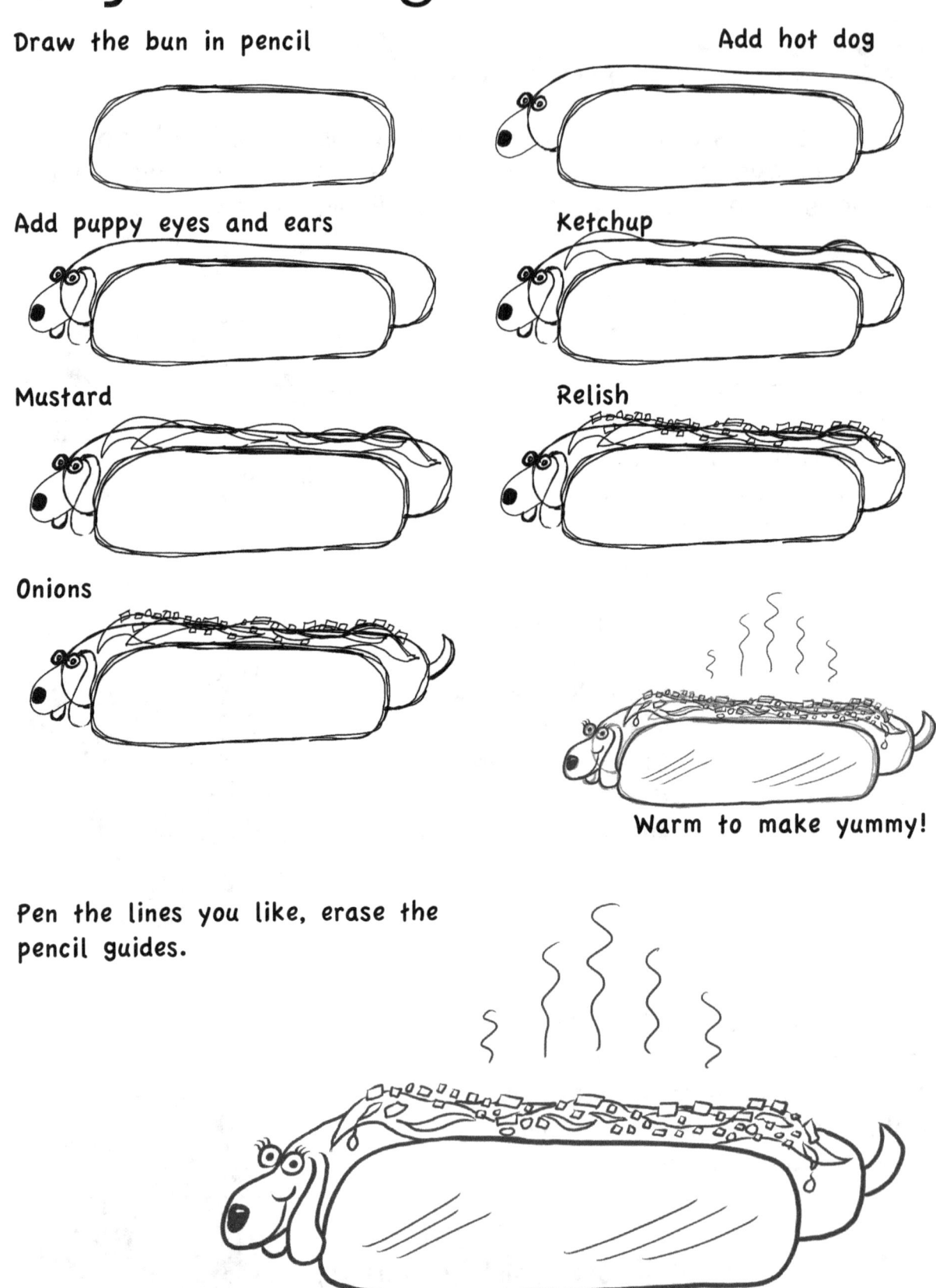

Chapter 18
Funny dog cartoons

Mary Beth's friend, Dr. Phil, likes to draw cartoons. Some cartoons are about dogs, others are about people in everyday life. Dr. Phil likes to put dogs and cats into his people cartoons. He figures that nice cartoon people tend to have fun pets.

Another way an artist can make money is to draw cartoons. For example, the following cartoons are sold in full color on lots of items like tee shirts, mugs, get well cards, and mouse pads. You can see over 1,000 of Dr. Phil's cartoons for free at, www.copitch.com

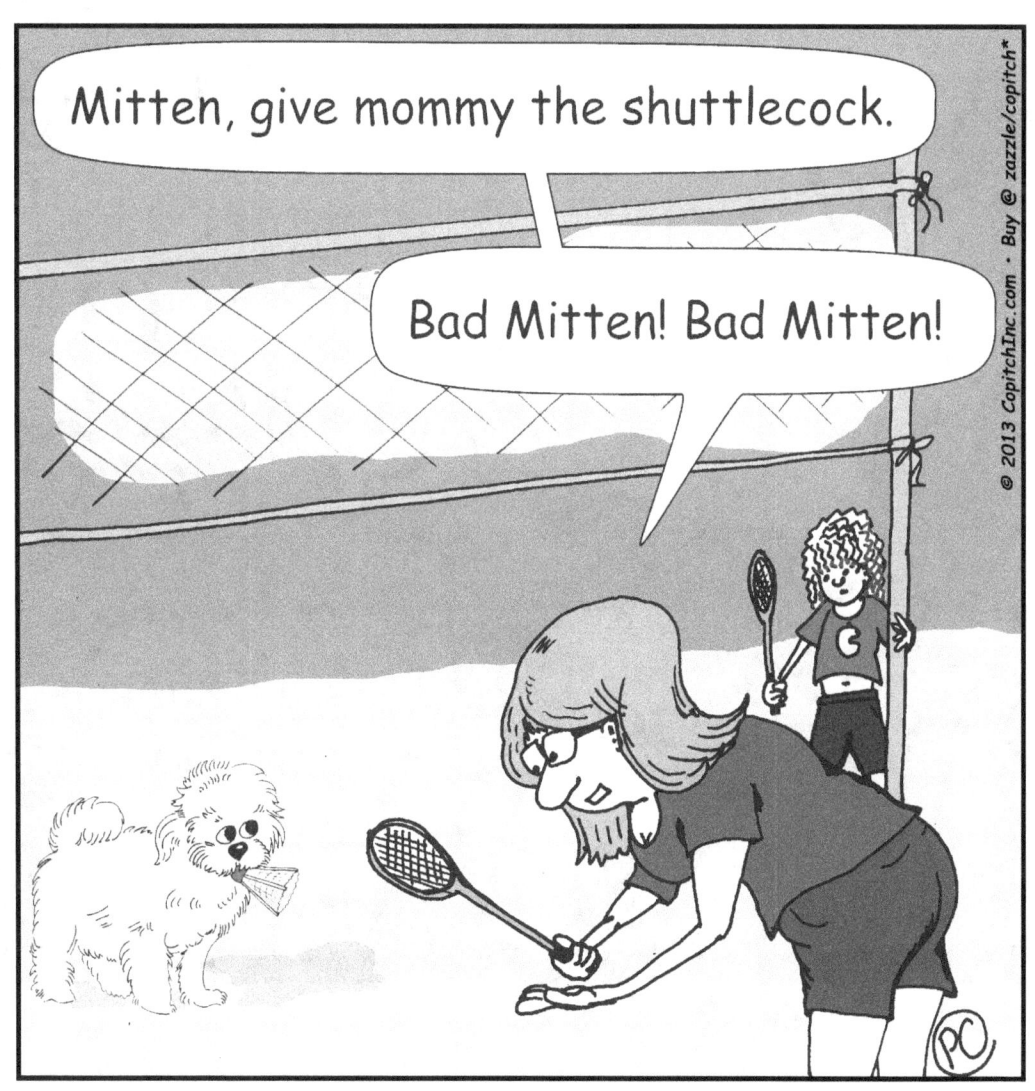

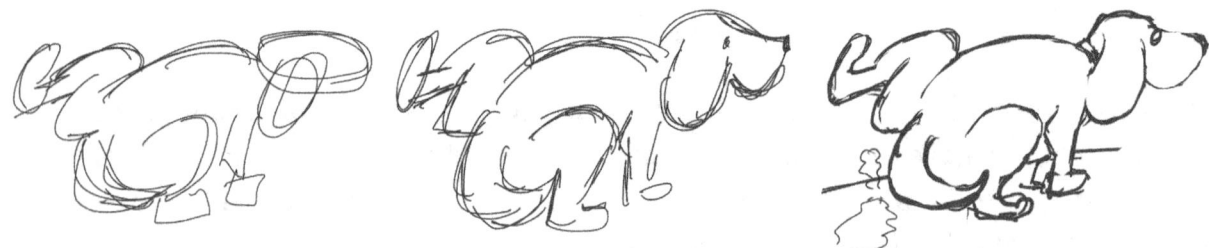

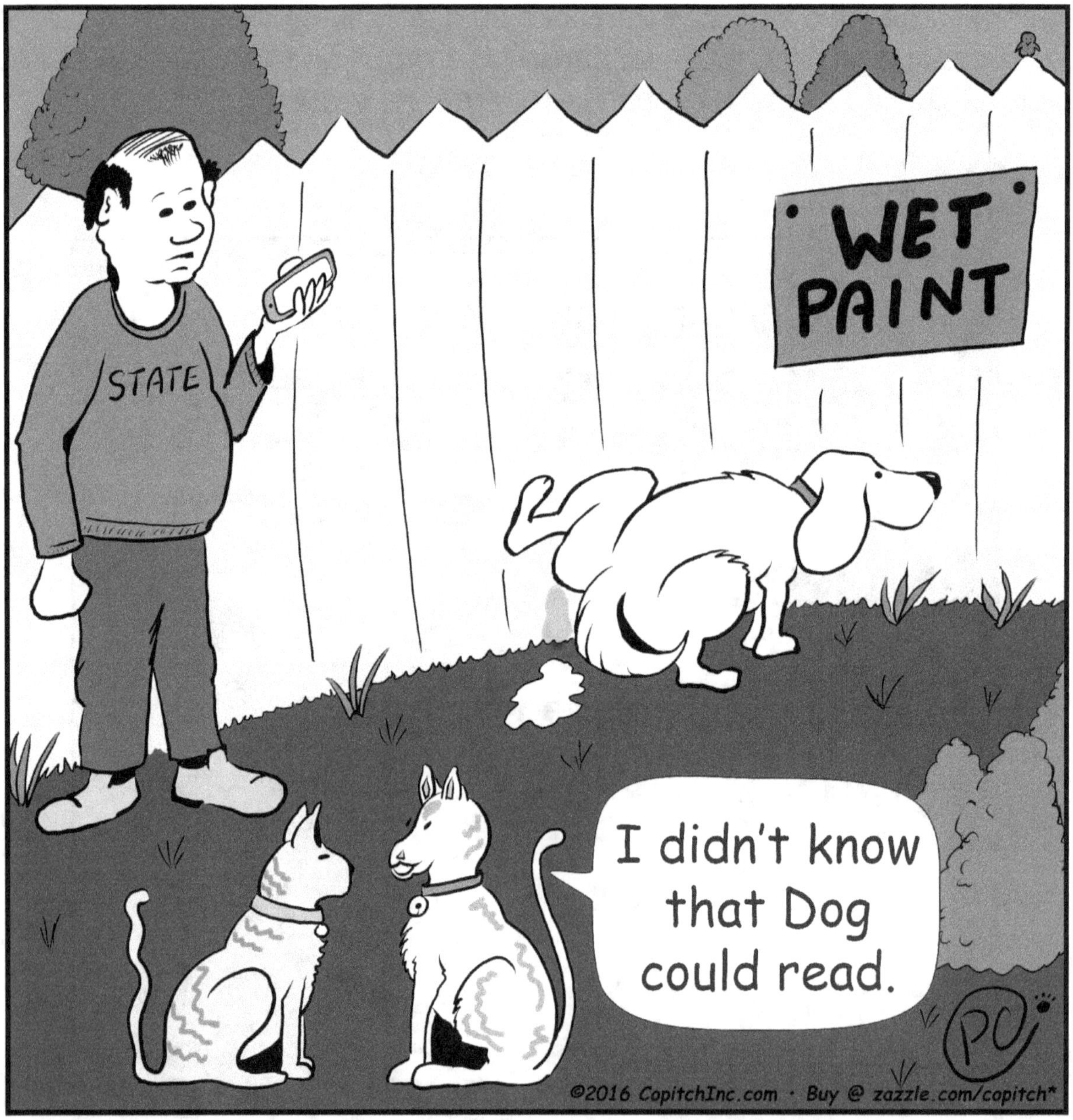

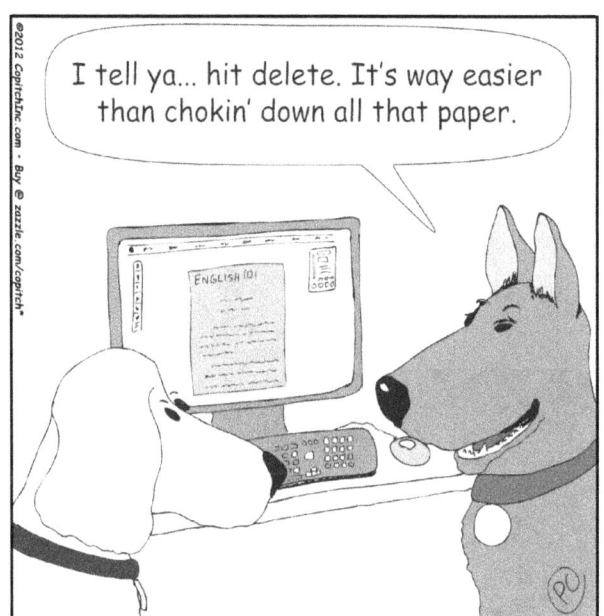

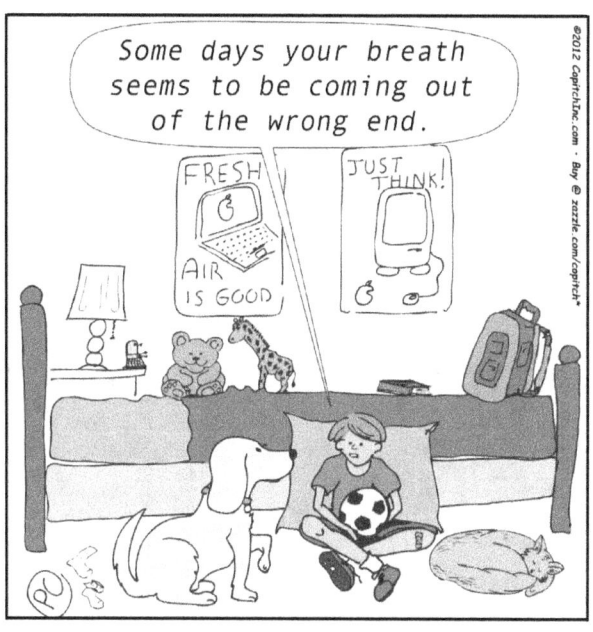

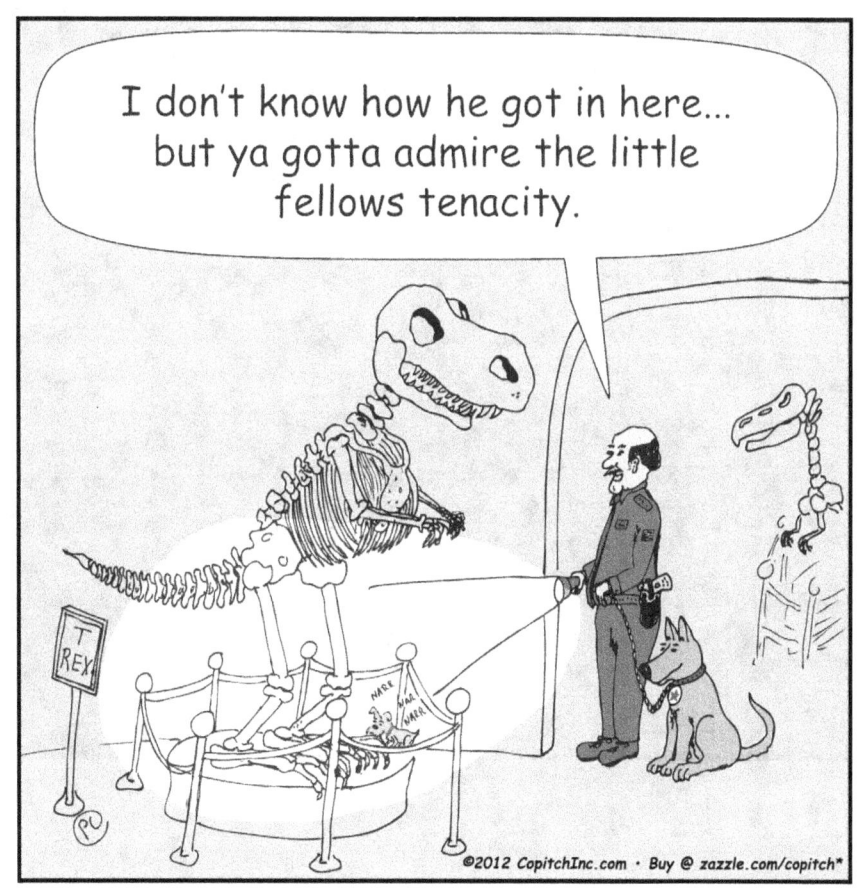

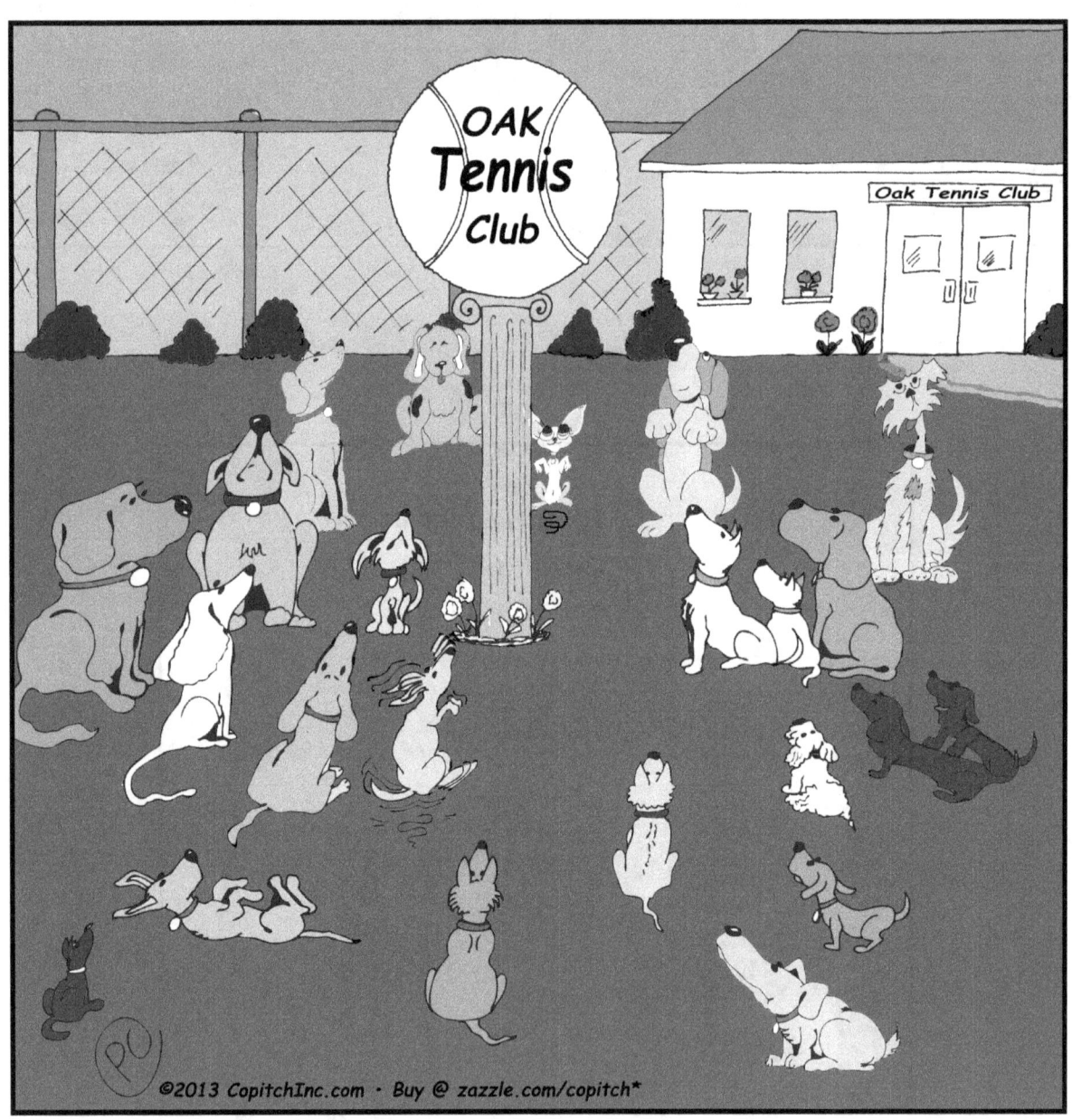

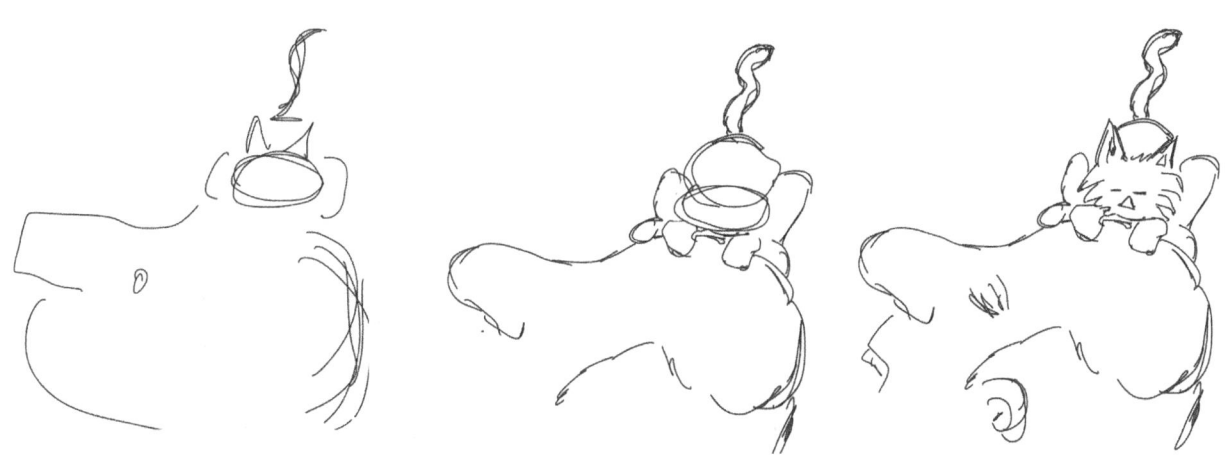

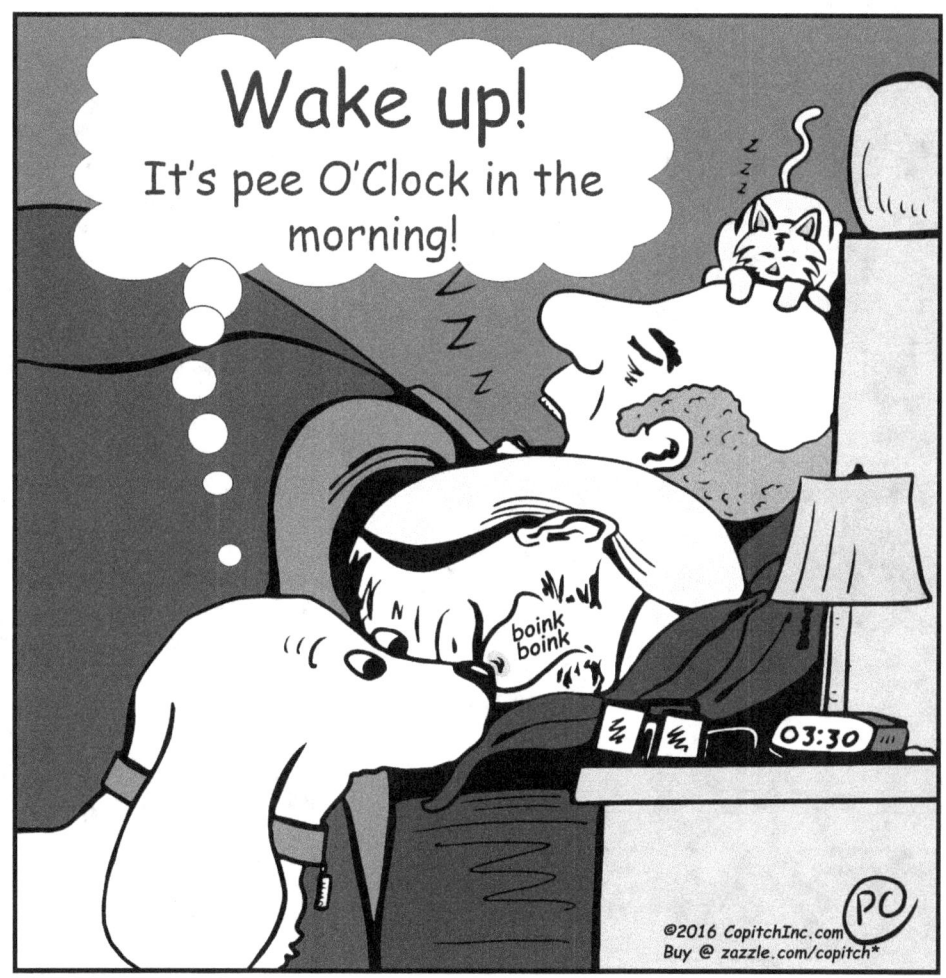

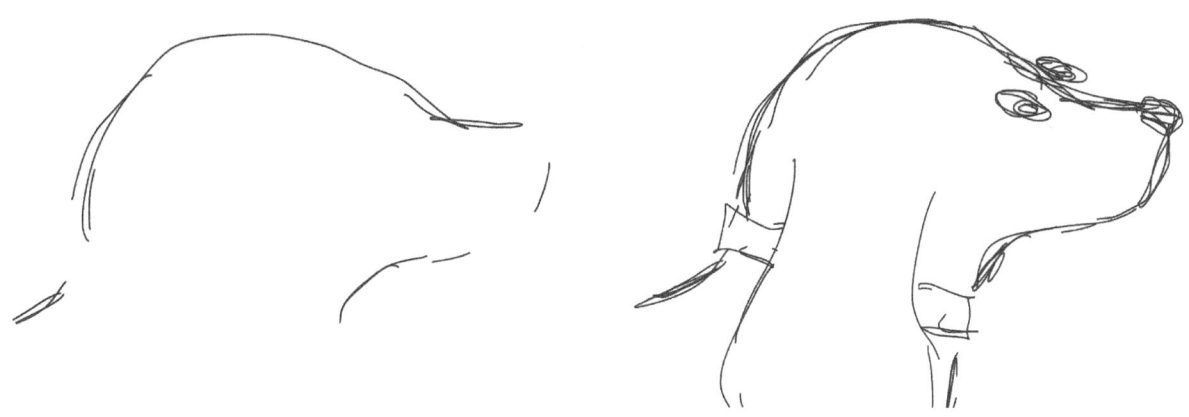

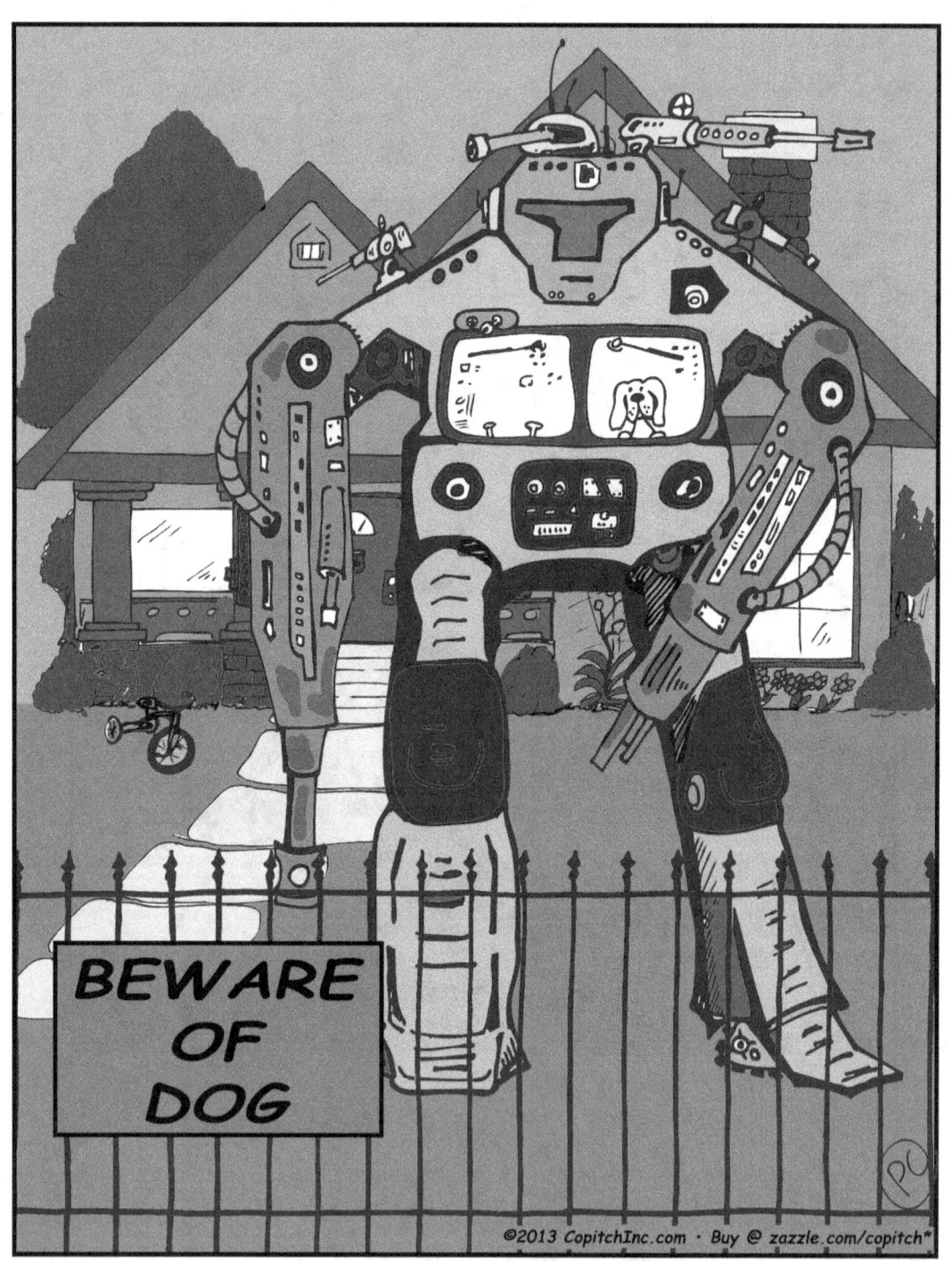

BEWARE
OF
DOG

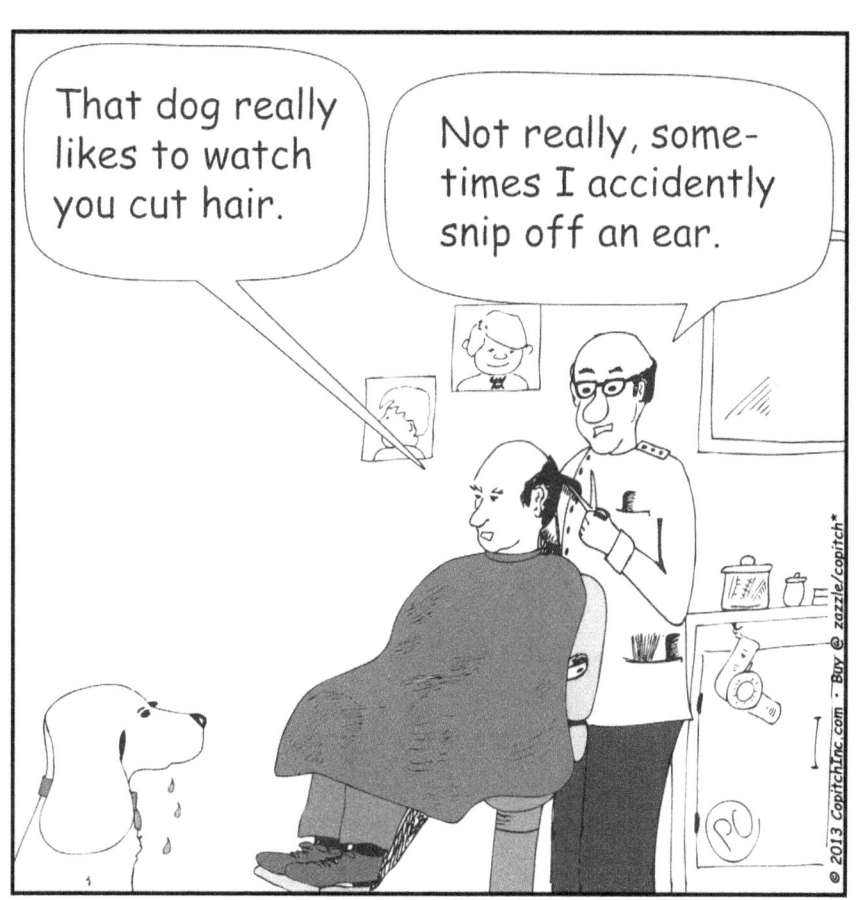

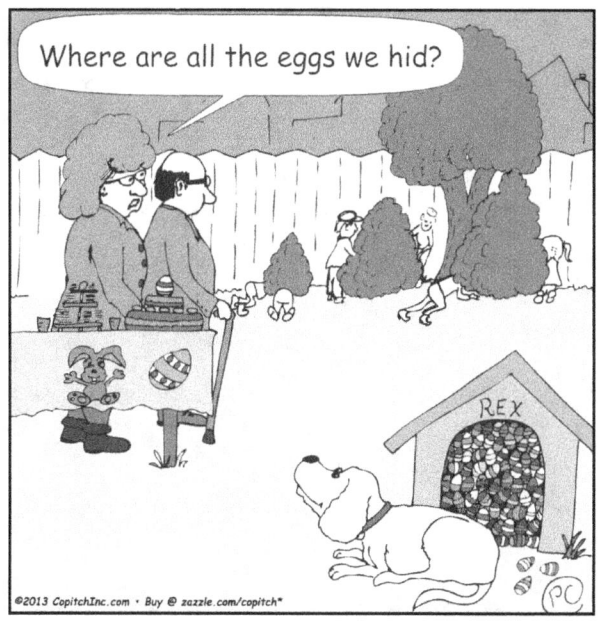

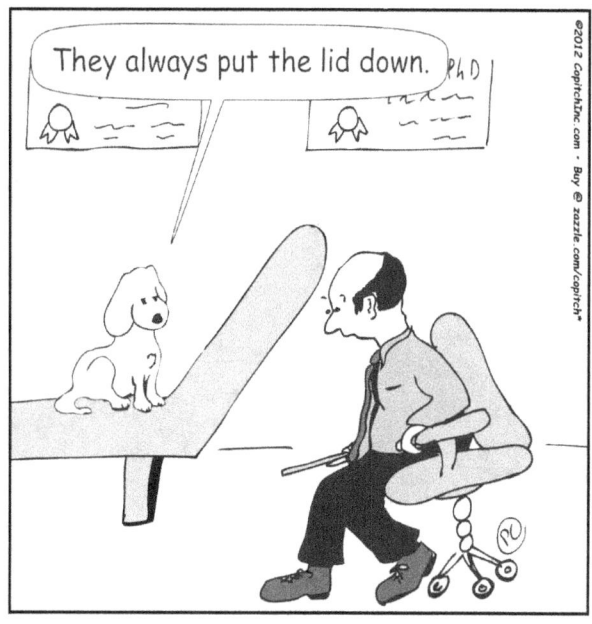

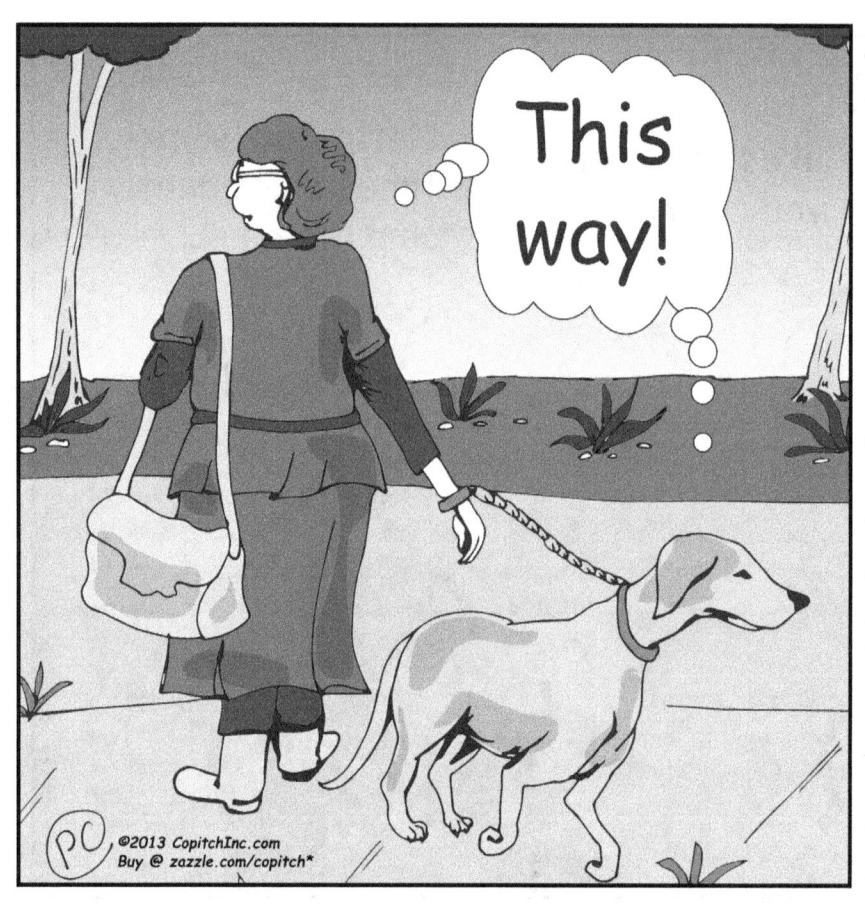

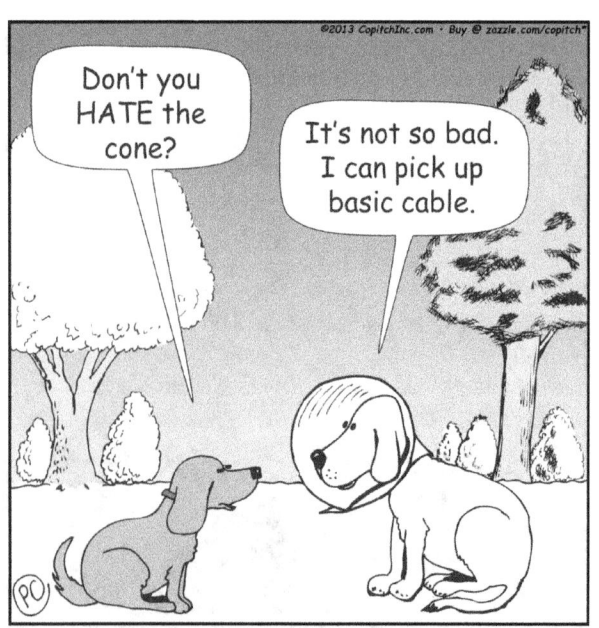

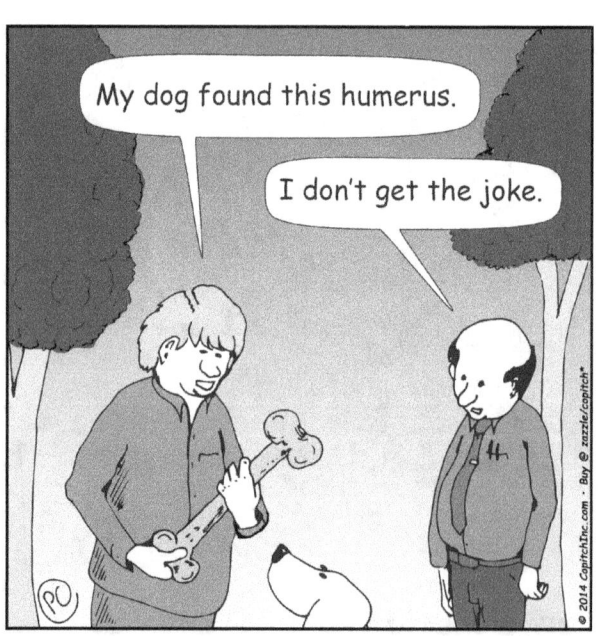

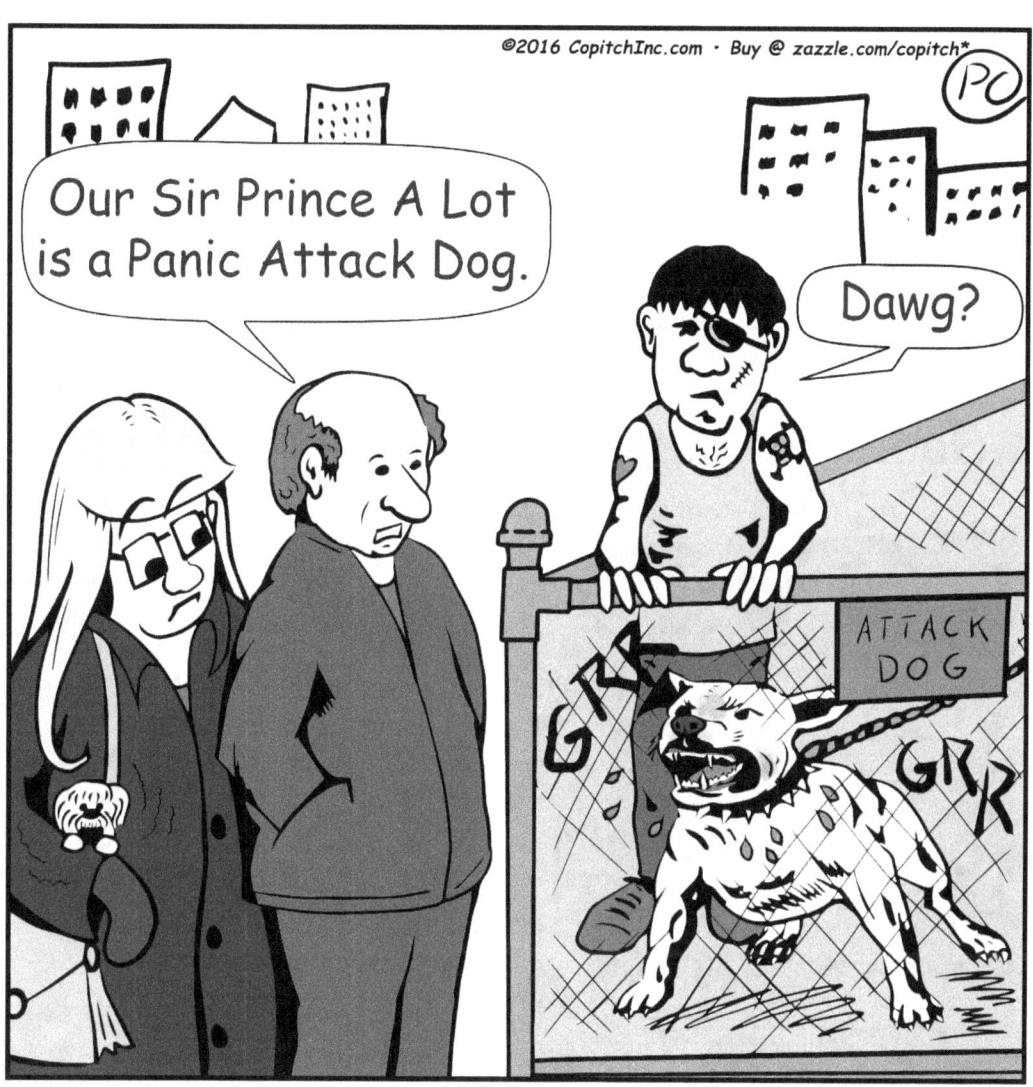

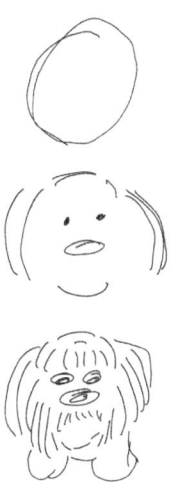

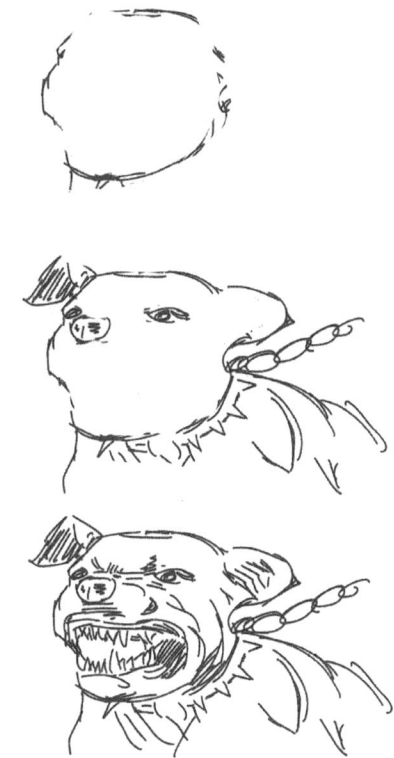

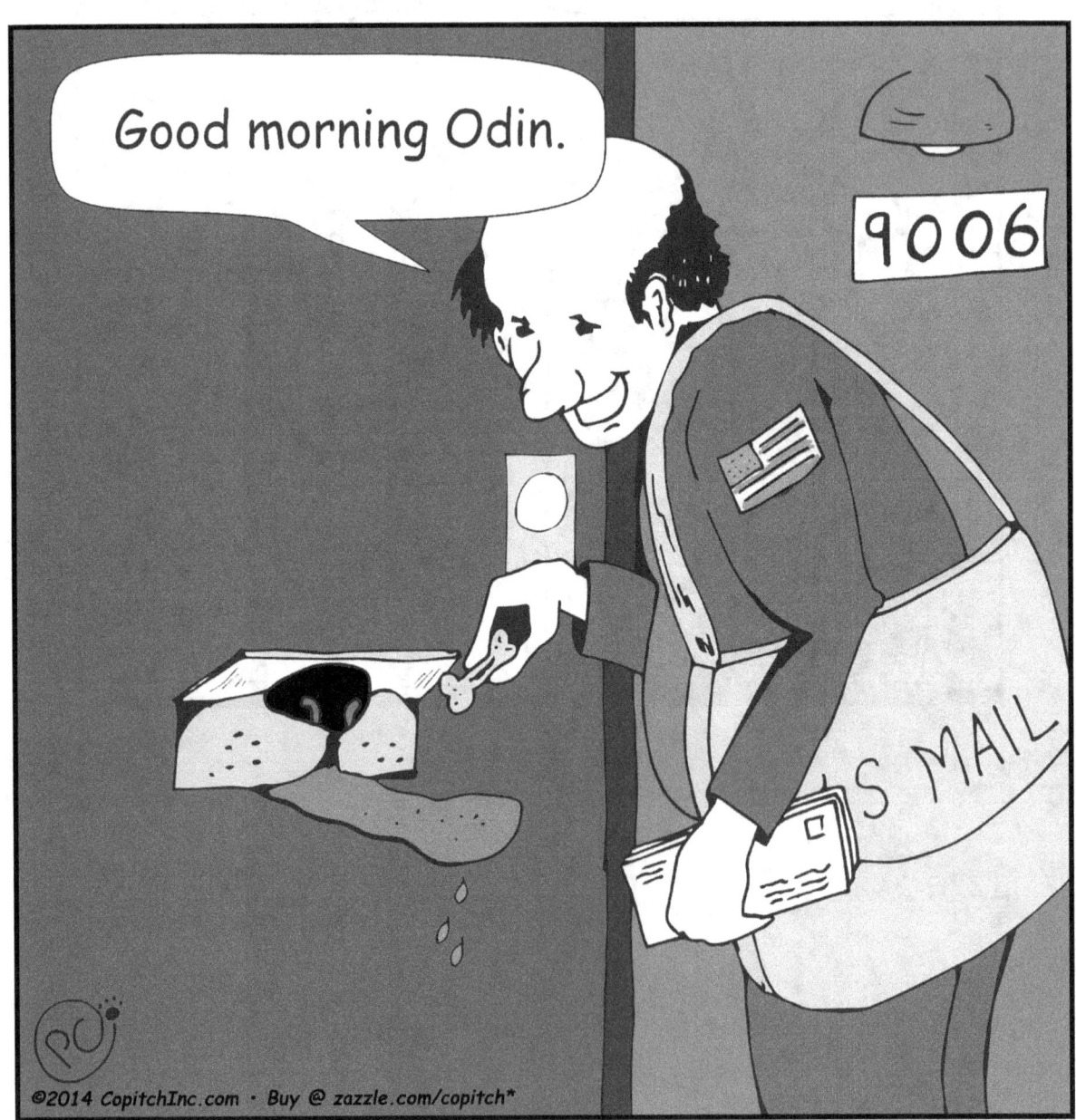

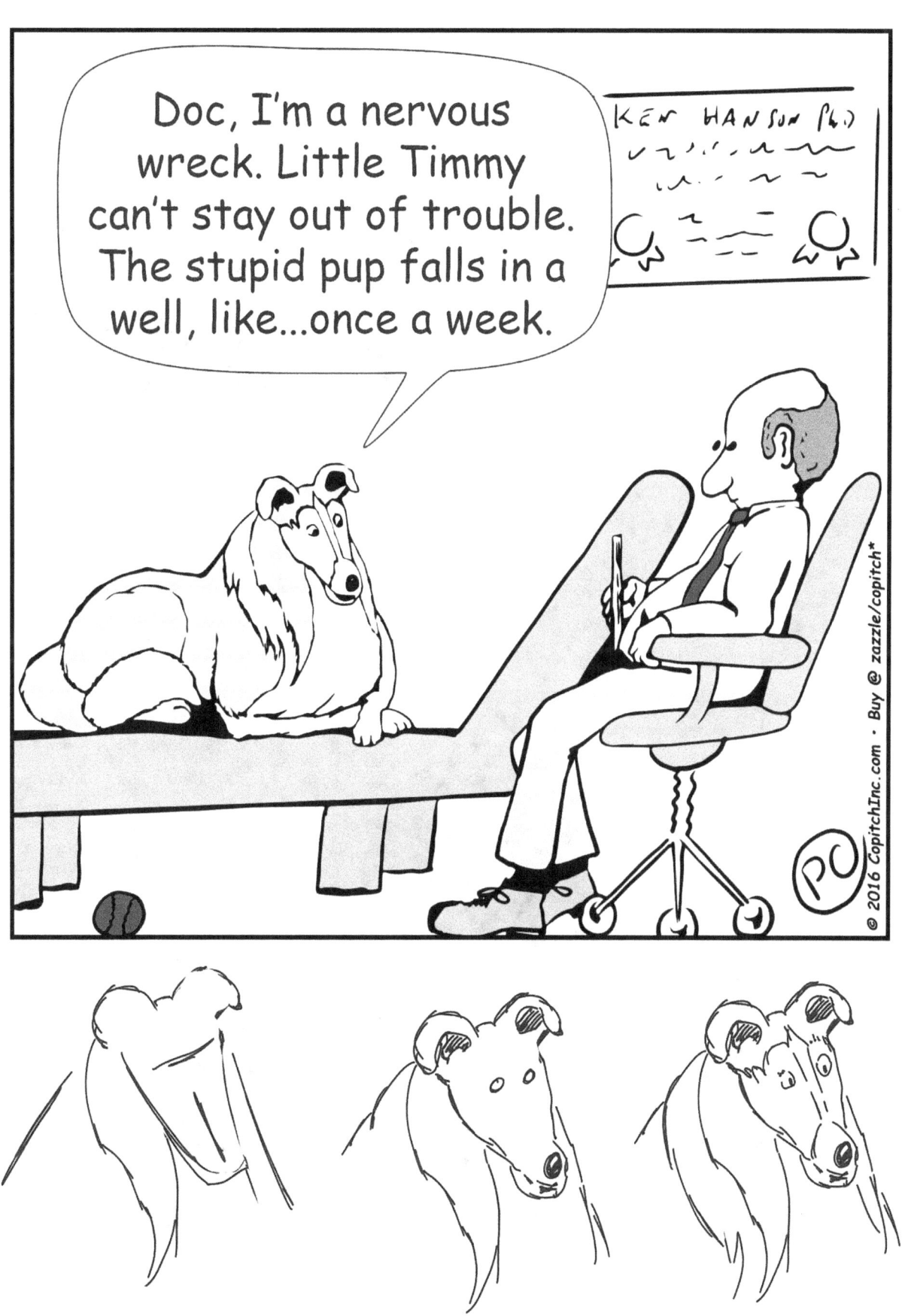

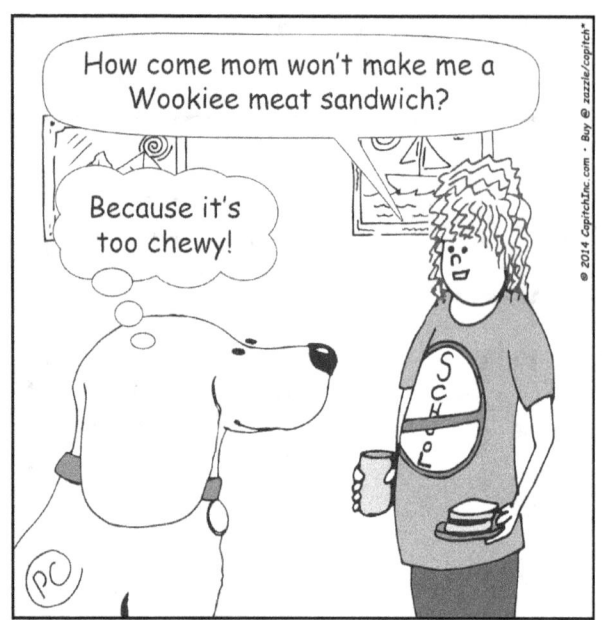

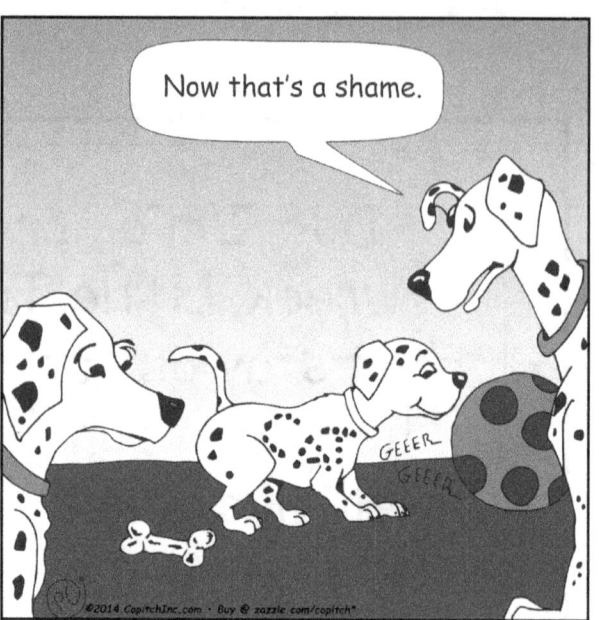

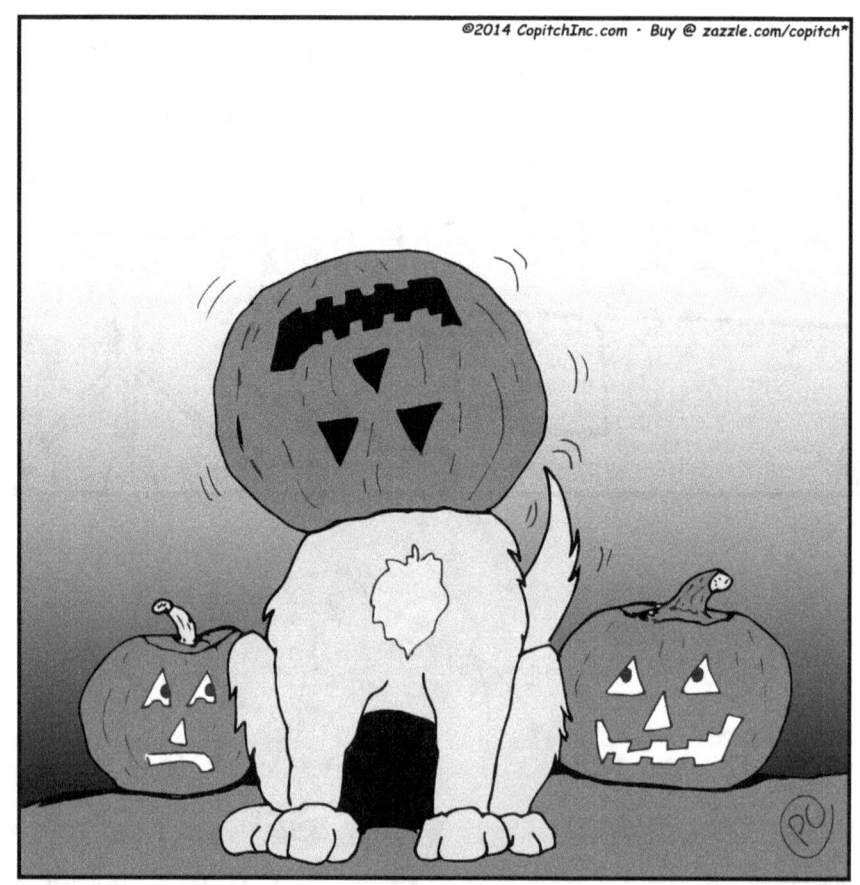

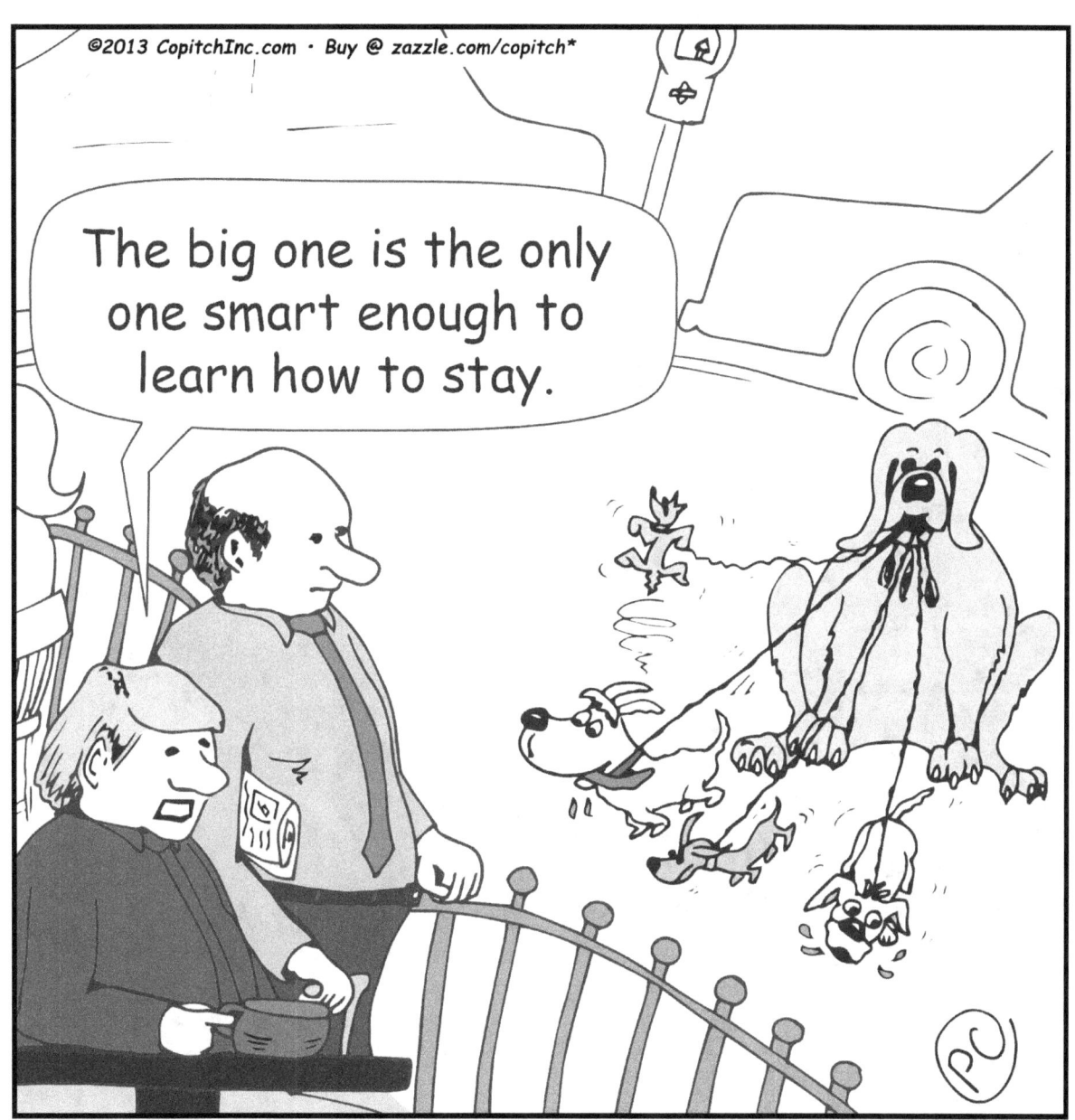

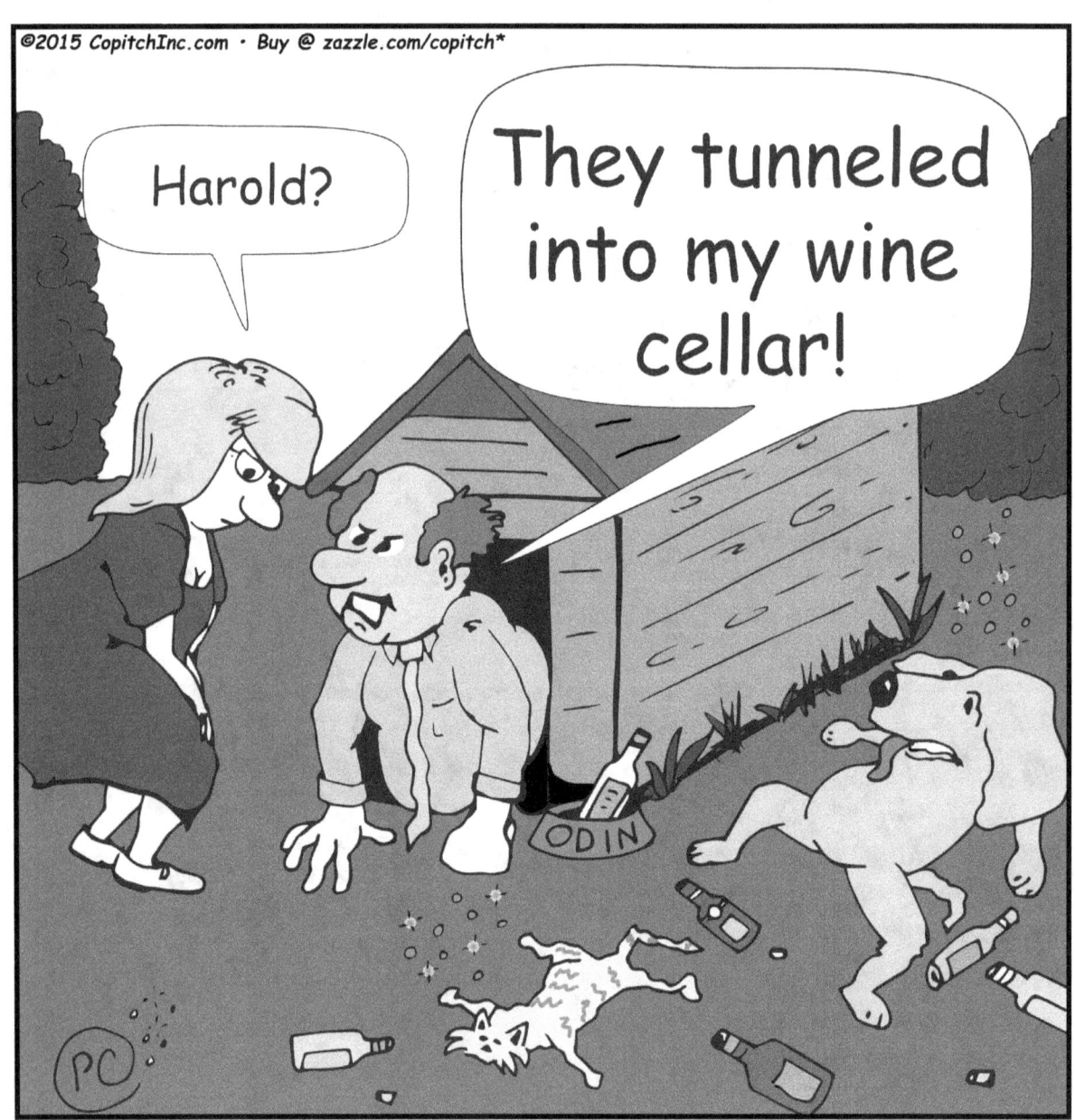

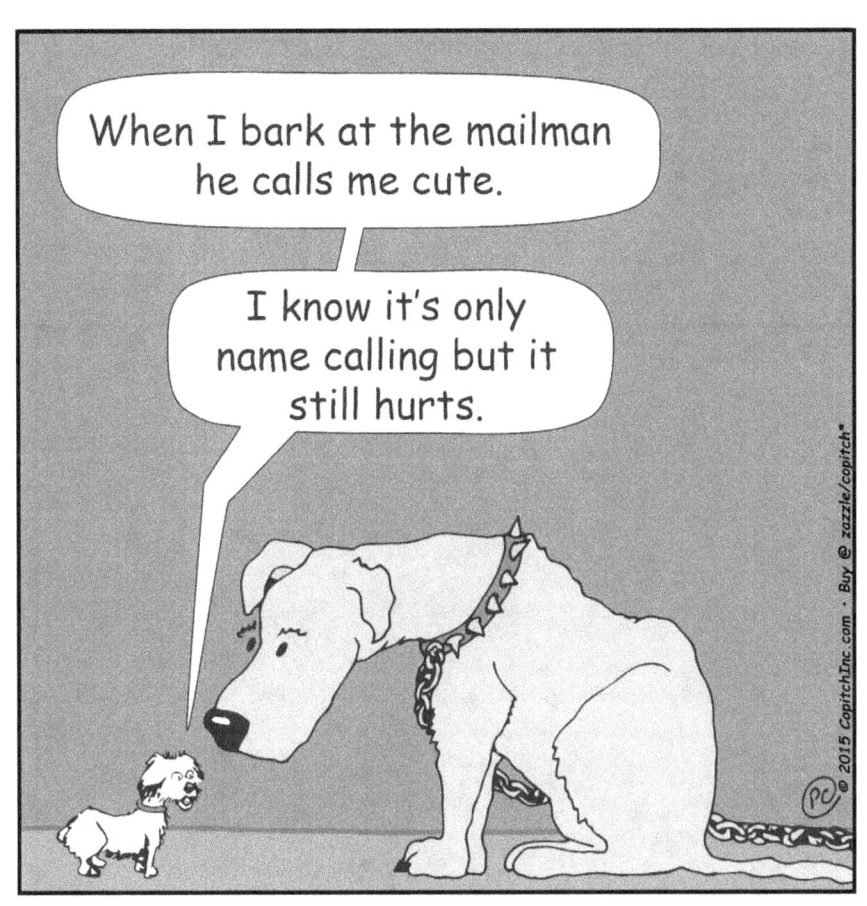

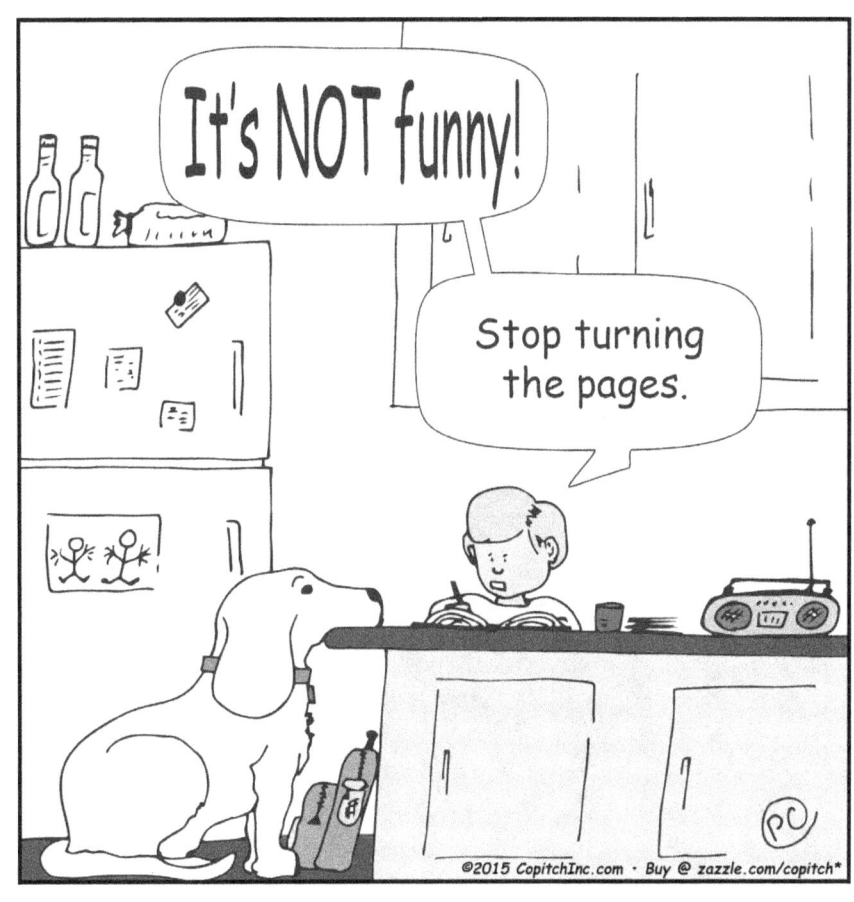

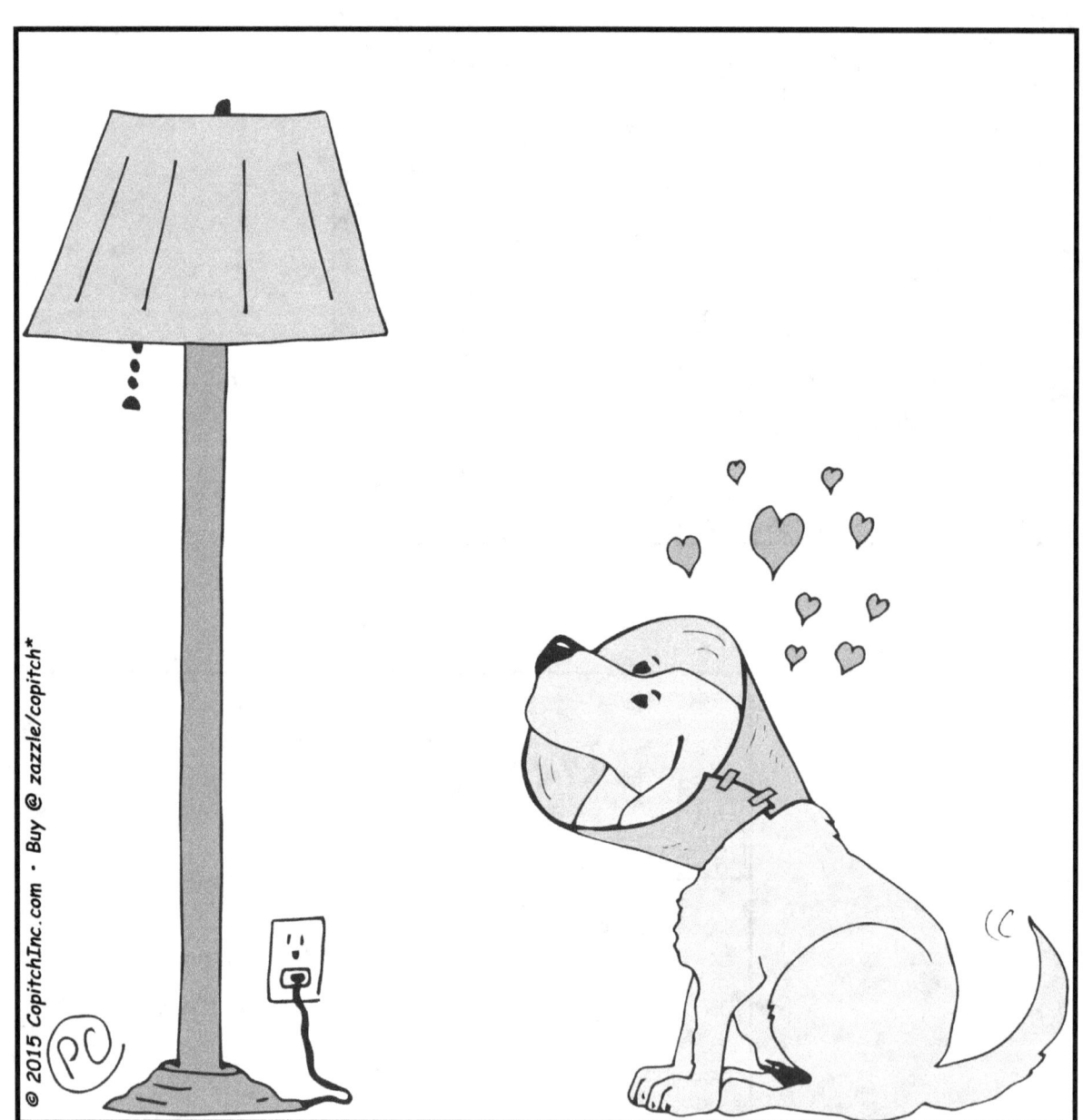

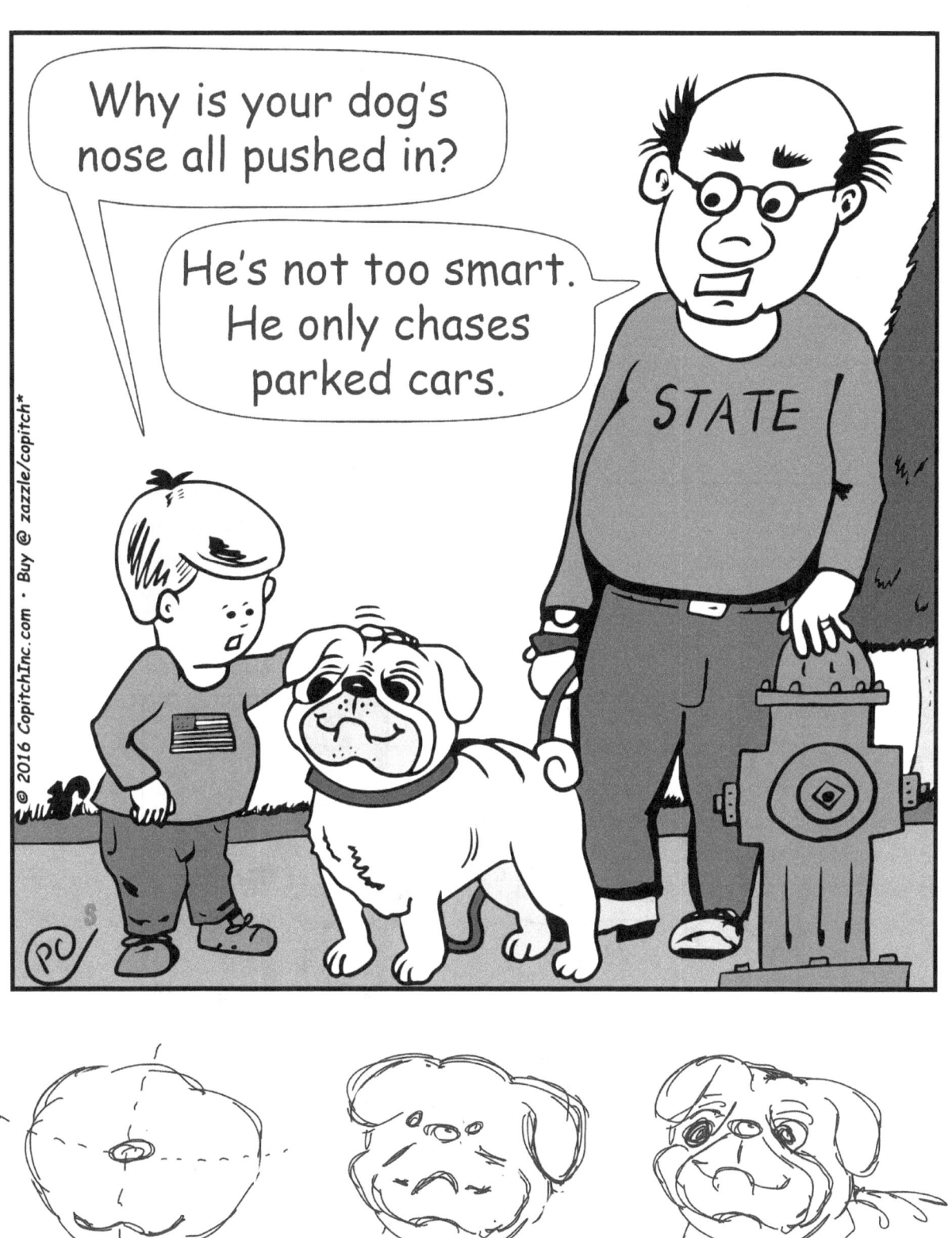

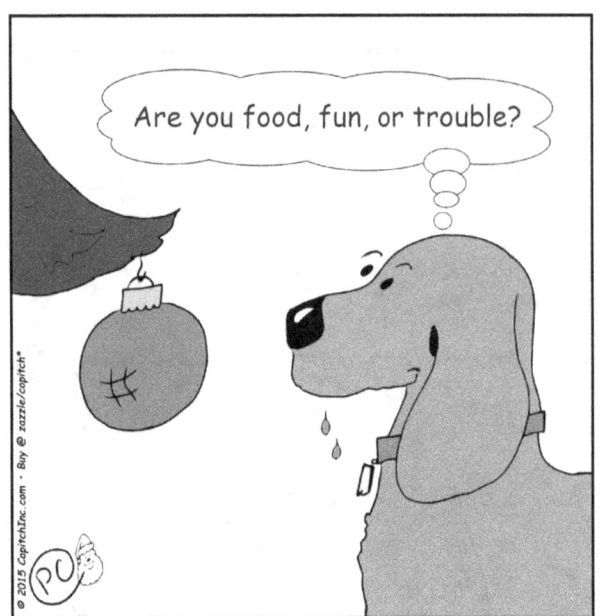

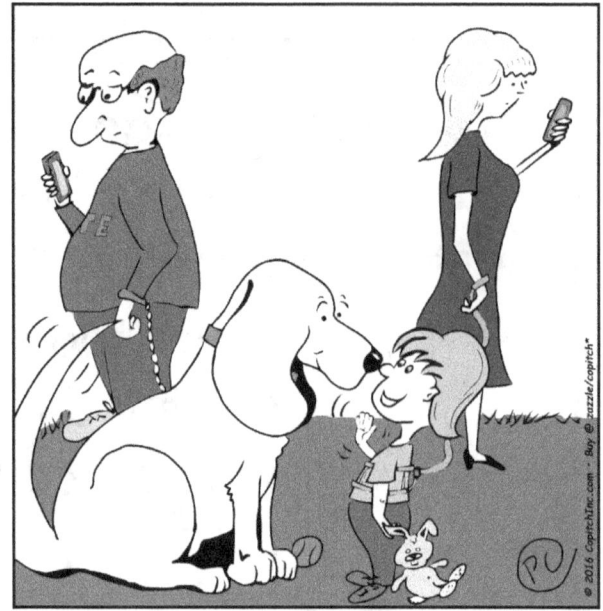

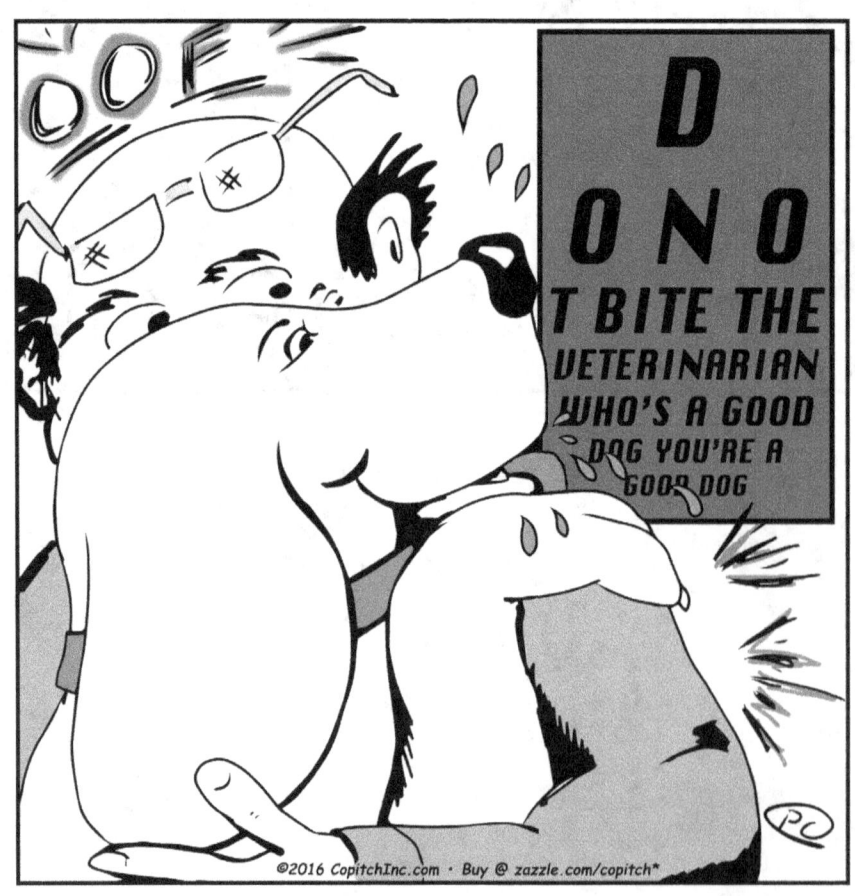

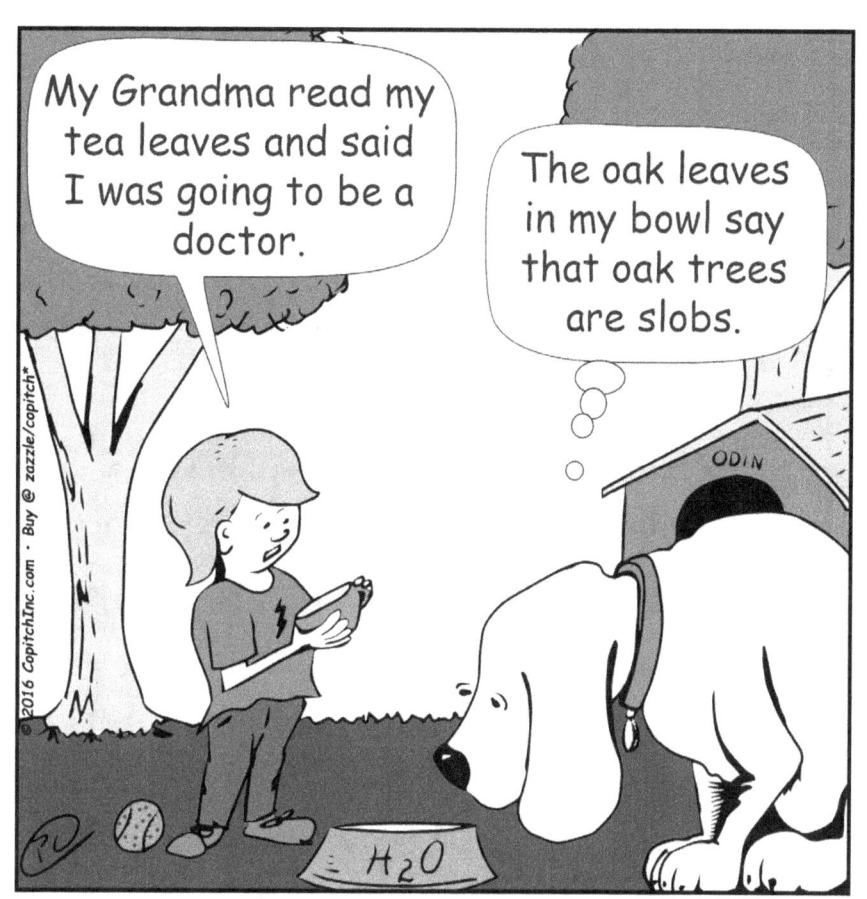

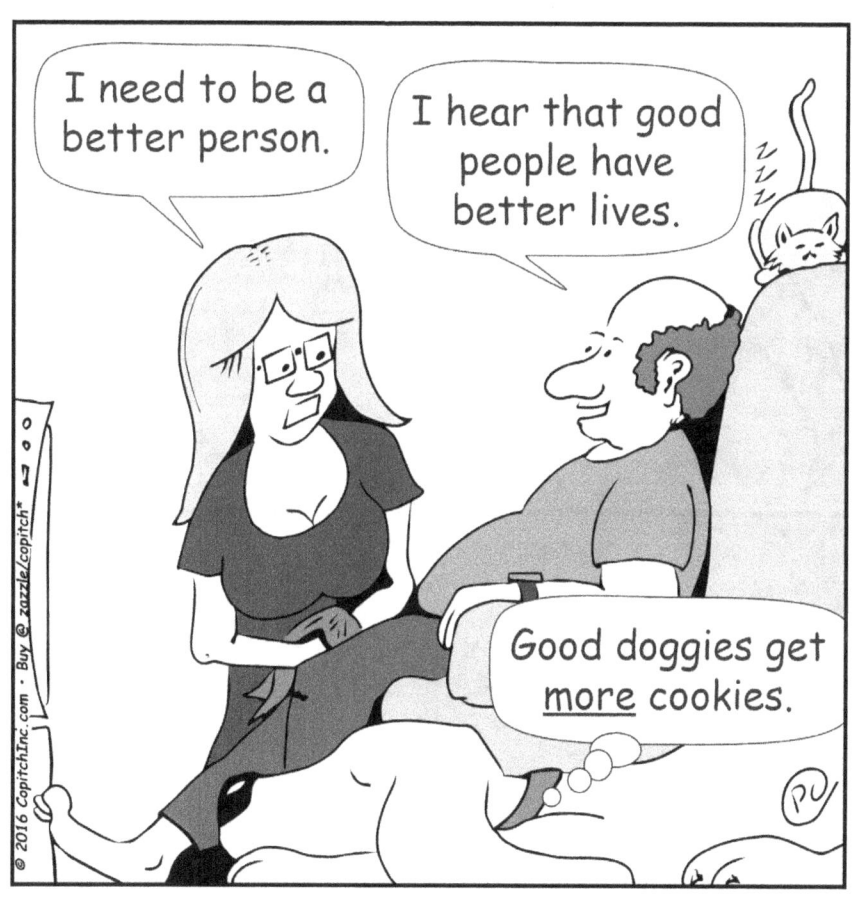

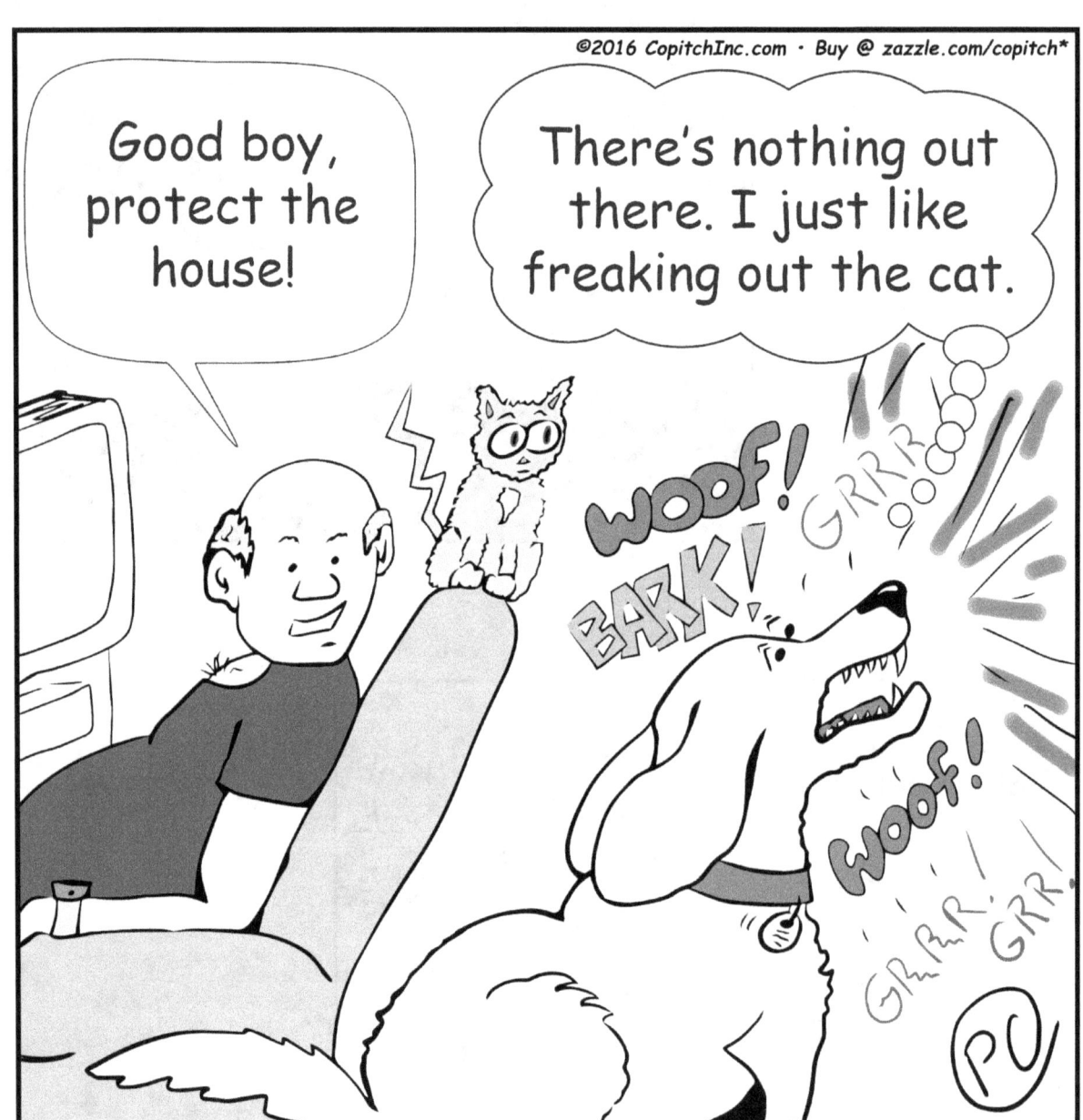

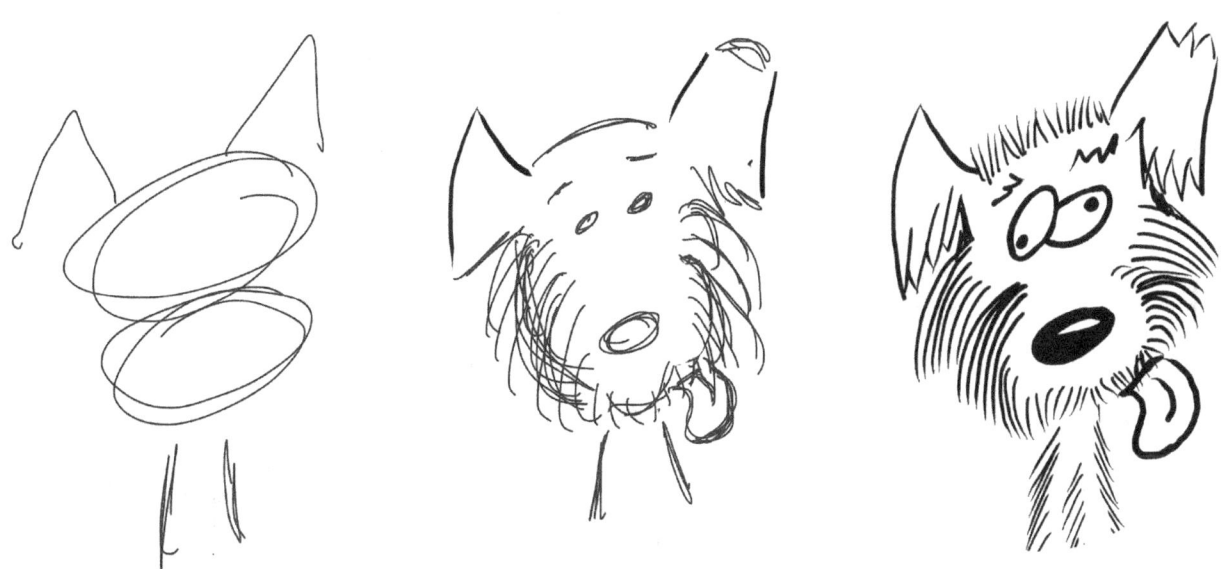

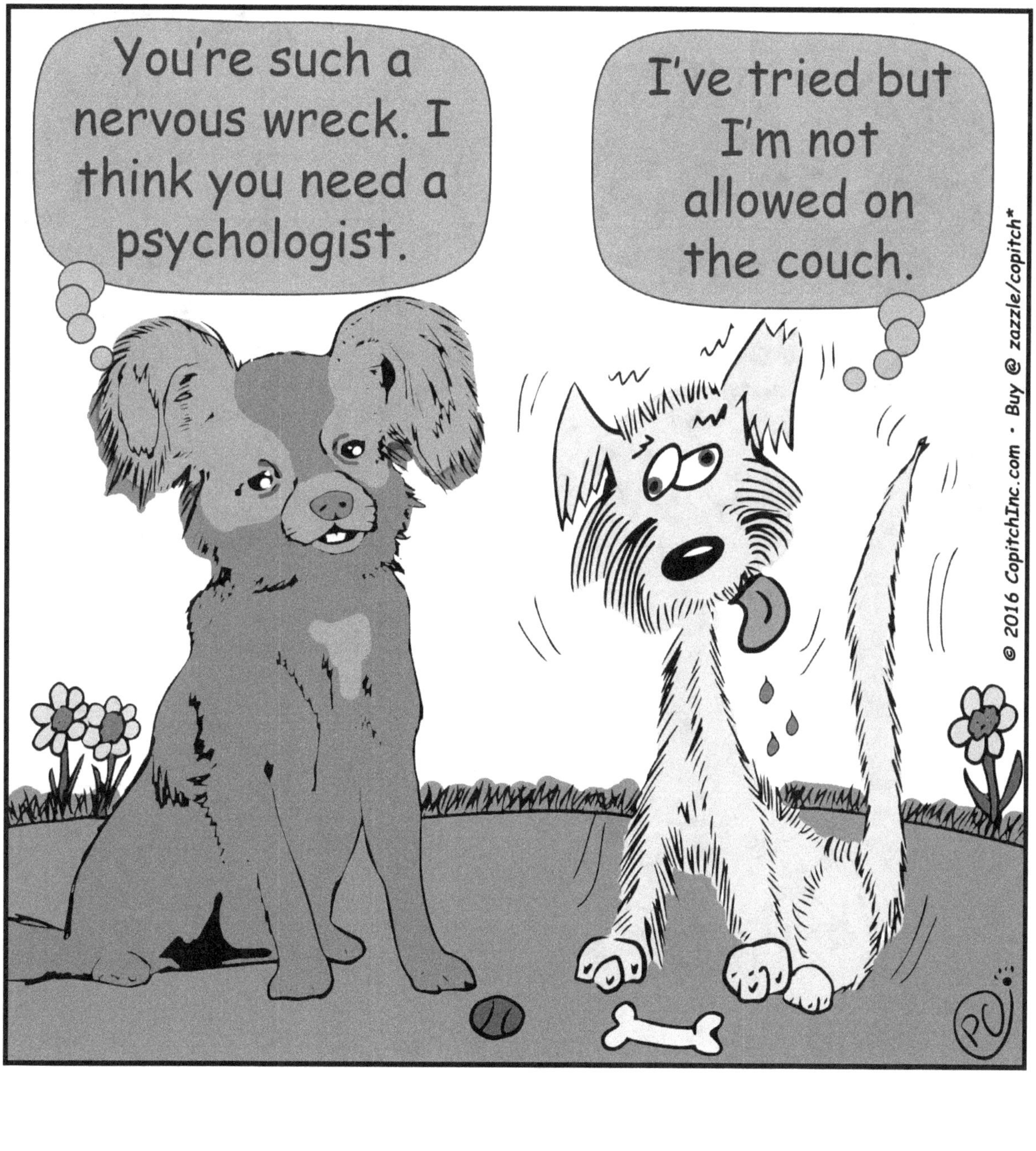

You're such a nervous wreck. I think you need a psychologist.

I've tried but I'm not allowed on the couch.

© 2016 CopitchInc.com · Buy @ zazzle/copitch*

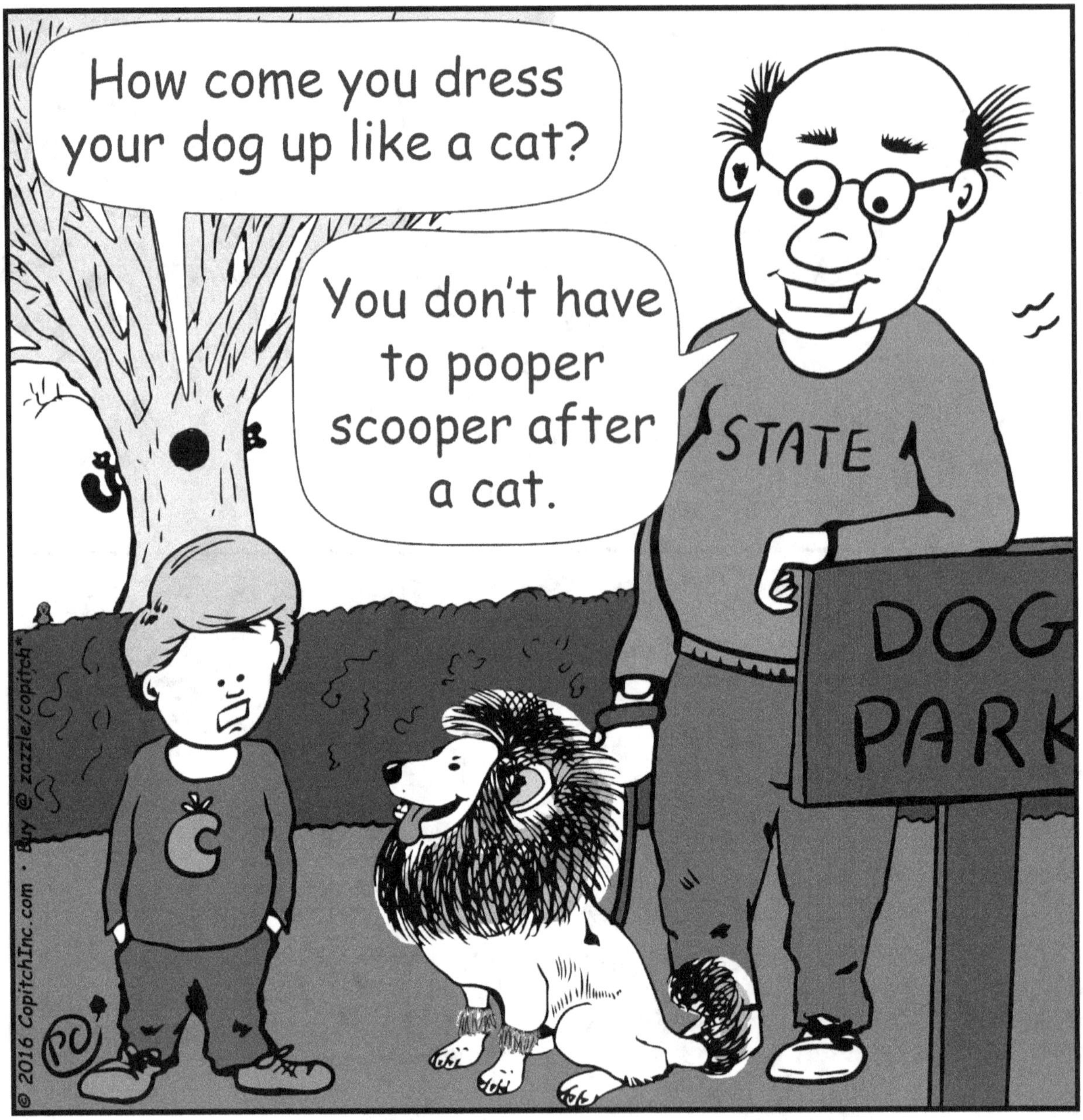

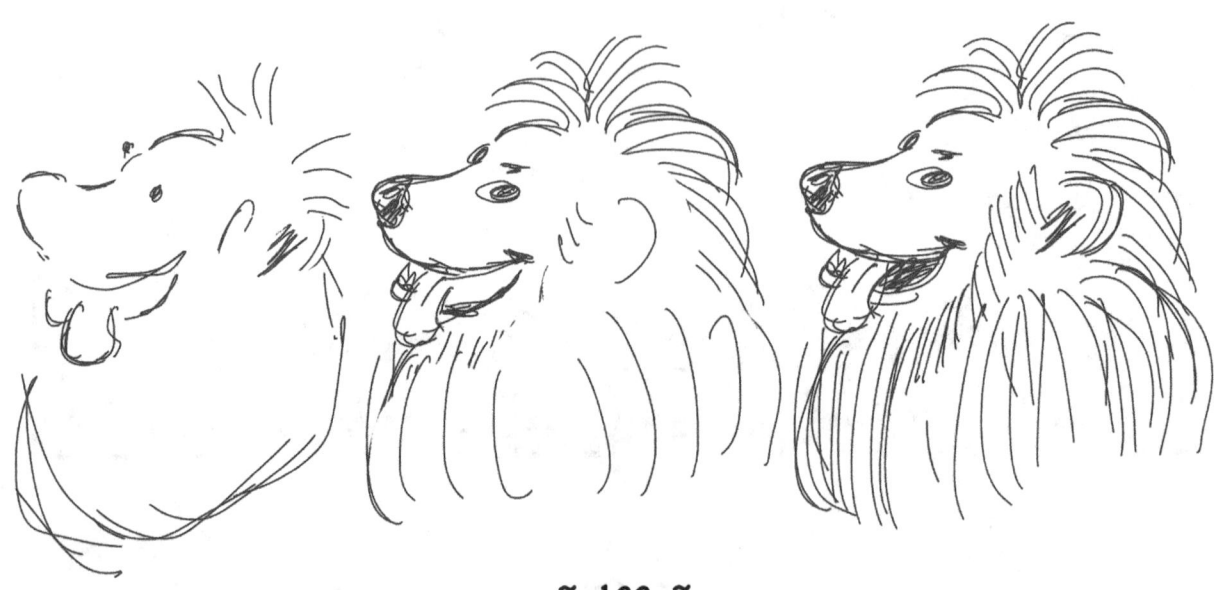

Chapter 19
Business advice

Before dinner, Mary Beth asked Mrs. Chapin for some advice about pricing her art.

"For now," Mrs. Chapin said, "you are doing it just right. You are pricing using the Cutie Pie method. You're so cute, and draw so well, people gush and throw money at you. I'd advise you to keep doing just that ... but at some point you'll need to expand your business. Have you ever thought about drawing cats, cars, or the people themselves? In this neighborhood alone there are lots of cats, you can easily have work for months."

"I get it, you want me to pivot to cats," Mary Beth said.

"You're a smart kid," Mrs. Chapin said. "Cats, goldfish, llamas. Draw what your customers love."

"I don't know about any llamas, but the janitor at school has a boa constrictor named Feather."

"Sell them what they want," Mrs. Chapin said, with a smile.

"OK," Mary Beth said. "From now on I will draw dogs <u>and</u> cats. And when school starts, maybe snakes."

The End

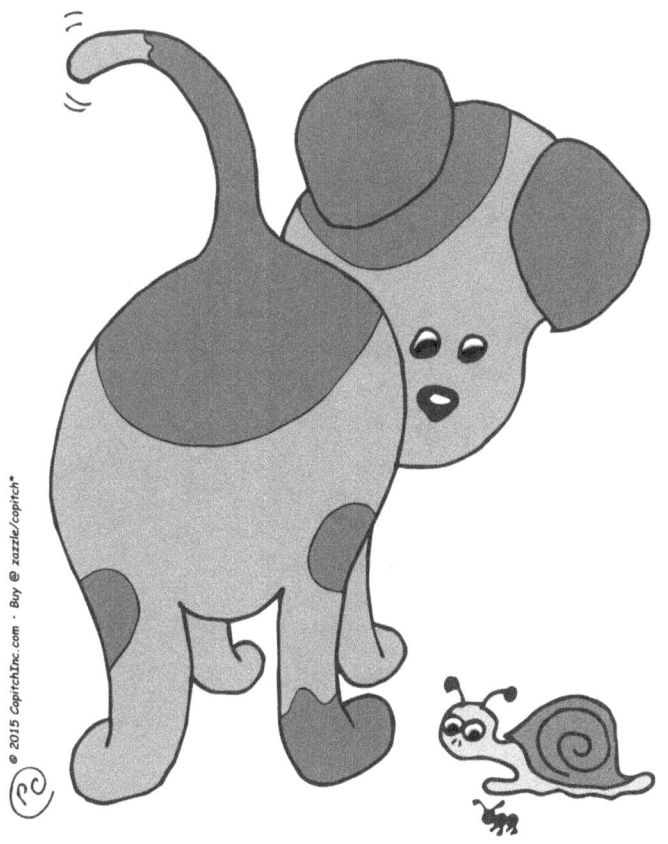

Books by Dr. Copitch (Available at Amazon.com)

Psychology/Self Help

- Basic Parenting 101: The Manual Your Child Should Have Been Born With
- Change: How to bring real change to your life: The psychology and secrets of highly effective people
- Life's Laws For New Adults: Mastering Your Social I.Q.

Business

- Chutzpah Marketing: Simple Low Cost Secrets For Building Your Business Fortune
- Phone Scripts For Mental Health Professionals That Fill Your How To Make Money From Your Website or Blog: From basics to money in five hours
- Chutzpah Marketing for Mental Health Professionals: The missing manual from your graduate school education

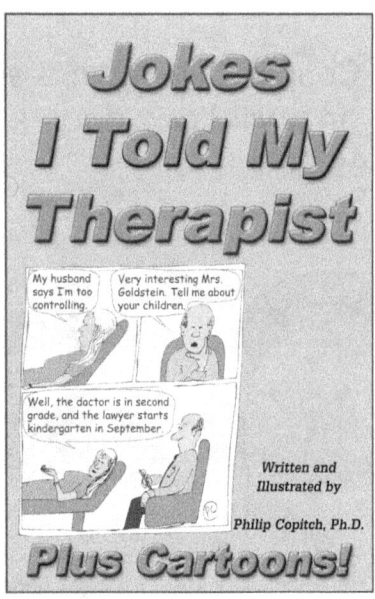
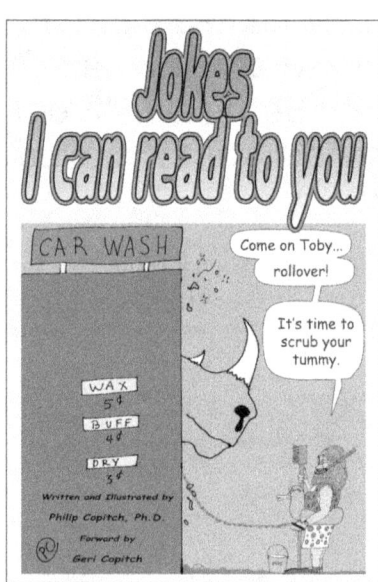

Jokes and funny

- Jokes I Told My Therapist, Plus Cartoons: Tall Tales, and Funny True Stories
- Christmas Cartoons
- Jokes I Can Read To You: Plus cartoons!
- Jokes Stories and Cartoons I can read to you
- Jokes, Cartoons, and Funny Stories I Can Read To You!

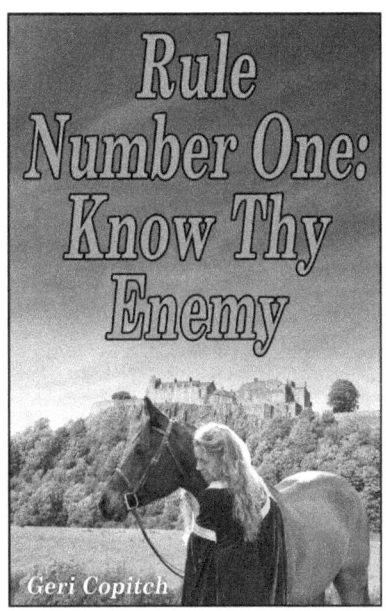

Geri Copitch, a novel (Dr. Phil's wife)

· Rule Number One—Know Thy Enemy

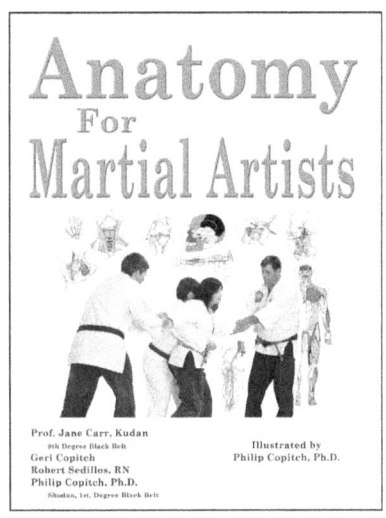

A Fundraiser

· Anatomy For Martial Artists - A fundraiser for Redding JuJitsu Academy, Redding, CA.

Websites

· CopitchInc.com - Dr. Phil's professional/business website

· copitch.com — Dr. Phil's free cartoon site. About 1000 free cartoons!

· funfreeclipart.com — Free clipart to spice up your school reports, newsletters, and posters

· Dr. Phil's cartoons available on shirts, mouse pads, cards, and lots more at https://www.zazzle.com/copitch

www.ingramcontent.com/pod-product-compliance
Lightning Source LLC
Chambersburg PA
CBHW081729220526
45468CB00008B/2033